The Third

251

Most Common
Chinese Characters

Book 8

An Introduction to the Stroke Order, Writing and Grammar

大毛猴子
Dà Máo Hóuzi
Big Hairy Monkey
www.SpeakandWriteChinese.com

Library and Archives Canada Cataloguing in Publication

Dà, Máo Hóuzi, 1969-

Title: The Third 251 Most Common Chinese Characters: An Introduction to the Stroke Order, Writing and Grammar / Dà Máo Hóuzi.

Subtitle: A Comprehensive Approach to Learning Chinese Language; Book 8

978-1-926564-03-6

1. Chinese Language-Writing. 2. Chinese Characters.
I. Title. II. Title: The Third Two Hundred and Fifty-One Most Common Chinese Characters. III. Series: A Comprehensive Approach to Learning Chinese Language; Book 8

PL1171.D37 2009a   495.1'11   C2009-901976-0

Author: Dà Máo Hóuzi
Editor-in-Chief: Dà Máo Hóuzi
Authentic Chinese Editor: Lu XueFeng
Copy Editor: Dà Máo Hóuzi
Graphics/Tables/Covers: Dà Máo Hóuzi

This is Book 8 in the Series;

A Comprehensive Approach to Learning Chinese Language

Monkey Monk Publications
Stoney Creek, Ontario, Canada

Published by Monkey Monk Publications

Office in Toronto, Ontario, Canada

Other publications by Monkey Monk Publications

1) Hanzi and the Kangxi Radicals

2) 425 Easy Chinese Characters

3) 425 Intermediate Chinese Characters

4) 425 Advanced Chinese Characters

5) 425 Chinese Characters Using 1 to 5 Strokes

6) The First 251 Most Common Chinese Characters

7) The Second 251 Most Common Chinese Characters

8) The Third 251 Most Common Chinese Characters

9) The Fourth 251 Most Common Chinese Characters

10) The First 1000 Most Common Chinese Characters

11) The Second 1000 Most Common Chinese Characters

12) The Third 1000 Most Common Chinese Characters

13) A Merciful Introduction to Chinese Grammar

14) Chinese Grammar for the Keener

15) Generally Clever Things to Say in Standard Mandarin Chinese

Preface to the General Introduction

Standard Mandarin is an official language of the United Nations. More people speak Mandarin than any other language. If you are a native English speaker you will need to turn on a part of your brain that is relatively dormant. This is the only language that exists that is not driven by a sound based signal system. A Chinese character is a logogram, a symbol. There are no consistent or reliable signals for meaning or sound in a character. After you learn a character you may be able to pick clues out of a small number of characters. If you never speak a word of Mandarin or travel to China you can still make a change in your brain that will open a whole new way to memorize.

The Chinese have always intrigued me. I was first exposed to them in university. I marvelled at how they could ace physics, math, chemistry, engineering and computer science yet barely speak English. It was not until I looked at their language that I began to understand. Their language is based on a system of a visual image representing meaning. Although each character has defined meanings, compiled together they may have totally different meanings. It would be nice if two characters beside each other as A and B equalled AB but in many situations it is more complex. A + B = AB exists but so does A + B = C. If you learn 200 characters in a paragraph and write all their meanings in an English sentence format, the product may be incomprehensible.

Initially you will struggle with learning complex characters. But like all skills you will improve. Many people lament the difficulty to me but my response is always, *2 billion people cannot be wrong*.

Table of Contents

Introduction

The Third 251 Most Common Chinese Characters is an introduction to the 3rd group of 251 statistically most common characters. These characters come from a list of the 3000 most common characters. This is list was compiled from a computer analysis of a recorded conversation database.

In writing this book I first looked to see what was available in the local English bookstore's titles. I bought all the books I could find and was surprised at books that missed some of the most common characters and books that presented some very uncommon characters. I did not find one book that presented accepted common characters.

Perhaps my biggest pleasure was finding books that published 250 characters. 250 is somewhat of an insult in the Chinese language. The story is long and ancient and involves four men who stole 1000 monies and history records that the ruling judge called them each (二百五, **èr bǎi wǔ**, **250**). Get it? 1000 divided by 4 = 250. Four idiots. Then he ordered them executed.

Most (外国人, **wài guó rén**, **outside country person**) or *foreigners* make little effort to learn the written script of China. Given the very long learning curve to develop a functional writing skill, it is wise to first learn the most common characters. Knowing the 251 most common characters will give you a very good start to understanding the basics you will need to survive in China.

This book is written as a compliment to my first 6 books, detailed in the front inside cover. My first book ***Hanzi and the Kangxi Radicals*** is a 568 page 8 1/2 by 11 book that I feel is the most comprehensive book in English that details the essential components to writing Chinese characters. That is, the 50 plus named strokes, the 214 essential characters known as the Kangxi Radicals and guided practice drills.

Writing Chinese characters requires skills and a form of memory that is under-utilized in English speakers. Like all skills it develops with practice. You will not learn by looking at the drills. Like billions of Chinese over thousands of years, you must practice, practice, practice. 大毛猴子

Using the Work Book

What lies ahead are 251 tables. At the upper left of each table is a large Chinese character. This is of course the topic character for the work sheet.

Immediately below the topic character is a small box with the alphabetic sound that represents the usual sound of this character. The method of representing the sound of the character is called (拼音, **Pīnyīn**, **spell sound**). This use of the Roman alphabet was developed and embraced by China so that school children across China would have a standardized sound for each character.

China historically was unified by the written language. The spoken language had and has over 200 recognized very distinct variations. (拼音, **Pīnyīn**, **spell sound**) helped China develop a universal literacy of spoken language. At the back of this work book is a guide to pronunciation.

The third box, below the (拼音, **Pīnyīn**, **spell sound**) box, is the common or usual English translation. Like English, a Chinese character can have more than one meaning.

To the right of these first three boxes is an area to write your own notes and also a brief explanation of the meaning of the character along with the character and the (拼音, **Pīnyīn**, **spell sound**).

Below all of these, making the fourth row and crossing the page, is a long box in which the stroke order of the character is shown. As you move from left to right across the box, one extra stroke is added until finally the entire character is drawn.

Then come the practice boxes. Photocopy, overwrite or use a clear acetate with a wipe off marker and get to work using the correct stroke and stroke order. Chant the (拼音, **Pīnyīn**, **spell sound**) and the meaning. You will find it more useful if you pick about 10 lesson tables and do one character on each of all ten lessons and repeat this cycle.

There is no easy way to do this. Practice, repetition, frustration are all part of learning any language.

证

Notes: Verb

(证, **zhèng**, **prove**, **testify**, **demonstrate**)

zhèng

prove

丶 讠 讠 讠 讠 讠 讠

证 证 证 证 证 证 证 证 证

证	证	证	证	证	证	证	证	证	证
zhèng	zhèng	zhèng	zhèng	zhèng	zhèng	zhèng	zhèng	zhèng	zhèng
prove	prove	prove	prove	prove	prove	prove	prove	prove	prove
证	证	证	证	证	证	证	证	证	证
zhèng	zhèng	zhèng	zhèng	zhèng	zhèng	zhèng	zhèng	zhèng	zhèng
prove	prove	prove	prove	prove	prove	prove	prove	prove	prove
证	证	证	证	证	证	证	证	证	证
证	证	证	证	证	证	证	证	证	证
证	证	证	证	证	证	证	证	证	证
证	证	证	证	证	证	证	证	证	证
证	证	证	证	证	证	证	证	证	证
证	证	证	证	证	证	证	证	证	证
证	证	证	证	证	证	证	证	证	证
证	证	证	证	证	证	证	证	证	证

苦	Notes: Adjective (苦, **kǔ**, **bitter**)
kǔ	
bitter	

一 十 艹 艹 芏 芢 芐 苦 苦

苦 苦 苦 苦 苦 苦 苦 苦 苦

苦	苦	苦	苦	苦	苦	苦	苦	苦	苦
kǔ	kǔ	kǔ	kǔ	kǔ	kǔ	kǔ	kǔ	kǔ	kǔ
bitter	bitter	bitter	bitter	bitter	bitter	bitter	bitter	bitter	bitter
苦	苦	苦	苦	苦	苦	苦	苦	苦	苦
kǔ	kǔ	kǔ	kǔ	kǔ	kǔ	kǔ	kǔ	kǔ	kǔ
bitter	bitter	bitter	bitter	bitter	bitter	bitter	bitter	bitter	bitter
苦	苦	苦	苦	苦	苦	苦	苦	苦	苦
苦	苦	苦	苦	苦	苦	苦	苦	苦	苦
苦	苦	苦	苦	苦	苦	苦	苦	苦	苦
苦	苦	苦	苦	苦	苦	苦	苦	苦	苦
苦	苦	苦	苦	苦	苦	苦	苦	苦	苦
苦	苦	苦	苦	苦	苦	苦	苦	苦	苦
苦	苦	苦	苦	苦	苦	苦	苦	苦	苦
苦	苦	苦	苦	苦	苦	苦	苦	苦	苦

照

zhào
shine

Notes: Verb

(照, zhào, shine, illuminate, reflect, mirror)

(照, zhào, take a picture or photograph)

(照, zhào, take care of, look after)

丨 冂 冃 日 日⸃ 日⸃⸃ 日⸃⸃⸃ 昭 昭 照 照 照 照

照 照 照 照 照 照 照 照 照

照	照	照	照	照	照	照	照	照	照
zhào	zhào	zhào	zhào	zhào	zhào	zhào	zhào	zhào	zhào
shine	shine	shine	shine	shine	shine	shine	shine	shine	shine
照	照	照	照	照	照	照	照	照	照
zhào	zhào	zhào	zhào	zhào	zhào	zhào	zhào	zhào	zhào
shine	shine	shine	shine	shine	shine	shine	shine	shine	shine
照	照	照	照	照	照	照	照	照	照
照	照	照	照	照	照	照	照	照	照
照	照	照	照	照	照	照	照	照	照
照	照	照	照	照	照	照	照	照	照
照	照	照	照	照	照	照	照	照	照
照	照	照	照	照	照	照	照	照	照
照	照	照	照	照	照	照	照	照	照
照	照	照	照	照	照	照	照	照	照

注

zhù

pour

Notes: Verb

(注, **zhù**, **pour, put a liquid into**)

(注, **zhù**, **annotate, record, register**)

丶 丶 氵 氵 广 产 汁 注

注 注 注 注 注 注 注 注 注

注	注	注	注	注	注	注	注	注	注
zhù	zhù	zhù	zhù	zhù	zhù	zhù	zhù	zhù	zhù
pour	pour	pour	pour	pour	pour	pour	pour	pour	pour
注	注	注	注	注	注	注	注	注	注
zhù	zhù	zhù	zhù	zhù	zhù	zhù	zhù	zhù	zhù
pour	pour	pour	pour	pour	pour	pour	pour	pour	pour
注	注	注	注	注	注	注	注		
注	注	注	注	注	注	注	注	注	
注	注	注	注	注	注	注	注	注	
注	注	注	注	注	注	注	注	注	
注	注	注	注	注	注	注	注	注	
注	注	注	注	注	注	注	注	注	
注	注	注	注	注	注	注	注		

费

fèi

spend

Notes: Verb

(费, fèi, spend, expend, charge)

(费, fèi, cost, fee, dues, expense)

(费, fèi, require a lot of talking or explaining)

フ ⼸ 弓 弔 弗 弗 弗 费 费

费 费 费 费 费 费 费 费 费

费	费	费	费	费	费	费	费	费	费
fèi	fèi	fèi	fèi	fèi	fèi	fèi	fèi	fèi	fèi
spend	spend	spend	spend	spend	spend	spend	spend	spend	spend
费	费	费	费	费	费	费	费	费	费
fèi	fèi	fèi	fèi	fèi	fèi	fèi	fèi	fèi	fèi
spend	spend	spend	spend	spend	spend	spend	spend	spend	spend
费	费	费	费	费	费	费	费	费	费
费	费	费	费	费	费	费	费	费	费
费	费	费	费	费	费	费	费	费	费
费	费	费	费	费	费	费	费	费	费
费	费	费	费	费	费	费	费	费	费
费	费	费	费	费	费	费	费	费	费
费	费	费	费	费	费	费	费	费	费
费	费	费	费	费	费	费	费	费	费

足

zú

foot

Notes: Common Noun

(足, **zú**, **foot**)

丨 冂 冂 口 吊 吊 足 足

足 足 足 足 足 足 足 足 足

足	足	足	足	足	足	足	足	足	足
zú	zú	zú	zú	zú	zú	zú	zú	zú	zú
foot	foot	foot	foot	foot	foot	foot	foot	foot	foot
足	足	足	足	足	足	足	足	足	足
zú	zú	zú	zú	zú	zú	zú	zú	zú	zú
foot	foot	foot	foot	foot	foot	foot	foot	foot	foot
足	足	足	足	足	足	足	足	足	足
足	足	足	足	足	足	足	足	足	足
足	足	足	足	足	足	足	足	足	足
足	足	足	足	足	足	足	足	足	足
足	足	足	足	足	足	足	足	足	足
足	足	足	足	足	足	足	足	足	足
足	足	足	足	足	足	足	足	足	足
足	足	足	足	足	足	足	足	足	足

尔

Notes: Personal Pronoun

(尔, ěr, you)

ěr

you

ノ 仒 仒 尔 尔

尔 尔 尔 尔 尔 尔 尔 尔 尔

尔	尔	尔	尔	尔	尔	尔	尔	尔	尔
ěr	ěr	ěr	ěr	ěr	ěr	ěr	ěr	ěr	ěr
you	you	you	you	you	you	you	you	you	you
尔	尔	尔	尔	尔	尔	尔	尔	尔	尔
ěr	ěr	ěr	ěr	ěr	ěr	ěr	ěr	ěr	ěr
you	you	you	you	you	you	you	you	you	you
尔	尔	尔	尔	尔	尔	尔	尔	尔	尔
尔	尔	尔	尔	尔	尔	尔	尔	尔	尔
尔	尔	尔	尔	尔	尔	尔	尔	尔	尔
尔	尔	尔	尔	尔	尔	尔	尔	尔	尔
尔	尔	尔	尔	尔	尔	尔	尔	尔	尔
尔	尔	尔	尔	尔	尔	尔	尔	尔	尔
尔	尔	尔	尔	尔	尔	尔	尔	尔	尔
尔	尔	尔	尔	尔	尔	尔	尔	尔	尔

招	Notes: Verb
	(招, **zhāo**, **beckon**, **recruit**, **attract**)
zhāo	
beckon	

一 十 扌 扩 护 护 招 招

招 招 招 招 招 招 招 招 招

招	招	招	招	招	招	招	招	招	招
zhāo	zhāo	zhāo	zhāo	zhāo	zhāo	zhāo	zhāo	zhāo	zhāo
beckon	beckon	beckon	beckon	beckon	beckon	beckon	beckon	beckon	beckon
招	招	招	招	招	招	招	招	招	招
zhāo	zhāo	zhāo	zhāo	zhāo	zhāo	zhāo	zhāo	zhāo	zhāo
beckon	beckon	beckon	beckon	beckon	beckon	beckon	beckon	beckon	beckon

招	招	招	招	招	招	招	招	招	招
招	招	招	招	招	招	招	招	招	招
招	招	招	招	招	招	招	招	招	招
招	招	招	招	招	招	招	招	招	招
招	招	招	招	招	招	招	招	招	招
招	招	招	招	招	招	招	招	招	招
招	招	招	招	招	招	招	招	招	招
招	招	招	招	招	招	招	招	招	招

群

Notes: Common Noun

(群, **qún**, **crowd, group**)

qún

crowd

ㄱ 于 尹 尹 君 君 君 君' 君" 群' 群' 群' 群

群 群 群 群 群 群 群 群 群

群	群	群	群	群	群	群	群	群	群
qún	qún	qún	qún	qún	qún	qún	qún	qún	qún
crowd	crowd	crowd	crowd	crowd	crowd	crowd	crowd	crowd	crowd
群	群	群	群	群	群	群	群	群	群
qún	qún	qún	qún	qún	qún	qún	qún	qún	qún
crowd	crowd	crowd	crowd	crowd	crowd	crowd	crowd	crowd	crowd
群	群	群	群	群	群	群	群	群	群
群	群	群	群	群	群	群	群	群	群
群	群	群	群	群	群	群	群	群	群
群	群	群	群	群	群	群	群	群	群
群	群	群	群	群	群	群	群	群	群
群	群	群	群	群	群	群	群	群	群
群	群	群	群	群	群	群	群	群	群
群	群	群	群	群	群	群	群	群	群

热

rè

hot

Notes: Adjective

(热, rè, hot)

一 十 扌 扌 扦 执 执 执 热 热 热

热 热 热 热 热 热 热 热 热

热	热	热	热	热	热	热	热	热	热
rè	rè	rè	rè	rè	rè	rè	rè	rè	rè
hot	hot	hot	hot	hot	hot	hot	hot	hot	hot
热	热	热	热	热	热	热	热	热	热
rè	rè	rè	rè	rè	rè	rè	rè	rè	rè
hot	hot	hot	hot	hot	hot	hot	hot	hot	hot
热	热	热	热	热	热	热	热	热	热
热	热	热	热	热	热	热	热	热	热
热	热	热	热	热	热	热	热	热	热
热	热	热	热	热	热	热	热	热	热
热	热	热	热	热	热	热	热	热	热
热	热	热	热	热	热	热	热	热	热
热	热	热	热	热	热	热	热	热	热
热	热	热	热	热	热	热	热	热	热

推	Notes: Verb (推, **tuī**, **push**)
tuī	
push	

一 十 才 扌 扩 扩 扩 护 抃 拚 拂 推 推

推 推 推 推 推 推 推 推 推

推	推	推	推	推	推	推	推	推	推
tuī	tuī	tuī	tuī	tuī	tuī	tuī	tuī	tuī	tuī
push	push	push	push	push	push	push	push	push	push
推	推	推	推	推	推	推	推	推	推
tuī	tuī	tuī	tuī	tuī	tuī	tuī	tuī	tuī	tuī
push	push	push	push	push	push	push	push	push	push
推	推	推	推	推	推	推	推	推	推
推	推	推	推	推	推	推	推	推	推
推	推	推	推	推	推	推	推	推	推
推	推	推	推	推	推	推	推	推	推
推	推	推	推	推	推	推	推	推	推
推	推	推	推	推	推	推	推	推	推
推	推	推	推	推	推	推	推	推	推

晚

Notes: Adjective

(晚, **wǎn**, **late**)

wǎn

late

丨 冂 冂 日 日 旷 旷 旷 睁 晚 晚 晚

晚 晚 晚 晚 晚 晚 晚 晚 晚

晚	晚	晚	晚	晚	晚	晚	晚	晚	晚
wǎn	wǎn	wǎn	wǎn	wǎn	wǎn	wǎn	wǎn	wǎn	wǎn
late	late	late	late	late	late	late	late	late	late
晚	晚	晚	晚	晚	晚	晚	晚	晚	晚
wǎn	wǎn	wǎn	wǎn	wǎn	wǎn	wǎn	wǎn	wǎn	wǎn
late	late	late	late	late	late	late	late	late	late
晚	晚	晚	晚	晚	晚	晚	晚	晚	
晚	晚	晚	晚	晚	晚	晚	晚	晚	
晚	晚	晚	晚	晚	晚	晚	晚	晚	
晚	晚	晚	晚	晚	晚	晚	晚	晚	
晚	晚	晚	晚	晚	晚	晚	晚	晚	
晚	晚	晚	晚	晚	晚	晚	晚	晚	
晚	晚	晚	晚	晚	晚	晚	晚	晚	

响	Notes: Common Noun (响, **xiǎng**, **sound**)
xiǎng	
sound	

丨 冂 冂 口 口′ 口″ 叮 叻 响 响

响 响 响 响 响 响 响 响 响

响	响	响	响	响	响	响	响	响	响
xiǎng	xiǎng	xiǎng	xiǎng	xiǎng	xiǎng	xiǎng	xiǎng	xiǎng	xiǎng
sound	sound	sound	sound	sound	sound	sound	sound	sound	sound
响	响	响	响	响	响	响	响	响	响
xiǎng	xiǎng	xiǎng	xiǎng	xiǎng	xiǎng	xiǎng	xiǎng	xiǎng	xiǎng
sound	sound	sound	sound	sound	sound	sound	sound	sound	sound
响	响	响	响	响	响	响	响	响	响
响	响	响	响	响	响	响	响	响	响
响	响	响	响	响	响	响	响	响	响
响	响	响	响	响	响	响	响	响	响
响	响	响	响	响	响	响	响	响	响
响	响	响	响	响	响	响	响	响	响
响	响	响	响	响	响	响	响	响	响
响	响	响	响	响	响	响	响	响	响

称

Notes: Verb

(称, **chēng**, **weigh**)

(称, **Chēng**, **surname Chēng**)

chēng
weigh

´ ⊂ 千 千 禾 秒 秒 秒 称 称

称 称 称 称 称 称 称 称 称

称	称	称	称	称	称	称	称	称	称
chēng	chēng	chēng	chēng	chēng	chēng	chēng	chēng	chēng	chēng
weigh	weigh	weigh	weigh	weigh	weigh	weigh	weigh	weigh	weigh
称	称	称	称	称	称	称	称	称	称
chēng	chēng	chēng	chēng	chēng	chēng	chēng	chēng	chēng	chēng
weigh	weigh	weigh	weigh	weigh	weigh	weigh	weigh	weigh	weigh
称	称	称	称	称	称	称	称	称	称
称	称	称	称	称	称	称	称	称	称
称	称	称	称	称	称	称	称	称	称
称	称	称	称	称	称	称	称	称	称
称	称	称	称	称	称	称	称	称	称
称	称	称	称	称	称	称	称	称	称
称	称	称	称	称	称	称	称	称	称
称	称	称	称	称	称	称	称	称	称

	Notes: Adjective
兴	(兴, **xìng**, **glad**, **happy**)
xìng	
happy	

丶　丷　业　业　业　兴

兴　兴　兴　兴　兴　兴　兴　兴　兴

兴	兴	兴	兴	兴	兴	兴	兴	兴	兴
xìng	xìng	xìng	xìng	xìng	xìng	xìng	xìng	xìng	xìng
happy	happy	happy	happy	happy	happy	happy	happy	happy	happy
兴	兴	兴	兴	兴	兴	兴	兴	兴	兴
xìng	xìng	xìng	xìng	xìng	xìng	xìng	xìng	xìng	xìng
happy	happy	happy	happy	happy	happy	happy	happy	happy	happy
兴	兴	兴	兴	兴	兴	兴	兴	兴	兴
兴	兴	兴	兴	兴	兴	兴	兴	兴	兴
兴	兴	兴	兴	兴	兴	兴	兴	兴	兴
兴	兴	兴	兴	兴	兴	兴	兴	兴	兴
兴	兴	兴	兴	兴	兴	兴	兴	兴	兴
兴	兴	兴	兴	兴	兴	兴	兴	兴	兴
兴	兴	兴	兴	兴	兴	兴	兴	兴	兴

待

dài
wait

Notes: Verb

(待, **dài**, **wait**, **wait for**)

(待, **dài**, **need**, **pending**)

(待, **dāi**, **stay**)

(待, **dài**, **treat**, **entertain**)

ノ ク イ 彳 彳 彳 彳 待 待

待 待 待 待 待 待 待 待 待

待	待	待	待	待	待	待	待	待	待
dài	dài	dài	dài	dài	dài	dài	dài	dài	dài
wait	wait	wait	wait	wait	wait	wait	wait	wait	wait
待	待	待	待	待	待	待	待	待	待
dài	dài	dài	dài	dài	dài	dài	dài	dài	dài
wait	wait	wait	wait	wait	wait	wait	wait	wait	wait
待	待	待	待	待	待	待	待	待	
待	待	待	待	待	待	待	待	待	
待	待	待	待	待	待	待	待	待	
待	待	待	待	待	待	待	待	待	
待	待	待	待	待	待	待	待	待	
待	待	待	待	待	待	待	待	待	
待	待	待	待	待	待	待	待	待	
待	待	待	待	待	待	待	待	待	

约	Notes: Verb
	(约, **yuē**, **ask, invite**)
	(约, **yuē**, **to make an appointment**)
	(约, **yuē**, **approximately, arrange**)
yuē invite	(约, **yuē**, **restrict, restrain**)

乡 乡 纟 纟 约 约

待 待 待 待 待 待 待 待 待

待	待	待	待	待	待	待	待	待	待
yuē invite	yuē invite	yuē invite	yuē invite	yuē invite	yuē invite	yuē invite	yuē invite	yuē invite	yuē invite
待	待	待	待	待	待	待	待	待	待
yuē invite	yuē invite	yuē invite	yuē invite	yuē invite	yuē invite	yuē invite	yuē invite	yuē invite	yuē invite
待	待	待	待	待	待	待	待	待	待
待	待	待	待	待	待	待	待	待	待
待	待	待	待	待	待	待	待	待	待
待	待	待	待	待	待	待	待	待	待
待	待	待	待	待	待	待	待	待	待
待	待	待	待	待	待	待	待	待	待
待	待	待	待	待	待	待	待	待	待
待	待	待	待	待	待	待	待	待	待

阴	Notes: Common Noun
	(阴, **yáng, male principle in nature**)
	(阴, **yáng, positive, active**)
yáng	
invite	

乛 阝 阝| 阝⊓ 阝∏ 阳

阴 阴 阴 阴 阴 阴 阴 阴 阴

阴	阴	阴	阴	阴	阴	阴	阴	阴	阴
yáng	yáng	yáng	yáng	yáng	yáng	yáng	yáng	yáng	yáng
invite	invite	invite	invite	invite	invite	invite	invite	invite	invite
阴	阴	阴	阴	阴	阴	阴	阴	阴	阴
yáng	yáng	yáng	yáng	yáng	yáng	yáng	yáng	yáng	yáng
invite	invite	invite	invite	invite	invite	invite	invite	invite	invite
阴	阴	阴	阴	阴	阴	阴	阴	阴	阴
阴	阴	阴	阴	阴	阴	阴	阴	阴	阴
阴	阴	阴	阴	阴	阴	阴	阴	阴	阴
阴	阴	阴	阴	阴	阴	阴	阴	阴	阴
阴	阴	阴	阴	阴	阴	阴	阴	阴	阴
阴	阴	阴	阴	阴	阴	阴	阴	阴	阴
阴	阴	阴	阴	阴	阴	阴	阴	阴	阴
阴	阴	阴	阴	阴	阴	阴	阴	阴	阴

哥

gē
brother

Notes: Common Noun

(哥, **gē**, **older brother**)

一 厂 丆 croplus 可 哥 哥 哥 哥 哥

哥 哥 哥 哥 哥 哥 哥 哥 哥

哥	哥	哥	哥	哥	哥	哥	哥	哥	哥
gē	gē	gē	gē	gē	gē	gē	gē	gē	gē
brother	brother	brother	brother	brother	brother	brother	brother	brother	brother
哥	哥	哥	哥	哥	哥	哥	哥	哥	哥
gē	gē	gē	gē	gē	gē	gē	gē	gē	gē
brother	brother	brother	brother	brother	brother	brother	brother	brother	brother

哥	哥	哥	哥	哥	哥	哥	哥	哥	哥
哥	哥	哥	哥	哥	哥	哥	哥	哥	哥
哥	哥	哥	哥	哥	哥	哥	哥	哥	哥
哥	哥	哥	哥	哥	哥	哥	哥	哥	哥
哥	哥	哥	哥	哥	哥	哥	哥	哥	哥
哥	哥	哥	哥	哥	哥	哥	哥	哥	哥
哥	哥	哥	哥	哥	哥	哥	哥	哥	哥
哥	哥	哥	哥	哥	哥	哥	哥	哥	哥

惊	Notes: Verb
	(惊, **jīng**, **to surprise**, **startle**, **to alarm**)
	(惊, **jīng**, **violent**, **fierce**)
jīng	(惊, **jīng**, **shy**)
alarm	

丶 丶 忄 忄 广 忄 忄 忄 惊 惊 惊

惊 惊 惊 惊 惊 惊 惊 惊 惊

惊	惊	惊	惊	惊	惊	惊	惊	惊	惊
jīng	jīng	jīng	jīng	jīng	jīng	jīng	jīng	jīng	jīng
alarm	alarm	alarm	alarm	alarm	alarm	alarm	alarm	alarm	alarm
惊	惊	惊	惊	惊	惊	惊	惊	惊	惊
jīng	jīng	jīng	jīng	jīng	jīng	jīng	jīng	jīng	jīng
alarm	alarm	alarm	alarm	alarm	alarm	alarm	alarm	alarm	alarm

惊	惊	惊	惊	惊	惊	惊	惊	惊	
惊	惊	惊	惊	惊	惊	惊	惊	惊	
惊	惊	惊	惊	惊	惊	惊	惊	惊	
惊	惊	惊	惊	惊	惊	惊	惊	惊	
惊	惊	惊	惊	惊	惊	惊	惊	惊	
惊	惊	惊	惊	惊	惊	惊	惊	惊	
惊	惊	惊	惊	惊	惊	惊	惊	惊	
惊	惊	惊	惊	惊	惊	惊	惊	惊	

吗	Notes: Grammatical Particle
	(吗, **ma**, **interrogative particle**) acts as a sentence final grammatical particle to show that the sentence is a question.
	(吗, **má**, **what**)
ma	
?	

| 丨 | 冂 | 口 | 口⁊ | 吗 | 吗 |

吗 吗 吗 吗 吗 吗 吗 吗 吗

吗	吗	吗	吗	吗	吗	吗	吗	吗	吗
ma	ma	ma	ma	ma	ma	ma	ma	ma	ma
?	?	?	?	?	?	?	?	?	?
吗	吗	吗	吗	吗	吗	吗	吗	吗	吗
ma	ma	ma	ma	ma	ma	ma	ma	ma	ma
?	?	?	?	?	?	?	?	?	?
吗	吗	吗	吗	吗	吗	吗	吗	吗	吗
吗	吗	吗	吗	吗	吗	吗	吗	吗	吗
吗	吗	吗	吗	吗	吗	吗	吗	吗	吗
吗	吗	吗	吗	吗	吗	吗	吗	吗	吗
吗	吗	吗	吗	吗	吗	吗	吗	吗	吗
吗	吗	吗	吗	吗	吗	吗	吗	吗	吗
吗	吗	吗	吗	吗	吗	吗	吗	吗	吗
吗	吗	吗	吗	吗	吗	吗	吗	吗	吗

整	Notes: Adjective
	(整, zhěng, entire, whole, full)
	(整, zhěng, neat, tidy)
zhěng	
entire	

一 厂 厂 万 束 束 束 束 束 敕 敕 敕 敕 敕 整 整 整 整

整 整 整 整 整 整 整 整 整

整	整	整	整	整	整	整	整	整	整
zhěng	zhěng	zhěng	zhěng	zhěng	zhěng	zhěng	zhěng	zhěng	zhěng
entire	entire	entire	entire	entire	entire	entire	entire	entire	entire
整	整	整	整	整	整	整	整	整	整
zhěng	zhěng	zhěng	zhěng	zhěng	zhěng	zhěng	zhěng	zhěng	zhěng
entire	entire	entire	entire	entire	entire	entire	entire	entire	entire
整	整	整	整	整	整	整	整	整	
整	整	整	整	整	整	整	整	整	
整	整	整	整	整	整	整	整	整	
整	整	整	整	整	整	整	整	整	
整	整	整	整	整	整	整	整	整	
整	整	整	整	整	整	整	整	整	
整	整	整	整	整	整	整	整	整	
整	整	整	整	整	整	整	整	整	

支

zhī

support

Notes: Verb

(支, zhī, support, sustain, bear)

(支, zhī, dispatch, send away, put somebody off)

(支, zhī, pay, draw, money)

(支, zhī, protrude, raise

(支, Zhī, surname Zhī)

一 十 ㄎ 支

支 支 支 支 支 支 支 支 支

支	支	支	支	支	支	支	支	支	支
zhī	zhī	zhī	zhī	zhī	zhī	zhī	zhī	zhī	zhī
support	support	support	support	support	support	support	support	support	support
支	支	支	支	支	支	支	支	支	支
zhī	zhī	zhī	zhī	zhī	zhī	zhī	zhī	zhī	zhī
support	support	support	support	support	support	support	support	support	support
支	支	支	支	支	支	支	支	支	支
支	支	支	支	支	支	支	支	支	支
支	支	支	支	支	支	支	支	支	支
支	支	支	支	支	支	支	支	支	支
支	支	支	支	支	支	支	支	支	支
支	支	支	支	支	支	支	支	支	支
支	支	支	支	支	支	支	支	支	支

	Notes: Adjective
古	(古, **gǔ**, **ancient, age- old, old**)
gǔ	(古, **gǔ**, **not following current customs or practice**)
old	

一 十 十 古 古

古 古 古 古 古 古 古 古 古

古	古	古	古	古	古	古	古	古	古
gǔ	gǔ	gǔ	gǔ	gǔ	gǔ	gǔ	gǔ	gǔ	gǔ
old	old	old	old	old	old	old	old	old	old
古	古	古	古	古	古	古	古	古	古
gǔ	gǔ	gǔ	gǔ	gǔ	gǔ	gǔ	gǔ	gǔ	gǔ
old	old	old	old	old	old	old	old	old	old
古	古	古				古			
古	古	古				古			
古	古	古				古			
古	古	古				古			
古	古	古				古			
古	古	古				古			
古	古	古				古			
古	古	古				古			

汉	Notes: Proper Noun (汉, **Hàn**, **Chinese ethnicity, Chinese ethnic majority**) x
gǔ old	

丶 丶 氵 汋 汉

汉 汉 汉 汉 汉 汉 汉 汉 汉

汉	汉	汉	汉	汉	汉	汉	汉	汉	汉
gǔ old	gǔ old	gǔ old	gǔ old	gǔ old	gǔ old	gǔ old	gǔ old	gǔ old	gǔ old
汉	汉	汉	汉	汉	汉	汉	汉	汉	汉
gǔ old	gǔ old	gǔ old	gǔ old	gǔ old	gǔ old	gǔ old	gǔ old	gǔ old	gǔ old
汉	汉	汉	汉	汉	汉	汉	汉	汉	汉
汉	汉	汉	汉	汉	汉	汉	汉	汉	汉
汉	汉	汉	汉	汉	汉	汉	汉	汉	汉
汉	汉	汉	汉	汉	汉	汉	汉	汉	汉
汉	汉	汉	汉	汉	汉	汉	汉	汉	汉
汉	汉	汉	汉	汉	汉	汉	汉	汉	汉
汉	汉	汉	汉	汉	汉	汉	汉	汉	汉
汉	汉	汉	汉	汉	汉	汉	汉	汉	汉

突	Notes: Verb (突, tū, charge forward, stick out) x
tū	
charge	

丶 丷 宀 宀 宀 空 空 突 突

突 突 突 突 突 突 突 突 突

突	突	突	突	突	突	突	突	突	突
tū	tū	tū	tū	tū	tū	tū	tū	tū	tū
charge	charge	charge	charge	charge	charge	charge	charge	charge	charge
突	突	突	突	突	突	突	突	突	突
tū	tū	tū	tū	tū	tū	tū	tū	tū	tū
charge	charge	charge	charge	charge	charge	charge	charge	charge	charge
突	突	突	突	突	突	突	突	突	
突	突	突	突	突	突	突	突	突	
突	突	突	突	突	突	突	突	突	
突	突	突	突	突	突	突	突	突	
突	突	突	突	突	突	突	突	突	
突	突	突	突	突	突	突	突	突	
突	突	突	突	突	突	突	突	突	

号	Notes: Common Noun (号, **hào, name, number, mark, number in a series**) (号, **háo, yell**)
hào number	

丨 冂 口 므 号

号 号 号 号 号 号 号 号 号

号	号	号	号	号	号	号	号	号	号
hào number	hào number	hào number	hào number	hào number	hào number	hào number	hào number	hào number	hào number
号	号	号	号	号	号	号	号	号	号
hào number	hào number	hào number	hào number	hào number	hào number	hào number	hào number	hào number	hào number
号	号	号	号	号	号	号	号	号	
号	号	号	号	号	号	号	号	号	
号	号	号	号	号	号	号	号	号	
号	号	号	号	号	号	号	号	号	
号	号	号	号	号	号	号	号	号	
号	号	号	号	号	号	号	号	号	
号	号	号	号	号	号	号	号	号	
号	号	号	号	号	号	号	号	号	

绝	Notes: Verb
	(绝, **jué**, **cut off**, **sever**)
	(绝, **jué**, **exhausted**, **used up**, **finished**)
	(绝, **jué**, **unique**, **superb**, **matchless**, **absolute**)
jué	(绝, **jué**, **extremely**, **most**, **absolutely**, **at the least**, **by any means**,
sever	**on any account**)

𡿨 乡 纟 纟 纠 纺 纺 纺 绝

绝 绝 绝 绝 绝 绝 绝 绝 绝

绝	绝	绝	绝	绝	绝	绝	绝	绝	绝
jué	jué	jué	jué	jué	jué	jué	jué	jué	jué
sever	sever	sever	sever	sever	sever	sever	sever	sever	sever
绝	绝	绝	绝	绝	绝	绝	绝	绝	绝
jué	jué	jué	jué	jué	jué	jué	jué	jué	jué
sever	sever	sever	sever	sever	sever	sever	sever	sever	sever

绝	绝	绝	绝	绝	绝	绝	绝	绝	
绝	绝	绝	绝	绝	绝	绝	绝	绝	
绝	绝	绝	绝	绝	绝	绝	绝	绝	
绝	绝	绝	绝	绝	绝	绝	绝	绝	
绝	绝	绝	绝	绝	绝	绝	绝	绝	
绝	绝	绝	绝	绝	绝	绝	绝	绝	
绝	绝	绝	绝	绝	绝	绝	绝	绝	
绝	绝	绝	绝	绝	绝	绝	绝	绝	

选	Notes: Verb (选, **xuǎn**, **select**, **choose**, **elect**)
xuǎn	
select	

丿 丄 丄 屵 生 先 先 选 选

选 选 选 选 选 选 选 选 选

选	选	选	选	选	选	选	选	选	选
xuǎn	xuǎn	xuǎn	xuǎn	xuǎn	xuǎn	xuǎn	xuǎn	xuǎn	xuǎn
select	select	select	select	select	select	select	select	select	select
选	选	选	选	选	选	选	选	选	选
xuǎn	xuǎn	xuǎn	xuǎn	xuǎn	xuǎn	xuǎn	xuǎn	xuǎn	xuǎn
select	select	select	select	select	select	select	select	select	select

选	选	选	选	选	选	选	选	选	选
选	选	选	选	选	选	选	选	选	选
选	选	选	选	选	选	选	选	选	选
选	选	选	选	选	选	选	选	选	选
选	选	选	选	选	选	选	选	选	选
选	选	选	选	选	选	选	选	选	选
选	选	选	选	选	选	选	选	选	选
选	选	选	选	选	选	选	选	选	选

吧	Notes: Grammatical Particle (吧, **ba**, sentence final particle indicates suggestion) (吧, **bā**, snap)
ba	

丨 丨丨 口 叮 叮 叮 吧

吧 吧 吧 吧 吧 吧 吧 吧 吧

吧	吧	吧	吧	吧	吧	吧	吧	吧	吧
ba	ba	ba	ba	ba	ba	ba	ba	ba	ba
吧	吧	吧	吧	吧	吧	吧	吧	吧	吧
ba	ba	ba	ba	ba	ba	ba	ba	ba	ba

吧	吧	吧	吧	吧	吧	吧	吧	吧	
吧	吧	吧	吧	吧	吧	吧	吧	吧	
吧	吧	吧	吧	吧	吧	吧	吧	吧	
吧	吧	吧	吧	吧	吧	吧	吧	吧	
吧	吧	吧	吧	吧	吧	吧	吧	吧	
吧	吧	吧	吧	吧	吧	吧	吧	吧	
吧	吧	吧	吧	吧	吧	吧	吧	吧	
吧	吧	吧	吧	吧	吧	吧	吧	吧	

参

cān
join

Notes: Verb

(参, **cān**, **participate**, **join**, **enter**, **take part in**)

(参, **shēn**, **ginseng**)

(参, **cēn**)

ㄥ ㄙ ㄙ ㄘ 纟 矢 叒 参 参

参 参 参 参 参 参 参 参 参

参	参	参	参	参	参	参	参	参	参
cān	cān	cān	cān	cān	cān	cān	cān	cān	cān
join	join	join	join	join	join	join	join	join	join
参	参	参	参	参	参	参	参	参	参
cān	cān	cān	cān	cān	cān	cān	cān	cān	cān
join	join	join	join	join	join	join	join	join	join

参	参	参	参	参	参	参	参	参	参
参	参	参	参	参	参	参	参	参	参
参	参	参	参	参	参	参	参	参	参
参	参	参	参	参	参	参	参	参	参
参	参	参	参	参	参	参	参	参	参
参	参	参	参	参	参	参	参	参	参
参	参	参	参	参	参	参	参	参	参
参	参	参	参	参	参	参	参	参	参

刊	
	Notes: Verb
	(刊, **kān**, **print**, **publish**)
	(刊, **kān**, **periodical**, **publication**)
kān	
print	

一　二　千　刊　刊

刊　刊　刊　刊　刊　刊　刊　刊　刊

刊	刊	刊	刊	刊	刊	刊	刊	刊	刊
kān	kān	kān	kān	kān	kān	kān	kān	kān	kān
print	print	print	print	print	print	print	print	print	print
刊	刊	刊	刊	刊	刊	刊	刊	刊	刊
kān	kān	kān	kān	kān	kān	kān	kān	kān	kān
print	print	print	print	print	print	print	print	print	print

	Notes: Adjective (亚, **yà**, **inferior, second**)
亚	
yà	
second	

一 丁 丌 丌 亞 亚

亚 亚 亚 亚 亚 亚 亚 亚 亚

亚	亚	亚	亚	亚	亚	亚	亚	亚	亚
yà	yà	yà	yà	yà	yà	yà	yà	yà	yà
second	second	second	second	second	second	second	second	second	second
亚	亚	亚	亚	亚	亚	亚	亚	亚	亚
yà	yà	yà	yà	yà	yà	yà	yà	yà	yà
second	second	second	second	second	second	second	second	second	second
亚	亚	亚	亚	亚	亚	亚	亚	亚	亚
亚	亚	亚	亚	亚	亚	亚	亚	亚	亚
亚	亚	亚	亚	亚	亚	亚	亚	亚	亚
亚	亚	亚	亚	亚	亚	亚	亚	亚	亚
亚	亚	亚	亚	亚	亚	亚	亚	亚	亚
亚	亚	亚	亚	亚	亚	亚	亚	亚	亚
亚	亚	亚	亚	亚	亚	亚	亚	亚	亚
亚	亚	亚	亚	亚	亚	亚	亚	亚	亚

复	Notes: Verb
	(复, **fù, turn round, turn over, return**)
	(复, **fù, recover, restore, avenge**)
	(复, **fù, compound, complex**)
fù	(复, **fù, again**)
return	

丿 𠂉 ㇒ 乍 𠂤 𠂤 夐 复 复

复 复 复 复 复 复 复 复 复

复	复	复	复	复	复	复	复	复	复
fù	fù	fù	fù	fù	fù	fù	fù	fù	fù
return	return	return	return	return	return	return	return	return	return
复	复	复	复	复	复	复	复	复	复
fù	fù	fù	fù	fù	fù	fù	fù	fù	fù
return	return	return	return	return	return	return	return	return	return

复	复	复	复	复	复	复	复	复	
复	复	复	复	复	复	复	复	复	
复	复	复	复	复	复	复	复	复	
复	复	复	复	复	复	复	复	复	
复	复	复	复	复	复	复	复	复	
复	复	复	复	复	复	复	复	复	
复	复	复	复	复	复	复	复	复	
复	复	复	复	复	复	复	复	复	

伤

shāng
wound

Notes: Verb

(伤, shāng, wound, injure)

(伤, shāng, fall ill from, damage, harm, injury)

ノ 亻 亻 仁 仿 伤

伤 伤 伤 伤 伤 伤 伤 伤 伤

伤	伤	伤	伤	伤	伤	伤	伤	伤	伤
shāng wound	shāng wound	shāng wound	shāng wound	shāng wound	shāng wound	shāng wound	shāng wound	shāng wound	shāng wound
伤	伤	伤	伤	伤	伤	伤	伤	伤	伤
shāng wound	shāng wound	shāng wound	shāng wound	shāng wound	shāng wound	shāng wound	shāng wound	shāng wound	shāng wound

类

Notes: Common Noun

(类, lèi, category, kind, type, class)

(类, lèi, resemble, be similar)

lèi

type

丶 丷 䒑 半 半 米 籿 籿 类

类 类 类 类 类 类 类 类 类

类	类	类	类	类	类	类	类	类	类
lèi	lèi	lèi	lèi	lèi	lèi	lèi	lèi	lèi	lèi
type	type	type	type	type	type	type	type	type	type
类	类	类	类	类	类	类	类	类	类
lèi	lèi	lèi	lèi	lèi	lèi	lèi	lèi	lèi	lèi
type	type	type	type	type	type	type	type	type	type
类	类	类	类	类	类	类	类	类	
类	类	类	类	类	类	类	类	类	
类	类	类	类	类	类	类	类	类	
类	类	类	类	类	类	类	类	类	
类	类	类	类	类	类	类	类	类	
类	类	类	类	类	类	类	类	类	
类	类	类	类	类	类	类	类	类	
类	类	类	类	类	类	类	类	类	

备
bèi
prepare

Notes: Verb

(备, bèi, get ready, prepare)

丿 ク タ タ 各 各 备 备

备 备 备 备 备 备 备 备 备

备	备	备	备	备	备	备	备	备	备
bèi	bèi	bèi	bèi	bèi	bèi	bèi	bèi	bèi	bèi
prepare	prepare	prepare	prepare	prepare	prepare	prepare	prepare	prepare	prepare
备	备	备	备	备	备	备	备	备	备
bèi	bèi	bèi	bèi	bèi	bèi	bèi	bèi	bèi	bèi
prepare	prepare	prepare	prepare	prepare	prepare	prepare	prepare	prepare	prepare
备	备	备	备	备	备	备	备	备	备
备	备	备	备	备	备	备	备	备	备
备	备	备	备	备	备	备	备	备	备
备	备	备	备	备	备	备	备	备	备
备	备	备	备	备	备	备	备	备	备
备	备	备	备	备	备	备	备	备	备
备	备	备	备	备	备	备	备	备	备
备	备	备	备	备	备	备	备	备	备

欢

Notes: Adjective

(欢, **huān**, **happy**, **cheerful**, **merry**)

(欢, **huān**, **dynamic**, **vigorous**

(欢, **Huān**, **surname Huān**)

huān

happy

フ ﾏ ﾏ ﾌ 欢 欢

欢 欢 欢 欢 欢 欢 欢 欢 欢

欢	欢	欢	欢	欢	欢	欢	欢	欢	欢
huān	huān	huān	huān	huān	huān	huān	huān	huān	huān
happy	happy	happy	happy	happy	happy	happy	happy	happy	happy
欢	欢	欢	欢	欢	欢	欢	欢	欢	欢
huān	huān	huān	huān	huān	huān	huān	huān	huān	huān
happy	happy	happy	happy	happy	happy	happy	happy	happy	happy
欢	欢	欢	欢	欢	欢	欢	欢	欢	
欢	欢	欢	欢	欢	欢	欢	欢	欢	
欢	欢	欢	欢	欢	欢	欢	欢	欢	
欢	欢	欢	欢	欢	欢	欢	欢	欢	
欢	欢	欢	欢	欢	欢	欢	欢	欢	
欢	欢	欢	欢	欢	欢	欢	欢	欢	
欢	欢	欢	欢	欢	欢	欢	欢	欢	
欢	欢	欢	欢	欢	欢	欢	欢	欢	

另									

Notes: Adjective

(另, lìng, other, another, separate, extra

(另, lìng, besides, in liàoition, besides)

lìng

other

丨 冂 口 马 另

另 另 另 另 另 另 另 另 另

另	另	另	另	另	另	另	另	另	另
lìng	lìng	lìng	lìng	lìng	lìng	lìng	lìng	lìng	lìng
other	other	other	other	other	other	other	other	other	other
另	另	另	另	另	另	另	另	另	另
lìng	lìng	lìng	lìng	lìng	lìng	lìng	lìng	lìng	lìng
other	other	other	other	other	other	other	other	other	other
另	另	另	另	另	另	另	另	另	
另	另	另	另	另	另	另	另	另	
另	另	另	另	另	另	另	另	另	
另	另	另	另	另	另	另	另	另	
另	另	另	另	另	另	另	另	另	
另	另	另	另	另	另	另	另	另	
另	另	另	另	另	另	另	另	另	
另	另	另	另	另	另	另	另	另	

港

gǎng

port

Notes: Common Noun

(港, **gǎng**, **port**, **harbour**)

丶 丶 氵 广 汁 泔 浐 浐 洪 洪 港 港

港 港 港 港 港 港 港 港 港

港	港	港	港	港	港	港	港	港	港
gǎng	gǎng	gǎng	gǎng	gǎng	gǎng	gǎng	gǎng	gǎng	gǎng
port	port	port	port	port	port	port	port	port	port
港	港	港	港	港	港	港	港	港	港
gǎng	gǎng	gǎng	gǎng	gǎng	gǎng	gǎng	gǎng	gǎng	gǎng
port	port	port	port	port	port	port	port	port	port
港	港	港	港	港	港	港	港	港	
港	港	港	港	港	港	港	港	港	
港	港	港	港	港	港	港	港	港	
港	港	港	港	港	港	港	港	港	
港	港	港	港	港	港	港	港	港	
港	港	港	港	港	港	港	港	港	
港	港	港	港	港	港	港	港	港	

势	Notes: Common Noun
	(势, shì, power, force, influence)
shì	
power	

一　十　扌　扌丿　执　执　势　势
丂　势

势　势　势　势　势　势　势　势　势

势	势	势	势	势	势	势	势	势	势
shì	shì	shì	shì	shì	shì	shì	shì	shì	shì
power	power	power	power	power	power	power	power	power	power
势	势	势	势	势	势	势	势	势	势
shì	shì	shì	shì	shì	shì	shì	shì	shì	shì
power	power	power	power	power	power	power	power	power	power
势	势	势	势	势	势	势	势	势	势
势	势	势	势	势	势	势	势	势	势
势	势	势	势	势	势	势	势	势	势
势	势	势	势	势	势	势	势	势	势
势	势	势	势	势	势	势	势	势	势
势	势	势	势	势	势	势	势	势	势
势	势	势	势	势	势	势	势	势	势
势	势	势	势	势	势	势	势	势	势

刻

kè
moment

Notes: Common Noun

(刻, kè, quarter hour, moment)

(刻, kè, set a time)

(刻, kè, carve, engrave, cut)

(刻, kè, edition)

丶 一 亠 亥 亥 亥 刻 刻

刻 刻 刻 刻 刻 刻 刻 刻 刻

刻	刻	刻	刻	刻	刻	刻	刻	刻	刻
kè	kè	kè	kè	kè	kè	kè	kè	kè	kè
moment	moment	moment	moment	moment	moment	moment	moment	moment	moment
刻	刻	刻	刻	刻	刻	刻	刻	刻	刻
kè	kè	kè	kè	kè	kè	kè	kè	kè	kè
moment	moment	moment	moment	moment	moment	moment	moment	moment	moment

星

xīng
star

Notes: Common Noun

(星, xīng, star, heavenly body)

(星, xīng, body, bit, particle)

丨 冂 冃 日 尸 旦 早 星 星

星 星 星 星 星 星 星 星

星	星	星	星	星	星	星	星	星	星
xīng	xīng	xīng	xīng	xīng	xīng	xīng	xīng	xīng	xīng
star	star	star	star	star	star	star	star	star	star
星	星	星	星	星	星	星	星	星	星
xīng	xīng	xīng	xīng	xīng	xīng	xīng	xīng	xīng	xīng
star	star	star	star	star	star	star	star	star	star
星	星	星	星	星	星	星	星	星	星
星	星	星	星	星	星	星	星	星	星
星	星	星	星	星	星	星	星	星	星
星	星	星	星	星	星	星	星	星	星
星	星	星	星	星	星	星	星	星	星
星	星	星	星	星	星	星	星	星	星
星	星	星	星	星	星	星	星	星	星
星	星	星	星	星	星	星	星	星	星

断	Notes: Verb
	(断, duàn, cut off, break)
	(断, duàn, give up)
	(断, duàn, decide)
duàn	(断, duàn, absolutely, decidedly)
break	

丶 丷 丛 半 半 米 迷 迷 断 断 断

断 断 断 断 断 断 断 断 断

断	断	断	断	断	断	断	断	断	断
duàn	duàn	duàn	duàn	duàn	duàn	duàn	duàn	duàn	duàn
break	break	break	break	break	break	break	break	break	break
断	断	断	断	断	断	断	断	断	断
duàn	duàn	duàn	duàn	duàn	duàn	duàn	duàn	duàn	duàn
break	break	break	break	break	break	break	break	break	break

陈		
chén old		

Notes: Adjective

(陈, **chén**, **old, stale, old and mellow**)

(陈, **Chén**, **Chén dynasty 557-589**)

(陈, **chén**, **lay out, put on display**)

(陈, **chén**, **state, explain**)

了 阝 阝 阰 阵 陈 陈

陈 陈 陈 陈 陈 陈 陈 陈 陈

陈	陈	陈	陈	陈	陈	陈	陈	陈	陈
chén old	chén old	chén old	chén old	chén old	chén old	chén old	chén old	chén old	chén old
陈	陈	陈	陈	陈	陈	陈	陈	陈	陈
chén old	chén old	chén old	chén old	chén old	chén old	chén old	chén old	chén old	chén old
陈	陈	陈	陈	陈	陈	陈	陈	陈	陈
陈	陈	陈	陈	陈	陈	陈	陈	陈	陈
陈	陈	陈	陈	陈	陈	陈	陈	陈	陈
陈	陈	陈	陈	陈	陈	陈	陈	陈	陈
陈	陈	陈	陈	陈	陈	陈	陈	陈	陈
陈	陈	陈	陈	陈	陈	陈	陈	陈	陈
陈	陈	陈	陈	陈	陈	陈	陈	陈	陈
陈	陈	陈	陈	陈	陈	陈	陈	陈	陈

掌

zhǎng
palm

Notes: Common Noun

(掌, **zhǎng, palm of the hand, palm**)

丨 丬 丬 丬 丬 丬 丬 当 当 堂 堂 掌

掌 掌 掌 掌 掌 掌 掌 掌 掌

掌	掌	掌	掌	掌	掌	掌	掌	掌	掌
zhǎng	zhǎng	zhǎng	zhǎng	zhǎng	zhǎng	zhǎng	zhǎng	zhǎng	zhǎng
palm	palm	palm	palm	palm	palm	palm	palm	palm	palm
掌	掌	掌	掌	掌	掌	掌	掌	掌	掌
zhǎng	zhǎng	zhǎng	zhǎng	zhǎng	zhǎng	zhǎng	zhǎng	zhǎng	zhǎng
palm	palm	palm	palm	palm	palm	palm	palm	palm	palm
掌	掌	掌	掌	掌	掌	掌	掌	掌	
掌	掌	掌	掌	掌	掌	掌	掌	掌	
掌	掌	掌	掌	掌	掌	掌	掌	掌	
掌	掌	掌	掌	掌	掌	掌	掌	掌	
掌	掌	掌	掌	掌	掌	掌	掌	掌	
掌	掌	掌	掌	掌	掌	掌	掌	掌	
掌	掌	掌	掌	掌	掌	掌	掌	掌	
掌	掌	掌	掌	掌	掌	掌	掌	掌	

农	
nóng	Notes: Common Noun (农, **nóng**, **farmer**, **peasant**) (农, **nóng**, **agriculture**, **farming**)
farmer	

丶 　 亠 　 ナ 　 农 　 农 　 农

农 农 农 农 农 农 农 农 农

农	农	农	农	农	农	农	农	农	农
nóng farmer	nóng farmer	nóng farmer	nóng farmer	nóng farmer	nóng farmer	nóng farmer	nóng farmer	nóng farmer	nóng farmer
农	农	农	农	农	农	农	农	农	农
nóng farmer	nóng farmer	nóng farmer	nóng farmer	nóng farmer	nóng farmer	nóng farmer	nóng farmer	nóng farmer	nóng farmer

夜

yè
night

Notes: Common Noun

(夜, yè, night, evening)

丶 亠 广 广 广 疒 夜 夜 夜

夜 夜 夜 夜 夜 夜 夜 夜 夜

夜	夜	夜	夜	夜	夜	夜	夜	夜	夜
yè	yè	yè	yè	yè	yè	yè	yè	yè	yè
night	night	night	night	night	night	night	night	night	night
夜	夜	夜	夜	夜	夜	夜	夜	夜	夜
yè	yè	yè	yè	yè	yè	yè	yè	yè	yè
night	night	night	night	night	night	night	night	night	night

般

bān

type

Notes: Adjective

(般, bān, type, sort, kind)

(般, pán, happy)

(般, bō, buddhist wisdom)

丿 丆 丬 甪 甪 舟 舟 舟 舟 般 般

般 般 般 般 般 般 般 般 般

般	般	般	般	般	般	般	般	般	般
bān	bān	bān	bān	bān	bān	bān	bān	bān	bān
type	type	type	type	type	type	type	type	type	type
般	般	般	般	般	般	般	般	般	般
bān	bān	bān	bān	bān	bān	bān	bān	bān	bān
type	type	type	type	type	type	type	type	type	type
般	般	般	般	般	般	般	般	般	般
般	般	般	般	般	般	般	般	般	般
般	般	般	般	般	般	般	般	般	般
般	般	般	般	般	般	般	般	般	般
般	般	般	般	般	般	般	般	般	般
般	般	般	般	般	般	般	般	般	般
般	般	般	般	般	般	般	般	般	般
般	般	般	般	般	般	般	般	般	般

念	Notes: Verb
	(念, **niàn**, read aloud)
	(念, **niàn**, think of, miss, ponder)
	(念, **niàn**, study, attend school)
niàn	
miss	

丿 人 人 今 今 念 念 念

念 念 念 念 念 念 念 念 念

念	念	念	念	念	念	念	念	念	念
niàn	niàn	niàn	niàn	niàn	niàn	niàn	niàn	niàn	niàn
miss	miss	miss	miss	miss	miss	miss	miss	miss	miss
念	念	念	念	念	念	念	念	念	念
niàn	niàn	niàn	niàn	niàn	niàn	niàn	niàn	niàn	niàn
miss	miss	miss	miss	miss	miss	miss	miss	miss	miss
念	念	念	念	念	念	念	念	念	
念	念	念	念	念	念	念	念	念	
念	念	念	念	念	念	念	念	念	
念	念	念	念	念	念	念	念	念	
念	念	念	念	念	念	念	念	念	
念	念	念	念	念	念	念	念	念	
念	念	念	念	念	念	念	念	念	
念	念	念	念	念	念	念	念	念	

58

价

jià
price

Notes: Common Noun

(价, **jià**, **price**)

(价, **jiè**, **servant**)

丿 亻 仁 价 价 价

价 价 价 价 价 价 价 价 价

价	价	价	价	价	价	价	价	价	价
jià	jià	jià	jià	jià	jià	jià	jià	jià	jià
price	price	price	price	price	price	price	price	price	price
价	价	价	价	价	价	价	价	价	价
jià	jià	jià	jià	jià	jià	jià	jià	jià	jià
price	price	price	price	price	price	price	price	price	price
价	价	价	价	价	价	价	价	价	价
价	价	价	价	价	价	价	价	价	价
价	价	价	价	价	价	价	价	价	价
价	价	价	价	价	价	价	价	价	价
价	价	价	价	价	价	价	价	价	价
价	价	价	价	价	价	价	价	价	价
价	价	价	价	价	价	价	价	价	价
价	价	价	价	价	价	价	价	价	价

脑	Notes: Common Noun
	(脑, **nǎo**, **brain**)

nǎo
brain

丿 刀 刀 月 月` 肛 肼 脑 脑 脑

脑 脑 脑 脑 脑 脑 脑 脑 脑

脑	脑	脑	脑	脑	脑	脑	脑	脑	脑
nǎo	nǎo	nǎo	nǎo	nǎo	nǎo	nǎo	nǎo	nǎo	nǎo
brain	brain	brain	brain	brain	brain	brain	brain	brain	brain
脑	脑	脑	脑	脑	脑	脑	脑	脑	脑
nǎo	nǎo	nǎo	nǎo	nǎo	nǎo	nǎo	nǎo	nǎo	nǎo
brain	brain	brain	brain	brain	brain	brain	brain	brain	brain

規

guī
dividers

Notes: Common Noun

(规, **guī**, **compasses**, **dividers**)

一　二　丰　夫　邦　扫　规　规

规　规　规　规　规　规　规　规　规

规	规	规	规	规	规	规	规	规	规
guī	guī	guī	guī	guī	guī	guī	guī	guī	guī
dividers	dividers	dividers	dividers	dividers	dividers	dividers	dividers	dividers	dividers
规	规	规	规	规	规	规	规	规	规
guī	guī	guī	guī	guī	guī	guī	guī	guī	guī
dividers	dividers	dividers	dividers	dividers	dividers	dividers	dividers	dividers	dividers
规	规	规	规	规	规	规	规	规	规
规	规	规	规	规	规	规	规	规	规
规	规	规	规	规	规	规	规	规	规
规	规	规	规	规	规	规	规	规	规
规	规	规	规	规	规	规	规	规	规
规	规	规	规	规	规	规	规	规	规
规	规	规	规	规	规	规	规	规	规
规	规	规	规	规	规	规	规	规	规

底	Notes: Common Noun
	(底, **dǐ**, **underside, bottom, base**)
	(底, **dǐ**, **ins and outs**)
	(底, **dǐ**, **rough draft**)
dǐ	(底, **dǐ**, **end**)
bottom	

丶 亠 广 广 庄 庄 底 底

底 底 底 底 底 底 底 底 底

底	底	底	底	底	底	底	底	底	底
dǐ	dǐ	dǐ	dǐ	dǐ	dǐ	dǐ	dǐ	dǐ	dǐ
bottom	bottom	bottom	bottom	bottom	bottom	bottom	bottom	bottom	bottom
底	底	底	底	底	底	底	底	底	底
dǐ	dǐ	dǐ	dǐ	dǐ	dǐ	dǐ	dǐ	dǐ	dǐ
bottom	bottom	bottom	bottom	bottom	bottom	bottom	bottom	bottom	bottom

故	Notes: Common Noun (故, **gù, cause, reason**) (故, **gù, therefore**)
gù	
reason	

一 十 十 古 古 古 故 故 故

故 故 故 故 故 故 故 故 故

故	故	故	故	故	故	故	故	故	故
gù	gù	gù	gù	gù	gù	gù	gù	gù	gù
reason	reason	reason	reason	reason	reason	reason	reason	reason	reason
故	故	故	故	故	故	故	故	故	故
gù	gù	gù	gù	gù	gù	gù	gù	gù	gù
reason	reason	reason	reason	reason	reason	reason	reason	reason	reason
故	故	故	故	故	故	故	故	故	故
故	故	故	故	故	故	故	故	故	故
故	故	故	故	故	故	故	故	故	故
故	故	故	故	故	故	故	故	故	故
故	故	故	故	故	故	故	故	故	故
故	故	故	故	故	故	故	故	故	故
故	故	故	故	故	故	故	故	故	故
故	故	故	故	故	故	故	故	故	故

省

63

Notes: Verb

(省, **shěng**, **save**, **economize**)

(省, **shěng**, **omit**, **leave**)

(省, **shěng**, **province**, **provincial capital**)

(省, **xǐng**, **be introspective**)

shěng

save

丿 丄 亅 少 少 省 省 省 省

省 省 省 省 省 省 省 省 省

省	省	省	省	省	省	省	省	省	省
shěng	shěng	shěng	shěng	shěng	shěng	shěng	shěng	shěng	shěng
save	save	save	save	save	save	save	save	save	save
省	省	省	省	省	省	省	省	省	省
shěng	shěng	shěng	shěng	shěng	shěng	shěng	shěng	shěng	shěng
save	save	save	save	save	save	save	save	save	save
省	省	省	省	省	省	省	省	省	省
省	省	省	省	省	省	省	省	省	省
省	省	省	省	省	省	省	省	省	省
省	省	省	省	省	省	省	省	省	省
省	省	省	省	省	省	省	省	省	省
省	省	省	省	省	省	省	省	省	省
省	省	省	省	省	省	省	省	省	省
省	省	省	省	省	省	省	省	省	省

妈

mā
mother

Notes: Common Noun

(妈, **mā**, **mother**, **mom**)

乙 夕 女 女 妈 妈

妈 妈 妈 妈 妈 妈 妈 妈 妈

妈	妈	妈	妈	妈	妈	妈	妈	妈	妈
mā	mā	mā	mā	mā	mā	mā	mā	mā	mā
mother	mother	mother	mother	mother	mother	mother	mother	mother	mother
妈	妈	妈	妈	妈	妈	妈	妈	妈	妈
mā	mā	mā	mā	mā	mā	mā	mā	mā	mā
mother	mother	mother	mother	mother	mother	mother	mother	mother	mother

妈	妈	妈	妈	妈	妈	妈	妈	妈	妈
妈	妈	妈	妈	妈	妈	妈	妈	妈	妈
妈	妈	妈	妈	妈	妈	妈	妈	妈	妈
妈	妈	妈	妈	妈	妈	妈	妈	妈	妈
妈	妈	妈	妈	妈	妈	妈	妈	妈	妈
妈	妈	妈	妈	妈	妈	妈	妈	妈	妈
妈	妈	妈	妈	妈	妈	妈	妈	妈	妈
妈	妈	妈	妈	妈	妈	妈	妈	妈	妈

刚

gāng
firm

Notes: Adjective

(刚, **gāng**, **firm**)

丨 冂 冈 冈 刚 刚

刚 刚 刚 刚 刚 刚 刚 刚 刚

刚	刚	刚	刚	刚	刚	刚	刚	刚	刚
gāng	gāng	gāng	gāng	gāng	gāng	gāng	gāng	gāng	gāng
firm	firm	firm	firm	firm	firm	firm	firm	firm	firm
刚	刚	刚	刚	刚	刚	刚	刚	刚	刚
gāng	gāng	gāng	gāng	gāng	gāng	gāng	gāng	gāng	gāng
firm	firm	firm	firm	firm	firm	firm	firm	firm	firm
刚	刚	刚	刚	刚	刚	刚	刚	刚	
刚	刚	刚	刚	刚	刚	刚	刚	刚	
刚	刚	刚	刚	刚	刚	刚	刚	刚	
刚	刚	刚	刚	刚	刚	刚	刚	刚	
刚	刚	刚	刚	刚	刚	刚	刚	刚	
刚	刚	刚	刚	刚	刚	刚	刚	刚	
刚	刚	刚	刚	刚	刚	刚	刚	刚	

句

jù

sentence

Notes: Common Noun

(句, **jù**, **sentence**)

丿 勹 勹 句 句

句 句 句 句 句 句 句 句 句

句	句	句	句	句	句	句	句	句	句
jù	jù	jù	jù	jù	jù	jù	jù	jù	jù
sentence	sentence	sentence	sentence	sentence	sentence	sentence	sentence	sentence	sentence
句	句	句	句	句	句	句	句	句	句
jù	jù	jù	jù	jù	jù	jù	jù	jù	jù
sentence	sentence	sentence	sentence	sentence	sentence	sentence	sentence	sentence	sentence
句	句	句	句	句	句	句	句	句	句
句	句	句	句	句	句	句	句	句	句
句	句	句	句	句	句	句	句	句	句
句	句	句	句	句	句	句	句	句	句
句	句	句	句	句	句	句	句	句	句
句	句	句	句	句	句	句	句	句	句
句	句	句	句	句	句	句	句	句	句

显

xiǎn
show

Notes: Verb

(显, **xiǎn**, **appear, be obvious, demonstrate, show, display, appear**)

丨 冂 冃 日 旦 昌 昂 昂 显

显 显 显 显 显 显 显 显 显

显	显	显	显	显	显	显	显	显	显
xiǎn	xiǎn	xiǎn	xiǎn	xiǎn	xiǎn	xiǎn	xiǎn	xiǎn	xiǎn
show	show	show	show	show	show	show	show	show	show
显	显	显	显	显	显	显	显	显	显
xiǎn	xiǎn	xiǎn	xiǎn	xiǎn	xiǎn	xiǎn	xiǎn	xiǎn	xiǎn
show	show	show	show	show	show	show	show	show	show
显	显	显	显	显	显	显	显	显	
显	显	显	显	显	显	显	显	显	
显	显	显	显	显	显	显	显	显	
显	显	显	显	显	显	显	显	显	
显	显	显	显	显	显	显	显	显	
显	显	显	显	显	显	显	显	显	
显	显	显	显	显	显	显	显	显	
显	显	显	显	显	显	显	显	显	

消

xiāo
remove

Notes: Verb

(消, xiāo, disappear, vanish, eliminate, dispel, remove)

、 冫 氵 氵 沪 沪 沪 消 消 消

消 消 消 消 消 消 消 消 消

消	消	消	消	消	消	消	消	消	消
xiāo	xiāo	xiāo	xiāo	xiāo	xiāo	xiāo	xiāo	xiāo	xiāo
remove	remove	remove	remove	remove	remove	remove	remove	remove	remove
消	消	消	消	消	消	消	消	消	消
xiāo	xiāo	xiāo	xiāo	xiāo	xiāo	xiāo	xiāo	xiāo	xiāo
remove	remove	remove	remove	remove	remove	remove	remove	remove	remove

消	消	消	消	消	消	消	消	消	消
消	消	消	消	消	消	消	消	消	消
消	消	消	消	消	消	消	消	消	消
消	消	消	消	消	消	消	消	消	消
消	消	消	消	消	消	消	消	消	消
消	消	消	消	消	消	消	消	消	消
消	消	消	消	消	消	消	消	消	消
消	消	消	消	消	消	消	消	消	消

衣

yī
clothes

Notes: Common Noun

(衣, yī, clothing, clothes, garment)

(衣, yì, wear clothing, give clothing to others to wear)

丶 亠 宀 衣 衣 衣

衣 衣 衣 衣 衣 衣 衣 衣 衣

衣	衣	衣	衣	衣	衣	衣	衣	衣	衣
yī	yī	yī	yī	yī	yī	yī	yī	yī	yī
clothes	clothes	clothes	clothes	clothes	clothes	clothes	clothes	clothes	clothes
衣	衣	衣	衣	衣	衣	衣	衣	衣	衣
yī	yī	yī	yī	yī	yī	yī	yī	yī	yī
clothes	clothes	clothes	clothes	clothes	clothes	clothes	clothes	clothes	clothes
衣	衣	衣	衣	衣	衣	衣	衣	衣	衣
衣	衣	衣	衣	衣	衣	衣	衣	衣	衣
衣	衣	衣	衣	衣	衣	衣	衣	衣	衣
衣	衣	衣	衣	衣	衣	衣	衣	衣	衣
衣	衣	衣	衣	衣	衣	衣	衣	衣	衣
衣	衣	衣	衣	衣	衣	衣	衣	衣	衣
衣	衣	衣	衣	衣	衣	衣	衣	衣	衣

陆	Notes: Common Noun
	(陆, lù, land)
	(陆, liù, six)
	(陆, Lù, surname Lù)
lù	
land	

3 阝 阝¯ 阝= 阡 陆 陆

陆 陆 陆 陆 陆 陆 陆 陆 陆

陆	陆	陆	陆	陆	陆	陆	陆	陆	陆
lù	lù	lù	lù	lù	lù	lù	lù	lù	lù
land	land	land	land	land	land	land	land	land	land
陆	陆	陆	陆	陆	陆	陆	陆	陆	陆
lù	lù	lù	lù	lù	lù	lù	lù	lù	lù
land	land	land	land	land	land	land	land	land	land

陆	陆	陆	陆	陆	陆	陆	陆	陆	陆
陆	陆	陆	陆	陆	陆	陆	陆	陆	陆
陆	陆	陆	陆	陆	陆	陆	陆	陆	陆
陆	陆	陆	陆	陆	陆	陆	陆	陆	陆
陆	陆	陆	陆	陆	陆	陆	陆	陆	陆
陆	陆	陆	陆	陆	陆	陆	陆	陆	陆
陆	陆	陆	陆	陆	陆	陆	陆	陆	陆
陆	陆	陆	陆	陆	陆	陆	陆	陆	陆

器

qì
vessel

Notes: Common Noun

(器, qì, vessel, utensil, ware)

丨 丨卜 日 日卜 日卜卜 日日 吅 罒 哭 哭 哭 哭 哭 器 器

器 器 器 器 器 器 器 器 器

器	器	器	器	器	器	器	器	器	器
qì	qì	qì	qì	qì	qì	qì	qì	qì	qì
vessel	vessel	vessel	vessel	vessel	vessel	vessel	vessel	vessel	vessel

器	器	器	器	器	器	器	器	器	器
qì	qì	qì	qì	qì	qì	qì	qì	qì	qì
vessel	vessel	vessel	vessel	vessel	vessel	vessel	vessel	vessel	vessel

器	器	器	器	器	器	器	器	器	器
器	器	器	器	器	器	器	器	器	器
器	器	器	器	器	器	器	器	器	器
器	器	器	器	器	器	器	器	器	器
器	器	器	器	器	器	器	器	器	器
器	器	器	器	器	器	器	器	器	
器	器	器	器	器	器	器	器	器	
器	器	器	器	器	器	器	器	器	

确

què
true

Notes: Adjective

(确, què, true, reliable, authentic)

一 厂 厂 石 石 石 矿 矿 矿 矿 矿 确 确

确 确 确 确 确 确 确 确 确

确	确	确	确	确	确	确	确	确	确
què true	què true	què true	què true	què true	què true	què true	què true	què true	què true
确	确	确	确	确	确	确	确	确	确
què true	què true	què true	què true	què true	què true	què true	què true	què true	què true
确	确	确	确	确	确	确	确	确	确
确	确	确	确	确	确	确	确	确	确
确	确	确	确	确	确	确	确	确	确
确	确	确	确	确	确	确	确	确	确
确	确	确	确	确	确	确	确	确	确
确	确	确	确	确	确	确	确	确	确
确	确	确	确	确	确	确	确	确	确
确	确	确	确	确	确	确	确	确	确

破

pò
broken

Notes: Adjective

(破, pò, broken, damaged, torn, run-down, inferior, poor)

(破, pò, smash, break, cleave, cut)

(破, pò, reveal the truth, expose a lie)

一 厂 丆 石 石 矿 矿 矿 砕 破

破 破 破 破 破 破 破 破 破

破	破	破	破	破	破	破	破	破	破
pò	pò	pò	pò	pò	pò	pò	pò	pò	pò
broken	broken	broken	broken	broken	broken	broken	broken	broken	broken
破	破	破	破	破	破	破	破	破	破
pò	pò	pò	pò	pò	pò	pò	pò	pò	pò
broken	broken	broken	broken	broken	broken	broken	broken	broken	broken

破	破	破	破	破	破	破	破	破	破
破	破	破	破	破	破	破	破	破	破
破	破	破	破	破	破	破	破	破	破
破	破	破	破	破	破	破	破	破	破
破	破	破	破	破	破	破	破	破	破
破	破	破	破	破	破	破	破	破	破
破	破	破	破	破	破	破	破	破	破
破	破	破	破	破	破	破	破	破	破

具

jù

tool

Notes: Common Noun

(具, **jù, utensil, tool, implement**)

丨 冂 冂 目 目 且 具 具

具 具 具 具 具 具 具 具 具

具	具	具	具	具	具	具	具	具	具
jù	jù	jù	jù	jù	jù	jù	jù	jù	jù
tool	tool	tool	tool	tool	tool	tool	tool	tool	tool
具	具	具	具	具	具	具	具	具	具
jù	jù	jù	jù	jù	jù	jù	jù	jù	jù
tool	tool	tool	tool	tool	tool	tool	tool	tool	tool
具	具	具	具	具	具	具	具	具	具
具	具	具	具	具	具	具	具	具	具
具	具	具	具	具	具	具	具	具	具
具	具	具	具	具	具	具	具	具	具
具	具	具	具	具	具	具	具	具	具
具	具	具	具	具	具	具	具	具	具
具	具	具	具	具	具	具	具	具	具
具	具	具	具	具	具	具	具	具	具

居

jū
reside

Notes: Verb

(居, **jū, reside, dwell, live,occupy a position or place**)

(居, **jū, claim, assert**)

(居, **jū, store up, lay by, stay put, be at a standstill**)

(居, **Jū, surname Jū**)

コ ユ 尸 尸 尸 尸 居 居

居 居 居 居 居 居 居 居

居	居	居	居	居	居	居	居	居	居
jū	jū	jū	jū	jū	jū	jū	jū	jū	jū
reside	reside	reside	reside	reside	reside	reside	reside	reside	reside
居	居	居	居	居	居	居	居	居	居
jū	jū	jū	jū	jū	jū	jū	jū	jū	jū
reside	reside	reside	reside	reside	reside	reside	reside	reside	reside

居	居	居	居	居	居	居	居	居	居
居	居	居	居	居	居	居	居	居	居
居	居	居	居	居	居	居	居	居	居
居	居	居	居	居	居	居	居	居	居
居	居	居	居	居	居	居	居	居	居
居	居	居	居	居	居	居	居	居	居
居	居	居	居	居	居	居	居	居	居
居	居	居	居	居	居	居	居	居	居

批	Notes: Grammatical Particle
	(批, pī, classifier for a batch or lot)
	(批, pī, batch, lot, group)
	(批, pī, slap somebodie's face)
pī batch	(批, pī, write comments on document, comment, criticize, refute)

一　丁　扌　扌　批　批′　批

批　批　批　批　批　批　批　批　批

批	批	批	批	批	批	批	批	批	批
pī	pī	pī	pī	pī	pī	pī	pī	pī	pī
batch	batch	batch	batch	batch	batch	batch	batch	batch	batch
批	批	批	批	批	批	批	批	批	批
pī	pī	pī	pī	pī	pī	pī	pī	pī	pī
batch	batch	batch	batch	batch	batch	batch	batch	batch	batch
批	批	批	批	批	批	批	批	批	批
批	批	批	批	批	批	批	批	批	批
批	批	批	批	批	批	批	批	批	批
批	批	批	批	批	批	批	批	批	批
批	批	批	批	批	批	批	批	批	批
批	批	批	批	批	批	批	批	批	批
批	批	批	批	批	批	批	批	批	批
批	批	批	批	批	批	批	批	批	批

送

sòng
deliver

Notes: Verb

(送, **sòng**, **see somebody off**, **deliver**, **give**)

(送, **sòng**, **carry**)

(送, **sòng**, **give as a present**)

丶 丷 丷 ⺍ 兰 关 关 送 送 送

送 送 送 送 送 送 送 送 送

送	送	送	送	送	送	送	送	送	送
sòng	sòng	sòng	sòng	sòng	sòng	sòng	sòng	sòng	sòng
deliver	deliver	deliver	deliver	deliver	deliver	deliver	deliver	deliver	deliver
送	送	送	送	送	送	送	送	送	送
sòng	sòng	sòng	sòng	sòng	sòng	sòng	sòng	sòng	sòng
deliver	deliver	deliver	deliver	deliver	deliver	deliver	deliver	deliver	deliver
送	送	送	送	送	送	送	送		
送	送	送	送	送	送	送	送		
送	送	送	送	送	送	送	送		
送	送	送	送	送	送	送	送		
送	送	送	送	送	送	送	送		
送	送	送	送	送	送	送	送		
送	送	送	送	送	送	送	送		
送	送	送	送	送	送	送	送		

泽 zé marsh	Notes: Common Noun (泽, **zé**, **marsh**, **swamp**)

丶 丶 氵 沪 沪 泽 泽 泽

泽 泽 泽 泽 泽 泽 泽 泽 泽

泽	泽	泽	泽	泽	泽	泽	泽	泽	泽
zé	zé	zé	zé	zé	zé	zé	zé	zé	zé
marsh	marsh	marsh	marsh	marsh	marsh	marsh	marsh	marsh	marsh
泽	泽	泽	泽	泽	泽	泽	泽	泽	泽
zé	zé	zé	zé	zé	zé	zé	zé	zé	zé
marsh	marsh	marsh	marsh	marsh	marsh	marsh	marsh	marsh	marsh

紧

jǐn

urgent

Notes: Adjective

(紧, jǐn, tight, taut)

(紧, jǐn, close at hand)

(紧, jǐn, urgent, tense)

(紧, jǐn, strict, stringent)

(紧, jǐn, hard up)

丨 刂 刂⁷ 刂又 刂又 刂又 刂又 刂又 刂又 刂又

紧 紧 紧 紧 紧 紧 紧 紧 紧

紧	紧	紧	紧	紧	紧	紧	紧	紧	紧
jǐn	jǐn	jǐn	jǐn	jǐn	jǐn	jǐn	jǐn	jǐn	jǐn
urgent	urgent	urgent	urgent	urgent	urgent	urgent	urgent	urgent.	urgent
紧	紧	紧	紧	紧	紧	紧	紧	紧	紧
jǐn	jǐn	jǐn	jǐn	jǐn	jǐn	jǐn	jǐn	jǐn	jǐn
urgent	urgent	urgent	urgent	urgent	urgent	urgent	urgent	urgent	urgent
紧	紧	紧	紧	紧	紧	紧	紧	紧	
紧	紧	紧	紧	紧	紧	紧	紧	紧	
紧	紧	紧	紧	紧	紧	紧	紧	紧	
紧	紧	紧	紧	紧	紧	紧	紧	紧	
紧	紧	紧	紧	紧	紧	紧	紧	紧	
紧	紧	紧	紧	紧	紧	紧	紧	紧	
紧	紧	紧	紧	紧	紧	紧	紧	紧	
紧	紧	紧	紧	紧	紧	紧	紧	紧	

帮	Notes: Verb (帮, **bāng, help, assist**)
bāng	
help	

一　⺊　⺕　尹　邦　邦　邦　帮　帮

帮　帮　帮　帮　帮　帮　帮　帮　帮

帮	帮	帮	帮	帮	帮	帮	帮	帮	帮
bāng	bāng	bāng	bāng	bāng	bāng	bāng	bāng	bāng	bāng
help	help	help	help	help	help	help	help	help	help
帮	帮	帮	帮	帮	帮	帮	帮	帮	帮
bāng	bāng	bāng	bāng	bāng	bāng	bāng	bāng	bāng	bāng
help	help	help	help	help	help	help	help	help	help

帮	帮	帮	帮	帮	帮	帮	帮	帮	帮
帮	帮	帮	帮	帮	帮	帮	帮	帮	帮
帮	帮	帮	帮	帮	帮	帮	帮	帮	帮
帮	帮	帮	帮	帮	帮	帮	帮	帮	帮
帮	帮	帮	帮	帮	帮	帮	帮	帮	帮
帮	帮	帮	帮	帮	帮	帮	帮	帮	帮
帮	帮	帮	帮	帮	帮	帮	帮	帮	帮
帮	帮	帮	帮	帮	帮	帮	帮	帮	帮

线

xiàn
line

Notes: Common Noun

(线, **xiàn**, **line**, **thread**, **string**, **wire**)

(线, **xiàn**, **route**, **line**, **demarcation line**, **boundary**)

(线, **xiàn**, **brink**, **verge**)

丨 𠄌 纟 纟 纟 纟 线 线 线

线 线 线 线 线 线 线 线 线

线	线	线	线	线	线	线	线	线	线
xiàn line	xiàn line	xiàn line	xiàn line	xiàn line	xiàn line	xiàn line	xiàn line	xiàn line	xiàn line
线	线	线	线	线	线	线	线	线	线
xiàn line	xiàn line	xiàn line	xiàn line	xiàn line	xiàn line	xiàn line	xiàn line	xiàn line	xiàn line
线	线	线	线	线	线	线	线		
线	线	线	线	线	线	线	线		
线	线	线	线	线	线	线	线		
线	线	线	线	线	线	线	线		
线	线	线	线	线	线	线	线		
线	线	线	线	线	线	线	线		
线	线	线	线	线	线	线	线		
线	线	线	线	线	线	线	线		

存

xiàn
line

Notes: Verb

(存, **cún**, **store, keep, preserve**)

(存, **cún**, **accumulate, collect, gather**)

(存, **cún**, **deposit money**) |

(存, **cún**, **reserve, retain, remain on balance, be in stock**)

一 ナ 𠂇 存 存 存

存 存 存 存 存 存 存 存 存

存	存	存	存	存	存	存	存	存	存
xiàn	xiàn	xiàn	xiàn	xiàn	xiàn	xiàn	xiàn	xiàn	xiàn
line	line	line	line	line	line	line	line	line	line
存	存	存	存	存	存	存	存	存	存
xiàn	xiàn	xiàn	xiàn	xiàn	xiàn	xiàn	xiàn	xiàn	xiàn
line	line	line	line	line	line	line	line	line	line
存	存	存	存	存	存	存	存	存	存
存	存	存	存	存	存	存	存	存	存
存	存	存	存	存	存	存	存	存	存
存	存	存	存	存	存	存	存	存	存
存	存	存	存	存	存	存	存	存	存
存	存	存	存	存	存	存	存	存	存
存	存	存	存	存	存	存	存	存	存

愿

Notes: Verb

(愿, **yuàn**, **wish**, **desire**)

(愿, **yuàn**, **willing to**, **want to**)

yuàn
wish

一 厂 厂 厂 厂 厍 庐 庐 原 原 原 原 原 愿 愿 愿

愿 愿 愿 愿 愿 愿 愿 愿 愿

愿	愿	愿	愿	愿	愿	愿	愿	愿	愿
yuàn	yuàn	yuàn	yuàn	yuàn	yuàn	yuàn	yuàn	yuàn	yuàn
wish	wish	wish	wish	wish	wish	wish	wish	wish	wish
愿	愿	愿	愿	愿	愿	愿	愿	愿	愿
yuàn	yuàn	yuàn	yuàn	yuàn	yuàn	yuàn	yuàn	yuàn	yuàn
wish	wish	wish	wish	wish	wish	wish	wish	wish	wish
愿	愿	愿	愿	愿	愿	愿	愿	愿	
愿	愿	愿	愿	愿	愿	愿	愿	愿	
愿	愿	愿	愿	愿	愿	愿	愿	愿	
愿	愿	愿	愿	愿	愿	愿	愿	愿	
愿	愿	愿	愿	愿	愿	愿	愿	愿	
愿	愿	愿	愿	愿	愿	愿	愿	愿	
愿	愿	愿	愿	愿	愿	愿	愿	愿	
愿	愿	愿	愿	愿	愿	愿	愿	愿	

	Notes: Adjective
奇 qí rare	(奇, **qí, marvellous, rare, strange, queer**) (奇, **jī, odd, not even**)

一　ナ　大　大　奄　奋　奇　奇

奇　奇　奇　奇　奇　奇　奇　奇　奇

奇	奇	奇	奇	奇	奇	奇	奇	奇	奇
qí	qí	qí	qí	qí	qí	qí	qí	qí	qí
rare	rare	rare	rare	rare	rare	rare	rare	rare	rare
奇	奇	奇	奇	奇	奇	奇	奇	奇	奇
qí	qí	qí	qí	qí	qí	qí	qí	qí	qí
rare	rare	rare	rare	rare	rare	rare	rare	rare	rare

奇	奇	奇	奇	奇	奇	奇	奇	奇	奇
奇	奇	奇	奇	奇	奇	奇	奇	奇	奇
奇	奇	奇	奇	奇	奇	奇	奇	奇	奇
奇	奇	奇	奇	奇	奇	奇	奇	奇	奇
奇	奇	奇	奇	奇	奇	奇	奇	奇	奇
奇	奇	奇	奇	奇	奇	奇	奇	奇	奇
奇	奇	奇	奇	奇	奇	奇	奇	奇	奇
奇	奇	奇	奇	奇	奇	奇	奇	奇	奇

害 hài injure	Notes: Verb (害, **hài**, **harm, injure, cause trouble**) (害, **hài**, **disaster, evil**) (害, **hài**, **harmful**) (害, **hài**, **kill**) (害, **hài**, **contract an illness**)

丶 宀 宀 宀 宇 宇 宇 害 害 害

害 害 害 害 害 害 害 害 害

害	害	害	害	害	害	害	害	害	害
hài injure	hài injure	hài injure	hài injure	hài injure	hài injure	hài injure	hài injure	hài injure	hài injure
害	害	害	害	害	害	害	害	害	害
hài injure	hài injure	hài injure	hài injure	hài injure	hài injure	hài injure	hài injure	hài injure	hài injure
害	害	害	害	害	害	害	害	害	害
害	害	害	害	害	害	害	害	害	害
害	害	害	害	害	害	害	害	害	害
害	害	害	害	害	害	害	害	害	害
害	害	害	害	害	害	害	害	害	害
害	害	害	害	害	害	害	害	害	害
害	害	害	害	害	害	害	害	害	害
害	害	害	害	害	害	害	害	害	害

增				
zēng				
zēng				

Notes: Verb

(增, zēng, increase, gain, add)

一 十 土 圵 圹 圹 圹 圹 圹 堆 堆 增 增 增

增 增 增 增 增 增 增 增

增	增	增	增	增	增	增	增	增	增
zēng	zēng	zēng	zēng	zēng	zēng	zēng	zēng	zēng	zēng
liào	liào	liào	liào	liào	liào	liào	liào	liào	liào

增	增	增	增	增	增	增	增	增	增
zēng	zēng	zēng	zēng	zēng	zēng	zēng	zēng	zēng	zēng
liào	liào	liào	liào	liào	liào	liào	liào	liào	liào

增 増 增 增 增 增 增 增 增 增

増 増 増 増 増 増 増 増 増 増

增 増 増 増 増 増 増 増 増 増

增 増 増 増 増 増 増 増 増 増

增 増 増 増 増 増 増 増 増 増

增 増 増 増 増 増 増 増 増 増

增 増 増 増 増 増 増 増 増 増

杨

Notes: Common Noun

(杨, **yáng**, **poplar tree**)

(杨, **Yáng**,**surname Yáng**)

yáng
poplar

一 十 才 才 朾 杨 杨 杨

杨 杨 杨 杨 杨 杨 杨 杨 杨

杨	杨	杨	杨	杨	杨	杨	杨	杨	杨
yáng	yáng	yáng	yáng	yáng	yáng	yáng	yáng	yáng	yáng
poplar	poplar	poplar	poplar	poplar	poplar	poplar	poplar	poplar	poplar
杨	杨	杨	杨	杨	杨	杨	杨	杨	杨
yáng	yáng	yáng	yáng	yáng	yáng	yáng	yáng	yáng	yáng
poplar	poplar	poplar	poplar	poplar	poplar	poplar	poplar	poplar	poplar
杨	杨	杨	杨	杨	杨	杨	杨	杨	杨
杨	杨	杨	杨	杨	杨	杨	杨	杨	杨
杨	杨	杨	杨	杨	杨	杨	杨	杨	杨
杨	杨	杨	杨	杨	杨	杨	杨	杨	杨
杨	杨	杨	杨	杨	杨	杨	杨	杨	杨
杨	杨	杨	杨	杨	杨	杨	杨	杨	杨
杨	杨	杨	杨	杨	杨	杨	杨	杨	杨
杨	杨	杨	杨	杨	杨	杨	杨	杨	杨

料

liào
expect

Notes: Verb

(料, liào, expect, anticipate, infer, foresee, consider)

(料, liào, calculate)

(料, liào, material)

丶 丷 丷 半 半 米 米 料 料 料

料 料 料 料 料 料 料 料 料

料	料	料	料	料	料	料	料	料	料
liào	liào	liào	liào	liào	liào	liào	liào	liào	liào
expect	expect	expect	expect	expect	expect	expect	expect	expect	expect
料	料	料	料	料	料	料	料	料	料
liào	liào	liào	liào	liào	liào	liào	liào	liào	liào
expect	expect	expect	expect	expect	expect	expect	expect	expect	expect
料	料	料	料	料	料	料	料	料	料
料	料	料	料	料	料	料	料	料	料
料	料	料	料	料	料	料	料	料	料
料	料	料	料	料	料	料	料	料	料
料	料	料	料	料	料	料	料	料	料
料	料	料	料	料	料	料	料	料	料
料	料	料	料	料	料	料	料	料	料
料	料	料	料	料	料	料	料	料	料

州

zhōu

prefect

Notes: Common Noun

(州, **zhōu**, **prefecture**, **prefect**, **administrative division**)

(州, **Zhōu**, **Zhōu**) forms part of a destination name.

丶　丿　少　州　州　州

州　州　州　州　州　州　州　州　州

州	州	州	州	州	州	州	州	州	州
zhōu	zhōu	zhōu	zhōu	zhōu	zhōu	zhōu	zhōu	zhōu	zhōu
prefect	prefect	prefect	prefect	prefect	prefect	prefect	prefect	prefect	prefect
州	州	州	州	州	州	州	州	州	州
zhōu	zhōu	zhōu	zhōu	zhōu	zhōu	zhōu	zhōu	zhōu	zhōu
prefect	prefect	prefect	prefect	prefect	prefect	prefect	prefect	prefect	prefect
州	州	州	州	州	州	州	州	州	州
州	州	州	州	州	州	州	州	州	州
州	州	州	州	州	州	州	州	州	州
州	州	州	州	州	州	州	州	州	州
州	州	州	州	州	州	州	州	州	州
州	州	州	州	州	州	州	州	州	州
州	州	州	州	州	州	州	州	州	州
州	州	州	州	州	州	州	州	州	州

节	Notes: Common Noun
jié	(节, **jié, joint, node, knot segment, part**)
part	(节, **jié, festival, holiday**)

一 十 艹 芐 节 节

节 节 节 节 节 节 节 节 节

节	节	节	节	节	节	节	节	节	节
jié	jié	jié	jié	jié	jié	jié	jié	jié	jié
part	part	part	part	part	part	part	part	part	part
节	节	节	节	节	节	节	节	节	节
jié	jié	jié	jié	jié	jié	jié	jié	jié	jié
part	part	part	part	part	part	part	part	part	part
节	节	节	节	节	节	节	节	节	节
节	节	节	节	节	节	节	节	节	节
节	节	节	节	节	节	节	节	节	节
节	节	节	节	节	节	节	节	节	节
节	节	节	节	节	节	节	节	节	节
节	节	节	节	节	节	节	节	节	节
节	节	节	节	节	节	节	节	节	节
节	节	节	节	节	节	节	节	节	节

左

zuǒ
left

Notes: Adjective

(左, **zuǒ**, **left**)

(左, **Zuǒ**, **surname Zuǒ**)

一 ナ 左 左 左

左 左 左 左 左 左 左 左 左

左	左	左	左	左	左	左	左	左	左
zuǒ	zuǒ	zuǒ	zuǒ	zuǒ	zuǒ	zuǒ	zuǒ	zuǒ	zuǒ
left	left	left	left	left	left	left	left	left	left
左	左	左	左	左	左	左	左	左	左
zuǒ	zuǒ	zuǒ	zuǒ	zuǒ	zuǒ	zuǒ	zuǒ	zuǒ	zuǒ
left	left	left	left	left	left	left	left	left	left
左	左	左	左	左	左	左	左	左	左
左	左	左	左	左	左	左	左	左	左
左	左	左	左	左	左	左	左	左	左
左	左	左	左	左	左	左	左	左	左
左	左	左	左	左	左	左	左	左	左
左	左	左	左	左	左	左	左	左	左
左	左	左	左	左	左	左	左	左	左
左	左	左	左	左	左	左	左	左	左

装

zhuāng
install

Notes: Verb

(装, **zhuāng, load, install**)

(装, **zhuāng, play the part of, act, dress up, pretend, feign**)

(装, **zhuāng, fit, assemble**)

(装, **zhuāng, load, pack, hold**)

丶　丷　丬　扌　十　卄　壮　壯　奘　奘　奘　装　装

装　装　装　装　装　装　装　装　装

装	装	装	装	装	装	装	装	装	装
zhuāng	zhuāng	zhuāng	zhuāng	zhuāng	zhuāng	zhuāng	zhuāng	zhuāng	zhuāng
install	install	install	install	install	install	install	install	install	install
装	装	装	装	装	装	装	装	装	装
zhuāng	zhuāng	zhuāng	zhuāng	zhuāng	zhuāng	zhuāng	zhuāng	zhuāng	zhuāng
install	install	install	install	install	install	install	install	install	install
装	装	装	装	装	装	装	装	装	装
装	装	装	装	装	装	装	装	装	装
装	装	装	装	装	装	装	装	装	装
装	装	装	装	装	装	装	装	装	装
装	装	装	装	装	装	装	装	装	装
装	装	装	装	装	装	装	装	装	装
装	装	装	装	装	装	装	装	装	装

易

yì

change

Notes: Verb

(易, yì, change)

(易, yì, easy)

(易, Yì, surname Yì)

丨 冂 冃 日 무 男 易 易

易 易 易 易 易 易 易 易 易

易	易	易	易	易	易	易	易	易	易
yì	yì	yì	yì	yì	yì	yì	yì	yì	yì
change	change	change	change	change	change	change	change	change	change
易	易	易	易	易	易	易	易	易	易
yì	yì	yì	yì	yì	yì	yì	yì	yì	yì
change	change	change	change	change	change	change	change	change	change
易	易	易	易	易	易	易	易	易	易
易	易	易	易	易	易	易	易	易	易
易	易	易	易	易	易	易	易	易	易
易	易	易	易	易	易	易	易	易	易
易	易	易	易	易	易	易	易	易	易
易	易	易	易	易	易	易	易	易	易
易	易	易	易	易	易	易	易	易	易
易	易	易	易	易	易	易	易	易	易

著

zhe

change

Notes: Grammatical Particle

(著, zhe, particle indicating continuing progressive state)

(著, zhù, write, book, show, manifest, prove)

(著, zháo, touch, come in contact with)

(著, zhuó, to put on clothes)

(著, zhāo, measure word, for tricks, devices, moves in chess)

一 十 丑 丑 芏 芏 芋 芋 著 著 著

著 著 著 著 著 著 著 著 著

著	著	著	著	著	著	著	著	著	著
zhe	zhe	zhe	zhe	zhe	zhe	zhe	zhe	zhe	zhe
change	change	change	change	change	change	change	change	change	change
著	著	著	著	著	著	著	著	著	著
zhe	zhe	zhe	zhe	zhe	zhe	zhe	zhe	zhe	zhe
change	change	change	change	change	change	change	change	change	change
著	著	著	著	著	著	著	著	著	著
著	著	著	著	著	著	著	著	著	著
著	著	著	著	著	著	著	著	著	著
著	著	著	著	著	著	著	著	著	著
著	著	著	著	著	著	著	著	著	著
著	著	著	著	著	著	著	著	著	著
著	著	著	著	著	著	著	著	著	著
著	著	著	著	著	著	著	著	著	著

急
jí
urgent

Notes: Adjective

(急, **jí**, **urgent**)

(急, **jí**, **impatient, anxious, irritated, annoyed**)

(急, **jí**, **rapid, fast, violent**)

ノ ア 亇 刍 刍 刍 刍 急 急 急

急 急 急 急 急 急 急 急 急

急	急	急	急	急	急	急	急	急	急
jí	jí	jí	jí	jí	jí	jí	jí	jí	jí
urgent	urgent	urgent	urgent	urgent	urgent	urgent	urgent	urgent	urgent
急	急	急	急	急	急	急	急	急	急
jí	jí	jí	jí	jí	jí	jí	jí	jí	jí
urgent	urgent	urgent	urgent	urgent	urgent	urgent	urgent	urgent	urgent
急	急	急	急	急	急	急	急	急	
急	急	急	急	急	急	急	急	急	
急	急	急	急	急	急	急	急	急	
急	急	急	急	急	急	急	急	急	
急	急	急	急	急	急	急	急	急	
急	急	急	急	急	急	急	急	急	
急	急	急	急	急	急	急	急	急	
急	急	急	急	急	急	急	急	急	

久

jiǔ

long time

Notes: Adverb

(久, **jiǔ**, **for a long time**, **long time**)

ノ ク 久

久 久 久 久 久 久 久 久 久

久	久	久	久	久	久	久	久	久	久
jiǔ	jiǔ	jiǔ	jiǔ	jiǔ	jiǔ	jiǔ	jiǔ	jiǔ	jiǔ
long time	long time	long time	long time	long time	long time	long time	long time	long time	long time
久	久	久	久	久	久	久	久	久	久
jiǔ	jiǔ	jiǔ	jiǔ	jiǔ	jiǔ	jiǔ	jiǔ	jiǔ	jiǔ
long time	long time	long time	long time	long time	long time	long time	long time	long time	long time
久	久	久	久	久	久	久	久	久	久
久	久	久	久	久	久	久	久	久	久
久	久	久	久	久	久	久	久	久	久
久	久	久	久	久	久	久	久	久	久
久	久	久	久	久	久	久	久	久	
久	久	久	久	久	久	久	久	久	
久	久	久	久	久	久	久	久	久	
久	久	久	久	久	久	久	久	久	

低

dī
lower

Notes: Verb

(低, **dī**, **let droop, hang down, lower**)

(低, **dī**, **low**)

丿 亻 仁 仾 低 低 低

低 低 低 低 低 低 低 低 低

低	低	低	低	低	低	低	低	低	低
dī	dī	dī	dī	dī	dī	dī	dī	dī	dī
lower	lower	lower	lower	lower	lower	lower	lower	lower	lower
低	低	低	低	低	低	低	低	低	低
dī	dī	dī	dī	dī	dī	dī	dī	dī	dī
lower	lower	lower	lower	lower	lower	lower	lower	lower	lower

低	低	低	低	低	低	低	低	低	低
低	低	低	低	低	低	低	低	低	低
低	低	低	低	低	低	低	低	低	低
低	低	低	低	低	低	低	低	低	低
低	低	低	低	低	低	低	低	低	低
低	低	低	低	低	低	低	低	低	低
低	低	低	低	低	低	低	低	低	低
低	低	低	低	低	低	低	低	低	低

岁

suì

years

Notes: Common Noun

(岁, suì, years old)

丨 屵 山 屵 岁 岁

岁 岁 岁 岁 岁 岁 岁 岁 岁

岁	岁	岁	岁	岁	岁	岁	岁	岁	岁
suì	suì	suì	suì	suì	suì	suì	suì	suì	suì
years	years	years	years	years	years	years	years	years	years
岁	岁	岁	岁	岁	岁	岁	岁	岁	岁
suì	suì	suì	suì	suì	suì	suì	suì	suì	suì
years	years	years	years	years	years	years	years	years	years

岁	岁	岁	岁	岁	岁	岁	岁	岁	
岁	岁	岁	岁	岁	岁	岁	岁	岁	
岁	岁	岁	岁	岁	岁	岁	岁	岁	
岁	岁	岁	岁	岁	岁	岁	岁	岁	
岁	岁	岁	岁	岁	岁	岁	岁	岁	
岁	岁	岁	岁	岁	岁	岁	岁	岁	
岁	岁	岁	岁	岁	岁	岁	岁	岁	
岁	岁	岁	岁	岁	岁	岁	岁	岁	

需	Notes: Verb
	(需, xū, to require, to need, to want, necessity, need)
xū	
need	

一 厂 户 币 币 雨 雨 雨 雷 雷 雪 雪 需 需

需 需 需 需 需 需 需 需 需

需	需	需	需	需	需	需	需	需	需
xū	xū	xū	xū	xū	xū	xū	xū	xū	xū
need	need	need	need	need	need	need	need	need	need
需	需	需	需	需	需	需	需	需	需
xū	xū	xū	xū	xū	xū	xū	xū	xū	xū
need	need	need	need	need	need	need	need	need	need

需	需	需	需	需	需	需	需	需	
需	需	需	需	需	需	需	需	需	
需	需	需	需	需	需	需	需	需	
需	需	需	需	需	需	需	需	需	
需	需	需	需	需	需	需	需	需	
需	需	需	需	需	需	需	需	需	
需	需	需	需	需	需	需	需	需	
需	需	需	需	需	需	需	需	需	

酒

Notes: Common Noun

(酒, **jiǔ**, **wine, liquor, spirits, alcohol**)

jiǔ
alcohol

丶 丶 氵 汀 汀 沔 洒 洒 酒

酒 酒 酒 酒 酒 酒 酒 酒 酒

酒	酒	酒	酒	酒	酒	酒	酒	酒	酒
jiǔ	jiǔ	jiǔ	jiǔ	jiǔ	jiǔ	jiǔ	jiǔ	jiǔ	jiǔ
alcohol	alcohol	alcohol	alcohol	alcohol	alcohol	alcohol	alcohol	alcohol	alcohol
酒	酒	酒	酒	酒	酒	酒	酒	酒	酒
jiǔ	jiǔ	jiǔ	jiǔ	jiǔ	jiǔ	jiǔ	jiǔ	jiǔ	jiǔ
alcohol	alcohol	alcohol	alcohol	alcohol	alcohol	alcohol	alcohol	alcohol	alcohol
酒	酒	酒	酒	酒	酒	酒	酒	酒	酒
酒	酒	酒	酒	酒	酒	酒	酒	酒	酒
酒	酒	酒	酒	酒	酒	酒	酒	酒	酒
酒	酒	酒	酒	酒	酒	酒	酒	酒	酒
酒	酒	酒	酒	酒	酒	酒	酒	酒	酒
酒	酒	酒	酒	酒	酒	酒	酒	酒	酒
酒	酒	酒	酒	酒	酒	酒	酒	酒	酒
酒	酒	酒	酒	酒	酒	酒	酒	酒	酒

河

hé
river

Notes: Common Noun

(河, **hé**, **river**)

丶 丶 氵 厂 厂 沂 河 河

河 河 河 河 河 河 河 河 河

河	河	河	河	河	河	河	河	河	河
hé	hé	hé	hé	hé	hé	hé	hé	hé	hé
river	river	river	river	river	river	river	river	river	river
河	河	河	河	河	河	河	河	河	河
hé	hé	hé	hé	hé	hé	hé	hé	hé	hé
river	river	river	river	river	river	river	river	river	river

河	河	河	河	河	河	河	河	河	河
河	河	河	河	河	河	河	河	河	河
河	河	河	河	河	河	河	河	河	河
河	河	河	河	河	河	河	河	河	河
河	河	河	河	河	河	河	河	河	河
河	河	河	河	河	河	河	河	河	河
河	河	河	河	河	河	河	河	河	河
河	河	河	河	河	河	河	河	河	河

初	Notes: Adverb (初,chū, at the beginning of, in the early part of, first in order, first, before, initially)
chū	
first	

丶 フ ラ 才 衤 ネ 初 初

初 初 初 初 初 初 初 初

初	初	初	初	初	初	初	初	初	初
chū	chū	chū	chū	chū	chū	chū	chū	chū	chū
first	first	first	first	first	first	first	first	first	first
初	初	初	初	初	初	初	初	初	初
chū	chū	chū	chū	chū	chū	chū	chū	chū	chū
first	first	first	first	first	first	first	first	first	first
初	初	初	初	初	初	初	初	初	初
初	初	初	初	初	初	初	初	初	初
初	初	初	初	初	初	初	初	初	初
初	初	初	初	初	初	初	初	初	初
初	初	初	初	初	初	初	初	初	初
初	初	初	初	初	初	初	初	初	初
初	初	初	初	初	初	初	初	初	初

游

Notes: Verb

(游, yóu, swim)

yóu
swim

丶　丶　氵　氵　广　方　汸　汸　浒　游　游

游 游 游 游 游 游 游 游

游	游	游	游	游	游	游	游	游	游
yóu	yóu	yóu	yóu	yóu	yóu	yóu	yóu	yóu	yóu
swim	swim	swim	swim	swim	swim	swim	swim	swim	swim
游	游	游	游	游	游	游	游	游	游
yóu	yóu	yóu	yóu	yóu	yóu	yóu	yóu	yóu	yóu
swim	swim	swim	swim	swim	swim	swim	swim	swim	swim
游	游	游	游	游	游	游	游		
游	游	游	游	游	游	游	游		
游	游	游	游	游	游	游	游		
游	游	游	游	游	游	游	游		
游	游	游	游	游	游	游	游		
游	游	游	游	游	游	游	游		
游	游	游	游	游	游	游	游		

严	Notes: Adjective
	(严, yán, severe, stern, tight, strict, rigorous)
	(严, yán, majestic, imposing)
	(严, Yán, surname Yán)
yán	
strict	

一 丅 丌 丌 严 严 严

严 严 严 严 严 严 严 严 严

严	严	严	严	严	严	严	严	严	严
yán	yán	yán	yán	yán	yán	yán	yán	yán	yán
strict	strict	strict	strict	strict	strict	strict	strict	strict	strict
严	严	严	严	严	严	严	严	严	严
yán	yán	yán	yán	yán	yán	yán	yán	yán	yán
strict	strict	strict	strict	strict	strict	strict	strict	strict	strict
严	严	严				严			
严	严	严				严			
严	严	严				严			
严	严	严				严			
严	严	严							
严	严	严				严			
严	严	严				严			
严	严	严				严			

铁

Notes: Common Noun

(铁, **tiě**, **iron, arms, weapon**)

(铁, **Tiě**, **surname Tiě**)

(铁, **tiě**, **firm, strong as iron**)

tiě

iron

丿 𠂉 𠂉 𠂊 年 钅 铂 铁 铁 铁

铁 铁 铁 铁 铁 铁 铁 铁 铁

铁	铁	铁	铁	铁	铁	铁	铁	铁	铁
tiě	tiě	tiě	tiě	tiě	tiě	tiě	tiě	tiě	tiě
iron	iron	iron	iron	iron	iron	iron	iron	iron	iron
铁	铁	铁	铁	铁	铁	铁	铁	铁	铁
tiě	tiě	tiě	tiě	tiě	tiě	tiě	tiě	tiě	tiě
iron	iron	iron	`iron	iron	iron	iron	iron	iron	iron
铁	铁	铁	铁	铁	铁	铁	铁	铁	
铁	铁	铁	铁	铁	铁	铁	铁	铁	
铁	铁	铁	铁	铁	铁	铁	铁	铁	
铁	铁	铁	铁	铁	铁	铁	铁	铁	
铁	铁	铁	铁	铁	铁	铁	铁	铁	
铁	铁	铁	铁	铁	铁	铁	铁	铁	
铁	铁	铁	铁	铁	铁	铁	铁	铁	
铁	铁	铁	铁	铁	铁	铁	铁	铁	

族

zú

clan

Notes: Common Noun

(族, zú, people, nationality)

(族, zú, clan, race, tribe, group)

(族, zú, family death penalty)

丶 亠 方 方 方 扩 扩 疒 庐 族 族

族 族 族 族 族 族 族 族 族

族	族	族	族	族	族	族	族	族	族
zú	zú	zú	zú	zú	zú	zú	zú	zú	zú
clan	clan	clan	clan	clan	clan	clan	clan	clan	clan
族	族	族	族	族	族	族	族	族	族
zú	zú	zú	zú	zú	zú	zú	zú	zú	zú
clan	clan	clan	clan	clan	clan	clan	clan	clan	clan
族	族	族	族	族	族	族	族	族	族
族	族	族	族	族	族	族	族	族	族
族	族	族	族	族	族	族	族	族	族
族	族	族	族	族	族	族	族	族	族
族	族	族	族	族	族	族	族	族	族
族	族	族	族	族	族	族	族	族	族
族	族	族	族	族	族	族	族	族	族
族	族	族	族	族	族	族	族	族	族

除

Notes: Verb

(除,**chú**, **get rid of, eliminate, remove**)

(除, **chú**, **divide**)

(除, **chú**, **except, besides**)

chú

remove

了 阝 阝 阝 阝 阝 阝 阝 除

除 除 除 除 除 除 除 除 除

除	除	除	除	除	除	除	除	除	除
chú	chú	chú	chú	chú	chú	chú	chú	chú	chú
remove	remove	remove	remove	remove	remove	remove	remove	remove	remove
除	除	除	除	除	除	除	除	除	除
chú	chú	chú	chú	chú	chú	chú	chú	chú	chú
remove	remove	remove	remove	remove	remove	remove	remove	remove	remove

除	除	除	除	除	除	除	除	除	除
除	除	除	除	除	除	除	除	除	除
除	除	除	除	除	除	除	除	除	除
除	除	除	除	除	除	除	除	除	除
除	除	除	除	除	除	除	除	除	除
除	除	除	除	除	除	除	除	除	除
除	除	除	除	除	除	除	除	除	除
除	除	除	除	除	除	除	除	除	除

份 fèn portion	Notes: Common Noun (份, fèn, a portion, a minute) (份, fèn, classifier for portions, shares, copies of newspapers) (份, fèn, to divide, share, copy) (份, fèn, a unit of length equalling 0.33 centimeter)

丿 亻 仆 份 份 份

份 份 份 份 份 份 份 份 份

份	份	份	份	份	份	份	份	份	份
fèn	fèn	fèn	fèn	fèn	fèn	fèn	fèn	fèn	fèn
portion	portion	portion	portion	portion	portion	portion	portion	portion	portion
份	份	份	份	份	份	份	份	份	份
fèn	fèn	fèn	fèn	fèn	fèn	fèn	fèn	fèn	fèn
portion	portion	portion	portion	portion	portion	portion	portion	portion	portion
份	份	份	份	份	份	份	份	份	份
份	份	份	份	份	份	份	份	份	份
份	份	份	份	份	份	份	份	份	份
份	份	份	份	份	份	份	份	份	份
份	份	份	份	份	份	份	份	份	份
份	份	份	份	份	份	份	份	份	份
份	份	份	份	份	份	份	份	份	份

敢	Notes: Adjective
	(敢, **gǎn**, **confidence, to be sure, courage**)
gǎn	(敢, **gǎn**, **to dare**)
dare	

フ コ マ 产 帝 帝 青 耳 耴 敢 敢 敢

敢 敢 敢 敢 敢 敢 敢 敢 敢

敢	敢	敢	敢	敢	敢	敢	敢	敢	敢
gǎn	gǎn	gǎn	gǎn	gǎn	gǎn	gǎn	gǎn	gǎn	gǎn
dare	dare	dare	dare	dare	dare	dare	dare	dare	dare
敢	敢	敢	敢	敢	敢	敢	敢	敢	敢
gǎn	gǎn	gǎn	gǎn	gǎn	gǎn	gǎn	gǎn	gǎn	gǎn
dare	dare	dare	dare	dare	dare	dare	dare	dare	dare

敢	敢	敢				敢			
敢	敢	敢				敢			
敢	敢	敢				敢			
敢	敢	敢				敢			
敢	敢	敢				敢			
敢	敢	敢				敢			
敢	敢	敢				敢			
敢	敢	敢				敢			

胡	Notes: Adjective
	(胡, hú, foreign)
	(胡, hú, recklessly, irrelevantly)
	(胡, hú, why, when, how)
hú	(胡, Hú, surname Hú)
foreign	(胡, hú, moustache, beard, whiskers)

一 十 十 古 古 却 胡 胡 胡

胡 胡 胡 胡 胡 胡 胡 胡 胡

胡	胡	胡	胡	胡	胡	胡	胡	胡	胡
hú	hú	hú	hú	hú	hú	hú	hú	hú	hú
foreign	foreign	foreign	foreign	foreign	foreign	foreign	foreign	foreign	foreign
胡	胡	胡	胡	胡	胡	胡	胡	胡	胡
hú	hú	hú	hú	hú	hú	hú	hú	hú	hú
foreign	foreign	foreign	foreign	foreign	foreign	foreign	foreign	foreign	foreign
胡	胡	胡	胡	胡	胡	胡	胡	胡	胡
胡	胡	胡	胡	胡	胡	胡	胡	胡	胡
胡	胡	胡	胡	胡	胡	胡	胡	胡	胡
胡	胡	胡	胡	胡	胡	胡	胡	胡	胡
胡	胡	胡	胡	胡	胡	胡	胡	胡	胡
胡	胡	胡	胡	胡	胡	胡	胡	胡	胡
胡	胡	胡	胡	胡	胡	胡	胡	胡	胡

Notes: Common Noun

(血, **xuè**, **blood**)

(血, **xiě**, **blood**)

(血, **xuè**, **related by blood**)

xuè
blood

xuè	xuè	xuè	xuè	xuè	xuè	xuè	xuè	xuè	xuè
blood	blood	blood	blood	blood	blood	blood	blood	blood	blood

xuè	xuè	xuè	xuè	xuè	xuè	xuè	xuè	xuè	xuè
blood	blood	blood	blood	blood	blood	blood	blood	blood	blood

企

qǐ
hope

Notes: Verb

(企, **qǐ, hope for, look forward to**)

(企, **qǐ, stand on tiptoe**)

丿 人 个 个 仐 企

企 企 企 企 企 企 企 企 企

企	企	企	企	企	企	企	企	企	企
qǐ	qǐ	qǐ	qǐ	qǐ	qǐ	qǐ	qǐ	qǐ	qǐ
hope	hope	hope	hope	hope	hope	hope	hope	hope	hope
企	企	企	企	企	企	企	企	企	企
qǐ	qǐ	qǐ	qǐ	qǐ	qǐ	qǐ	qǐ	qǐ	qǐ
hope	hope	hope	hope	hope	hope	hope	hope	hope	hope
企	企	企	企	企	企	企	企	企	企
企	企	企	企	企	企	企	企	企	企
企	企	企	企	企	企	企	企	企	企
企	企	企	企	企	企	企	企	企	企
企	企	企	企	企	企	企	企	企	企
企	企	企	企	企	企	企	企	企	企
企	企	企	企	企	企	企	企	企	企
企	企	企	企	企	企	企	企	企	企

仍

réng
still

Notes: Adverb

(仍, **réng, still, yet, as before**)

(仍, **réng, again and again, over and over**)

丿　亻　仍　仍

仍 仍 仍 仍 仍 仍 仍 仍 仍

仍	仍	仍	仍	仍	仍	仍	仍	仍	仍
réng still	réng still	réng still	réng still	réng still	réng still	réng still	réng still	réng still	réng still
仍	仍	仍	仍	仍	仍	仍	仍	仍	仍
réng still	réng still	réng still	réng still	réng still	réng still	réng still	réng still	réng still	réng still

仍	仍	仍	仍	仍	仍	仍	仍	仍	仍
仍	仍	仍	仍	仍	仍	仍	仍	仍	仍
仍	仍	仍	仍	仍	仍	仍	仍	仍	仍
仍	仍	仍	仍	仍	仍	仍	仍	仍	仍
仍	仍	仍	仍	仍	仍	仍	仍	仍	仍
仍	仍	仍	仍	仍	仍	仍	仍	仍	仍
仍	仍	仍	仍	仍	仍	仍	仍	仍	仍
仍	仍	仍	仍	仍	仍	仍	仍	仍	仍

投

tóu
throw

Notes: Verb

(投, tóu, throw, fling)

(投, tóu, send, deliver)

(投, tóu, before, prior to)

(投, tóu, go to, join)

一 十 扌 扩 护 扮 投

投 投 投 投 投 投 投 投 投

投	投	投	投	投	投	投	投	投	投
tóu	tóu	tóu	tóu	tóu	tóu	tóu	tóu	tóu	tóu
throw	throw	throw	throw	throw	throw	throw	throw	throw	throw
投	投	投	投	投	投	投	投	投	投
tóu	tóu	tóu	tóu	tóu	tóu	tóu	tóu	tóu	tóu
throw	throw	throw	throw	throw	throw	throw	throw	throw	throw
投	投	投	投	投	投	投	投	投	投
投	投	投	投	投	投	投	投	投	投
投	投	投	投	投	投	投	投	投	投
投	投	投	投	投	投	投	投	投	投
投	投	投	投	投	投	投	投	投	投
投	投	投	投	投	投	投	投	投	投
投	投	投	投	投	投	投	投	投	投

闻	Notes: Verb
	(闻, **wén**, **smell**, **hear**)
	(闻, **wén**, **news**, **story**)
	(闻, **wén**, **well-known**, **famous**)
wén	(闻, **Wén**, **surname Wén**)
smell	

丶 丶 门 门 门 闩 闰 闻 闻 闻

闻 闻 闻 闻 闻 闻 闻 闻 闻

闻	闻	闻	闻	闻	闻	闻	闻	闻	闻
wén	wén	wén	wén	wén	wén	wén	wén	wén	wén
smell	smell	smell	smell	smell	smell	smell	smell	smell	smell
闻	闻	闻	闻	闻	闻	闻	闻	闻	闻
wén	wén	wén	wén	wén	wén	wén	wén	wén	wén
smell	smell	smell	smell	smell	smell	smell	smell	smell	smell

闻	闻	闻	闻	闻	闻	闻	闻	闻	
闻	闻	闻	闻	闻	闻	闻	闻	闻	
闻	闻	闻	闻	闻	闻	闻	闻	闻	
闻	闻	闻	闻	闻	闻	闻	闻	闻	
闻	闻	闻	闻	闻	闻	闻	闻	闻	
闻	闻	闻	闻	闻	闻	闻	闻	闻	
闻	闻	闻	闻	闻	闻	闻	闻	闻	
闻	闻	闻	闻	闻	闻	闻	闻	闻	

斗

dǒu
fight

Notes: Verb

(斗, dòu, to fight, to battle, to struggle, to incite)

(斗, dǒu, 10 liters)

(斗, dòu, vie, denounce, purge)

(斗, dòu, make animals fight)

(斗, dòu, discuss, talk over, consult)

丶　丶　亠　斗

斗 斗 斗 斗 斗 斗 斗 斗 斗

斗	斗	斗	斗	斗	斗	斗	斗	斗	斗
dǒu	dǒu	dǒu	dǒu	dǒu	dǒu	dǒu	dǒu	dǒu	dǒu
fight	fight	fight	fight	fight	fight	fight	fight	fight	fight
斗	斗	斗	斗	斗	斗	斗	斗	斗	斗
dǒu	dǒu	dǒu	dǒu	dǒu	dǒu	dǒu	dǒu	dǒu	dǒu
fight	fight	fight	fight	fight	fight	fight	fight	fight	fight
斗	斗	斗	斗	斗	斗	斗	斗	斗	斗	斗
斗	斗	斗	斗	斗	斗	斗	斗	斗	斗
斗	斗	斗	斗	斗	斗	斗	斗	斗	斗
斗	斗	斗	斗	斗	斗	斗	斗	斗	斗
斗	斗	斗	斗	斗	斗	斗	斗	斗	斗
斗	斗	斗	斗	斗	斗	斗	斗	斗	斗
斗	斗	斗	斗	斗	斗	斗	斗	斗	斗

纪

jì
record

Notes: Verb

(纪, **jì**, **write down, record**)

(纪, **jì**, **historical record, annals, chronicles**)

(纪, **jì**, **age, era, period, period of 12 years**)

(纪, **Jǐ**, **surname Jǐ**)

乙　纟　纟　纟　纟　纪

纪 纪 纪 纪 纪 纪 纪 纪 纪

纪	纪	纪	纪	纪	纪	纪	纪	纪	纪
jì	jì	jì	jì	jì	jì	jì	jì	jì	jì
record	record	record	record	record	record	record	record	record	record
纪	纪	纪	纪	纪	纪	纪	纪	纪	纪
jì	jì	jì	jì	jì	jì	jì	jì	jì	jì
record	record	record	record	record	record	record	record	record	record
纪	纪	纪	纪	纪	纪	纪	纪	纪	
纪	纪	纪	纪	纪	纪	纪	纪	纪	
纪	纪	纪	纪	纪	纪	纪	纪	纪	
纪	纪	纪	纪	纪	纪	纪	纪	纪	
纪	纪	纪	纪	纪	纪	纪	纪	纪	
纪	纪	纪	纪	纪	纪	纪	纪	纪	
纪	纪	纪	纪	纪	纪	纪	纪	纪	
纪	纪	纪	纪	纪	纪	纪	纪	纪	

脚	
jiǎo	Notes: Common Noun
foot	(脚, **jiǎo**, **foot**, **leg**) (脚, **jué**, **role**, **part**, **character**, **actor**, **actress**)

丨 刀 刀 月 厂 肝 肝 胠 胠 脚 脚

脚 脚 脚 脚 脚 脚 脚 脚 脚

脚	脚	脚	脚	脚	脚	脚	脚	脚	脚
jiǎo	jiǎo	jiǎo	jiǎo	jiǎo	jiǎo	jiǎo	jiǎo	jiǎo	jiǎo
foot	foot	foot	foot	foot	foot	foot	foot	foot	foot
脚	脚	脚	脚	脚	脚	脚	脚	脚	脚
jiǎo	jiǎo	jiǎo	jiǎo	jiǎo	jiǎo	jiǎo	jiǎo	jiǎo	jiǎo
foot	foot	foot	foot	foot	foot	foot	foot	foot	foot
脚	脚	脚	脚	脚	脚	脚	脚	脚	脚
脚	脚	脚	脚	脚	脚	脚	脚	脚	脚
脚	脚	脚	脚	脚	脚	脚	脚	脚	脚
脚	脚	脚	脚	脚	脚	脚	脚	脚	脚
脚	脚	脚	脚	脚	脚	脚	脚	脚	脚
脚	脚	脚	脚	脚	脚	脚	脚	脚	脚
脚	脚	脚	脚	脚	脚	脚	脚	脚	脚
脚	脚	脚	脚	脚	脚	脚	脚	脚	脚

右
yòu
right

Notes: Adverb

(右, **yòu**, **right, right side**)

一 ナ オ 右 右

右 右 右 右 右 右 右 右 右

右	右	右	右	右	右	右	右	右	右
yòu	yòu	yòu	yòu	yòu	yòu	yòu	yòu	yòu	yòu
right	right	right	right	right	right	right	right	right	right
右	右	右	右	右	右	右	右	右	右
yòu	yòu	yòu	yòu	yòu	yòu	yòu	yòu	yòu	yòu
right	right	right	right	right	right	right	right	right	right

右	右	右	右	右	右	右	右	右	右
右	右	右	右	右	右	右	右	右	右
右	右	右	右	右	右	右	右	右	右
右	右	右	右	右	右	右	右	右	右
右	右	右	右	右	右	右	右	右	右
右	右	右	右	右	右	右	右	右	右
右	右	右	右	右	右	右	右	右	右
右	右	右	右	右	右	右	右	右	右

苏

sū
Suzhou

Notes: Proper Noun

(苏, **Sū, short for Suzhou, surname Sū**)

(苏, **sū, revive**)

一 十 艹 艹 芀 芀 苏 苏

苏 苏 苏 苏 苏 苏 苏 苏 苏

苏	苏	苏	苏	苏	苏	苏	苏	苏	苏
sū	sū	sū	sū	sū	sū	sū	sū	sū	sū
Suzhou	Suzhou	Suzhou	Suzhou	Suzhou	Suzhou	Suzhou	Suzhou	Suzhou	Suzhou
苏	苏	苏	苏	苏	苏	苏	苏	苏	苏
sū	sū	sū	sū	sū	sū	sū	sū	sū	sū
Suzhou	Suzhou	Suzhou	Suzhou	Suzhou	Suzhou	Suzhou	Suzhou	Suzhou	Suzhou
苏	苏	苏	苏	苏	苏	苏	苏	苏	苏
苏	苏	苏	苏	苏	苏	苏	苏	苏	苏
苏	苏	苏	苏	苏	苏	苏	苏	苏	苏
苏	苏	苏	苏	苏	苏	苏	苏	苏	苏
苏	苏	苏	苏	苏	苏	苏	苏	苏	苏
苏	苏	苏	苏	苏	苏	苏	苏	苏	苏
苏	苏	苏	苏	苏	苏	苏	苏	苏	苏
苏	苏	苏	苏	苏	苏	苏	苏	苏	苏

标

biāo
label

Notes: Common Noun

(标, **biāo**, **mark**, **label**, **symbol**)

(标, **biāo**, **prize**, **award**)

(标, **biāo**, **outward sign**)

(标, **biāo**, **superficiality**)

一 十 扌 木 朾 标 标 标 标

标 标 标 标 标 标 标 标 标

标	标	标	标	标	标	标	标	标	标
biāo	biāo	biāo	biāo	biāo	biāo	biāo	biāo	biāo	biāo
label	label	label	label	label	label	label	label	label	label
标	标	标	标	标	标	标	标	标	标
biāo	biāo	biāo	biāo	biāo	biāo	biāo	biāo	biāo	biāo
label	label	label	label	label	label	label	label	label	label

标	标	标	标	标	标	标	标	标	
标	标	标	标	标	标	标	标	标	
标	标	标	标	标	标	标	标	标	
标	标	标	标	标	标	标	标	标	
标	标	标	标	标	标	标	标	标	
标	标	标	标	标	标	标	标	标	
标	标	标	标	标	标	标	标	标	

饭

fàn
rice

Notes: Common Noun

(饭, **fàn**, **rice, food cooked rice or other cereals**)

(饭, **fàn**, **meal**)

丿 亻 𠂉 忄 𠂤 饣 饭 饭

饭 饭 饭 饭 饭 饭 饭 饭 饭

饭	饭	饭	饭	饭	饭	饭	饭	饭	饭
fàn	fàn	fàn	fàn	fàn	fàn	fàn	fàn	fàn	fàn
rice	rice	rice	rice	rice	rice	rice	rice	rice	rice
饭	饭	饭	饭	饭	饭	饭	饭	饭	饭
fàn	fàn	fàn	fàn	fàn	fàn	fàn	fàn	fàn	fàn
rice	rice	rice	rice	rice	rice	rice	rice	rice	rice
饭	饭	饭	饭	饭	饭	饭	饭	饭	饭
饭	饭	饭	饭	饭	饭	饭	饭	饭	饭
饭	饭	饭	饭	饭	饭	饭	饭	饭	饭
饭	饭	饭	饭	饭	饭	饭	饭	饭	饭
饭	饭	饭	饭	饭	饭	饭	饭	饭	饭
饭	饭	饭	饭	饭	饭	饭	饭	饭	饭
饭	饭	饭	饭	饭	饭	饭	饭	饭	饭
饭	饭	饭	饭	饭	饭	饭	饭	饭	饭

云	Notes: Common Noun
	(云, **yún**, **cloud**)
	(云, **yún**, **say**)
	(云, **Yún**, **short name for Yunnan**)
yún cloud	(云, **Yún**, **surname Yún**)

一　二　云　云

云　云　云　云　云　云　云　云　云

云	云	云	云	云	云	云	云	云	云
yún cloud	yún cloud	yún cloud	yún cloud	yún cloud	yún cloud	yún cloud	yún cloud	yún cloud	yún cloud
云	云	云	云	云	云	云	云	云	云
yún cloud	yún cloud	yún cloud	yún cloud	yún cloud	yún cloud	yún cloud	yún cloud	yún cloud	yún cloud

云	云	云	云	云	云	云	云	云	
云	云	云	云	云	云	云	云	云	
云	云	云	云	云	云	云	云	云	
云	云	云	云	云	云	云	云	云	
云	云	云	云	云	云	云	云	云	
云	云	云	云	云	云	云	云		
云	云	云	云	云	云	云	云		
云	云	云	云	云	云	云	云		

病

bìng
sick

Notes: Common Noun

(病, bìng, sick, disease)

(病, bìng, fall sick)

(病, bìng, fault, defect)

丶 亠 广 广 疒 疒 疒 疖 病 病

病 病 病 病 病 病 病 病 病

病	病	病	病	病	病	病	病	病	病
bìng	bìng	bìng	bìng	bìng	bìng	bìng	bìng	bìng	bìng
sick	sick	sick	sick	sick	sick	sick	sick	sick	sick
病	病	病	病	病	病	病	病	病	病
bìng	bìng	bìng	bìng	bìng	bìng	bìng	bìng	bìng	bìng
sick	sick	sick	sick	sick	sick	sick	sick	sick	sick

医	Notes: Common Noun
	(医, yī, doctor of medicine)
yī	
doctor	

一 厂 厂 三 丐 丐 医

医 医 医 医 医 医 医 医 医

医	医	医	医	医	医	医	医	医	医
yī	yī	yī	yī	yī	yī	yī	yī	yī	yī
doctor	doctor	doctor	doctor	doctor	doctor	doctor	doctor	doctor	doctor
医	医	医	医	医	医	医	医	医	医
yī	yī	yī	yī	yī	yī	yī	yī	yī	yī
doctor	doctor	doctor	doctor	doctor	doctor	doctor	doctor	doctor	doctor

阿 ā Ā	Notes: Grammatical Particle (阿, ā, an initial particle, prefix to names of people, an honorific address) (阿, Ā, birth-order number)

阝 阝 阝 阝 阝丁 阝口 阿

阿 阿 阿 阿 阿 阿 阿 阿 阿

阿	阿	阿	阿	阿	阿	阿	阿	阿	阿
ā Ā	ā Ā	ā Ā	ā Ā	ā Ā	ā Ā	ā Ā	ā Ā	ā Ā	ā Ā
阿	阿	阿	阿	阿	阿	阿	阿	阿	阿
ā Ā	ā Ā	ā Ā	ā Ā	ā Ā	ā Ā	ā Ā	ā Ā	ā Ā	ā Ā
阿	阿	阿	阿	阿	阿	阿	阿	阿	阿
阿	阿	阿	阿	阿	阿	阿	阿	阿	阿
阿	阿	阿	阿	阿	阿	阿	阿	阿	阿
阿	阿	阿	阿	阿	阿	阿	阿	阿	阿
阿	阿	阿	阿	阿	阿	阿	阿	阿	阿
阿	阿	阿	阿	阿	阿	阿	阿	阿	阿
阿	阿	阿	阿	阿	阿	阿	阿	阿	阿
阿	阿	阿	阿	阿	阿	阿	阿	阿	阿

答

Notes: Verb

(答, dá, answer, reply, return a call, reciprocate)

(答, dā, respond, reply, agree to, promise)

dá

reply

丿 𠂉 𠂇 𥤦 𥫗 𥫗 𥫗 𥫗 笁 笁 答 答

宀 户 答

答 答 答 答 答 答 答 答 答

答	答	答	答	答	答	答	答	答	答
dá	dá	dá	dá	dá	dá	dá	dá	dá	dá
reply	reply	reply	reply	reply	reply	reply	reply	reply	reply
答	答	答	答	答	答	答	答	答	答
dá	dá	dá	dá	dá	dá	dá	dá	dá	dá
reply	reply	reply	reply	reply	reply	reply	reply	reply	reply
答	答	答	答	答	答	答	答	答	
答	答	答	答	答	答	答	答	答	
答	答	答	答	答	答	答	答	答	
答	答	答	答	答	答	答	答	答	
答	答	答	答	答	答	答	答	答	
答	答	答	答	答	答	答	答	答	
答	答	答	答	答	答	答	答	答	

土	Notes: Common Noun
	(土, tǔ, soil, earth, clay)
tǔ	(土, tǔ, surname Tǔ)
soil	(土, tǔ, uncouth, crude, unsophisticated)

一　十　土

土 土 土 土 土 土 土 土 土

土	土	土	土	土	土	土	土	土	土
tǔ	tǔ	tǔ	tǔ	tǔ	tǔ	tǔ	tǔ	tǔ	tǔ
soil	soil	soil	soil	soil	soil	soil	soil	soil	soil
土	土	土	土	土	土	土	土	土	土
tǔ	tǔ	tǔ	tǔ	tǔ	tǔ	tǔ	tǔ	tǔ	tǔ
soil	soil	soil	soil	soil	soil	soil	soil	soil	soil
土	土	土	土	土		土	土	土	
土	土	土	土	土		土	土	土	
土	土	土	土	土		土	土	土	
土	土	土	土	土		土	土	土	
土	土	土	土	土		土	土	土	
土	土	土	土	土		土	土	土	
土	土	土	土	土		土	土	土	
土	土	土	土	土		土	土	土	

况

kuàng
situation

Notes: Common Noun

(况, **kuàng**, **circumstance**, **situation**)

(况, **kuàng**, **give**, **grant**)

况, **kuàng**, **besides**)

丶 冫 冴 冴 沪 沪 况

况 况 况 况 况 况 况 况 况

况	况	况	况	况	况	况	况	况	况
kuàng	kuàng	kuàng	kuàng	kuàng	kuàng	kuàng	kuàng	kuàng	kuàng
situation	situation	situation	situation	situation	situation	situation	situation	situation	situation
况	况	况	况	况	况	况	况	况	况
kuàng	kuàng	kuàng	kuàng	kuàng	kuàng	kuàng	kuàng	kuàng	kuàng
situation	situation	situation	situation	situation	situation	situation	situation	situation	situation

境	Notes: Common Noun (境, **jìng, border, territory**)
jìng	
border	

一 十 扌 扩 扩 扩 扩 护 培 培 培 境 境

境 境 境 境 境 境 境 境 境

境	境	境	境	境	境	境	境	境	境
jìng	jìng	jìng	jìng	jìng	jìng	jìng	jìng	jìng	jìng
border	border	border	border	border	border	border	border	border	border
境	境	境	境	境	境	境	境	境	境
jìng	jìng	jìng	jìng	jìng	jìng	jìng	jìng	jìng	jìng
border	border	border	border	border	border	border	border	border	border

软	Notes: Adjective
	(软, **ruǎn**, **soft, weak, pliant**)
	(软, **ruǎn**, **cowardly, timid**)
ruǎn	(软, **ruǎn**, **poor in quality, wrinkled**)
soft	

一 七 车 车 车 轫 轫 软

软 软 软 软 软 软 软 软 软

软	软	软	软	软	软	软	软	软	软
ruǎn	ruǎn	ruǎn	ruǎn	ruǎn	ruǎn	ruǎn	ruǎn	ruǎn	ruǎn
soft	soft	soft	soft	soft	soft	soft	soft	soft	soft
软	软	软	软	软	软	软	软	软	软
ruǎn	ruǎn	ruǎn	ruǎn	ruǎn	ruǎn	ruǎn	ruǎn	ruǎn	ruǎn
soft	soft	soft	soft	soft	soft	soft	soft	soft	soft
软	软	软	软	软	软	软	软	软	
软	软	软	软	软	软	软	软	软	
软	软	软	软	软	软	软	软	软	
软	软	软	软	软	软	软	软	软	
软	软	软	软	软	软	软	软	软	
软	软	软	软	软	软	软	软	软	
软	软	软	软	软	软	软	软	软	
软	软	软	软	软	软	软	软	软	

考	Notes: Verb
kǎo	(考, kǎo, give a test, take a test)
test	(考, kǎo, check, inspect, study, investigate, verify, examine)
	(考, kǎo, consider)

一　十　土　耂　耂　考

考 考 考 考 考 考 考 考 考

考	考	考	考	考	考	考	考	考	考
kǎo	kǎo	kǎo	kǎo	kǎo	kǎo	kǎo	kǎo	kǎo	kǎo
test	test	test	test	test	test	test	test	test	test
考	考	考	考	考	考	考	考	考	考
kǎo	kǎo	kǎo	kǎo	kǎo	kǎo	kǎo	kǎo	kǎo	kǎo
test	test	test	test	test	test	test	test	test	test
考	考	考	考	考	考	考	考	考	
考	考	考	考	考	考	考	考	考	
考	考	考	考	考	考	考	考	考	
考	考	考	考	考	考	考	考	考	
考	考	考	考	考	考	考	考	考	
考	考	考	考	考	考	考	考	考	
考	考	考	考	考	考	考	考	考	
考	考	考	考	考	考	考	考	考	

娘

niáng
mother

Notes: Common Noun

(娘, niáng, mother, aunt)

(娘, niáng, elderly married woman)

ㄑ 女 女 女ˋ 妒 妒 妒 娘 娘 娘

娘 娘 娘 娘 娘 娘 娘 娘 娘

娘	娘	娘	娘	娘	娘	娘	娘	娘	娘
niáng	niáng	niáng	niáng	niáng	niáng	niáng	niáng	niáng	niáng
mother	mother	mother	mother	mother	mother	mother	mother	mother	mother
娘	娘	娘	娘	娘	娘	娘	娘	娘	娘
niáng	niáng	niáng	niáng	niáng	niáng	niáng	niáng	niáng	niáng
mother	mother	mother	mother	mother	mother	mother	mother	mother	mother

娘	娘	娘	娘	娘	娘	娘	娘	娘	
娘	娘	娘	娘	娘	娘	娘	娘	娘	
娘	娘	娘	娘	娘	娘	娘	娘	娘	
娘	娘	娘	娘	娘	娘	娘	娘	娘	
娘	娘	娘	娘	娘	娘	娘	娘	娘	
娘	娘	娘	娘	娘	娘	娘	娘	娘	
娘	娘	娘	娘	娘	娘	娘	娘	娘	
娘	娘	娘	娘	娘	娘	娘	娘	娘	

村	Notes: Common Noun
	(村, **cūn**, **village, hamlet**)
cūn	(村, **cūn**, **rustic, boorish**)
village	

一　十　才　才　木　朾　村　村

村　村　村　村　村　村　村　村　村

村	村	村	村	村	村	村	村	村	村
cūn	cūn	cūn	cūn	cūn	cūn	cūn	cūn	cūn	cūn
village	village	village	village	village	village	village	village	village	village
村	村	村	村	村	村	村	村	村	村
cūn	cūn	cūn	cūn	cūn	cūn	cūn	cūn	cūn	cūn
village	village	village	village	village	village	village	village	village	village
村	村	村	村	村	村	村	村	村	村
村	村	村	村	村	村	村	村	村	村
村	村	村	村	村	村	村	村	村	村
村	村	村	村	村	村	村	村	村	村
村	村	村	村	村	村	村	村	村	
村	村	村	村	村	村	村	村	村	
村	村	村	村	村	村	村	村	村	

刀

Notes: Common Noun

(刀, **dāo**, **knife, sword, blade**)

(刀, **dāo**, **something shaped like a knife**)

(刀, **bǎ**, **measure word for 100 sheets of paper**)

dāo

knife

丁刀

刀 刀 刀 刀 刀 刀 刀 刀 刀

刀	刀	刀	刀	刀	刀	刀	刀	刀	刀
dāo	dāo	dāo	dāo	dāo	dāo	dāo	dāo	dāo	dāo
knife	knife	knife	knife	knife	knife	knife	knife	knife	knife
刀	刀	刀	刀	刀	刀	刀	刀	刀	刀
dāo	dāo	dāo	dāo	dāo	dāo	dāo	dāo	dāo	dāo
knife	knife	knife	knife	knife	knife	knife	knife	knife	knife
刀	刀	刀	刀	刀		刀	刀	刀	
刀	刀	刀	刀	刀		刀	刀	刀	
刀	刀	刀	刀	刀		刀	刀	刀	
刀	刀	刀	刀	刀		刀	刀	刀	
刀	刀	刀	刀	刀		刀	刀	刀	
刀	刀	刀	刀	刀		刀	刀	刀	
刀	刀	刀	刀	刀		刀	刀	刀	
刀	刀	刀	刀	刀		刀	刀	刀	

击

jī
beat

Notes: Verb

(击, jī, beat, hit, strike, knock)

一 二 キ 击 击

击 击 击 击 击 击 击 击 击

击	击	击	击	击	击	击	击	击	击
jī	jī	jī	jī	jī	jī	jī	jī	jī	jī
beat	beat	beat	beat	beat	beat	beat	beat	beat	beat
击	击	击	击	击	击	击	击	击	击
jī	jī	jī	jī	jī	jī	jī	jī	jī	jī
beat	beat	beat	beat	beat	beat	beat	beat	beat	beat
击	击	击	击	击	击	击	击	击	
击	击	击	击	击	击	击	击	击	
击	击	击	击	击	击	击	击	击	
击	击	击	击	击	击	击	击	击	
击	击	击	击	击	击	击	击	击	
击	击	击	击	击	击	击	击	击	
击	击	击	击	击	击	击	击	击	
击	击	击	击	击	击	击	击	击	

仅

jǐn

only

Notes: Adverb

(仅, **jǐn**, **only, merely, barely**)

ノ 亻 仉 仅

仅 仅 仅 仅 仅 仅 仅 仅 仅

仅	仅	仅	仅	仅	仅	仅	仅	仅	仅
jǐn	jǐn	jǐn	jǐn	jǐn	jǐn	jǐn	jǐn	jǐn	jǐn
only	only	only	only	only	only	only	only	only	only
仅	仅	仅	仅	仅	仅	仅	仅	仅	仅
jǐn	jǐn	jǐn	jǐn	jǐn	jǐn	jǐn	jǐn	jǐn	jǐn
only	only	only	only	only	only	only	only	only	only

查

chá
check

Notes: Verb

(查, chá, examine, investigate, check, look up)

(查, Zhā, surname Zhā)

一 十 才 木 杢 杏 杳 查 查

查 查 查 查 查 查 查 查 查

查	查	查	查	查	查	查	查	查	查
chá	chá	chá	chá	chá	chá	chá	chá	chá	chá
check	check	check	check	check	check	check	check	check	check
查	查	查	查	查	查	查	查	查	查
chá	chá	chá	chá	chá	chá	chá	chá	chá	chá
check	check	check	check	check	check	check	check	check	check
查	查	查	查	查	查	查	查	查	查
查	查	查	查	查	查	查	查	查	查
查	查	查	查	查	查	查	查	查	查
查	查	查	查	查	查	查	查	查	查
查	查	查	查	查	查	查	查	查	查
查	查	查	查	查	查	查	查	查	查
查	查	查	查	查	查	查	查	查	查
查	查	查	查	查	查	查	查	查	查

引	Notes: Verb
	(引, yǐn, lead, guide)
	(引, yǐn, draw, stretch, pull)
	(引, yǐn, unit of length of 33 1/3 meters)
yǐn guide	(引, yǐn, number of units of salt certificates)

フ　コ　弓　引

引　引　引　引　引　引　引　引　引

引	引	引	引	引	引	引	引	引	引
yǐn	yǐn	yǐn	yǐn	yǐn	yǐn	yǐn	yǐn	yǐn	yǐn
guide	guide	guide	guide	guide	guide	guide	guide	guide	guide
引	引	引	引	引	引	引	引	引	引
yǐn	yǐn	yǐn	yǐn	yǐn	yǐn	yǐn	yǐn	yǐn	yǐn
guide	guide	guide	guide	guide	guide	guide	guide	guide	guide

引	引	引	引	引	引	引	引	引	
引	引	引	引	引	引	引	引	引	
引	引	引	引	引	引	引	引	引	
引	引	引	引	引	引	引	引	引	
引	引	引	引	引	引	引	引	引	
引	引	引	引	引	引	引	引	引	
引	引	引	引	引	引	引	引	引	
引	引	引	引	引	引	引	引	引	

朝

cháo
towards

Notes: Verb

(朝, **cháo**, **towards**)

(朝, **cháo**, **court**, **government**)

(朝, **zhāo**, **morning**)

(朝, **Cháo**, **Cháo dynasty**)

一 十 产 吉 吉 吉 直 卓 朝 朝 朝 朝

朝 朝 朝 朝 朝 朝 朝 朝

朝	朝	朝	朝	朝	朝	朝	朝	朝	朝
cháo	cháo	cháo	cháo	cháo	cháo	cháo	cháo	cháo	cháo
towards	towards	towards	towards	towards	towards	towards	towards	towards	towards
朝	朝	朝	朝	朝	朝	朝	朝	朝	朝
cháo	cháo	cháo	cháo	cháo	cháo	cháo	cháo	cháo	cháo
towards	towards	towards	towards	towards	towards	towards	towards	towards	towards
朝	朝	朝	朝	朝	朝	朝	朝	朝	朝
朝	朝	朝	朝	朝	朝	朝	朝	朝	朝
朝	朝	朝	朝	朝	朝	朝	朝	朝	朝
朝	朝	朝	朝	朝	朝	朝	朝	朝	朝
朝	朝	朝	朝	朝	朝	朝	朝	朝	朝
朝	朝	朝	朝	朝	朝	朝	朝	朝	朝
朝	朝	朝	朝	朝	朝	朝	朝	朝	朝
朝	朝	朝	朝	朝	朝	朝	朝	朝	朝

育		
yù		Notes: Verb
raise		(育, yù, raise, educate, train) (育, yù, give birth to) (育, yō, heave-ho, yo-ho)

丶 一 亠 云 产 产 育 育

育 育 育 育 育 育 育 育 育

育	育	育	育	育	育	育	育	育	育
yù	yù	yù	yù	yù	yù	yù	yù	yù	yù
raise	raise	raise	raise	raise	raise	raise	raise	raise	raise
育	育	育	育	育	育	育	育	育	育
yù	yù	yù	yù	yù	yù	yù	yù	yù	yù
raise	raise	raise	raise	raise	raise	raise	raise	raise	raise

育	育	育	育	育	育	育	育	育	育
育	育	育	育	育	育	育	育	育	育
育	育	育	育	育	育	育	育	育	育
育	育	育	育	育	育	育	育	育	育
育	育	育	育	育	育	育	育	育	育
育	育	育	育	育	育	育	育	育	育
育	育	育	育	育	育	育	育	育	育
育	育	育	育	育	育	育	育	育	育

继

jì
continue

Notes: Verb

(继, jì, continue, extend, join)

(继, jì, add, supply more)

(继, jì, be continuous or successive)

丿 ㄥ 纟 纟' 纟'' 纟ˊ 纰 绊 继 继

继 继 继 继 继 继 继 继 继

继	继	继	继	继	继	继	继	继	继
jì	jì	jì	jì	jì	jì	jì	jì	jì	jì
continue	continue	continue	continue	continue	continue	continue	continue	continue	continue

继	继	继	继	继	继	继	继	继	继
jì	jì	jì	jì	jì	jì	jì	jì	jì	jì
continue	continue	continue	continue	continue	continue	continue	continue	continue	continue

继	继	继	继	继	继	继	继	继	继
继	继	继	继	继	继	继	继	继	继
继	继	继	继	继	继	继	继	继	继
继	继	继	继	继	继	继	继	继	继
继	继	继	继	继	继	继	继	继	继
继	继	继	继	继	继	继	继	继	继
继	继	继	继	继	继	继	继	继	继
继	继	继	继	继	继	继	继	继	继

独

dú
alone

Notes: Adverb

(独, **dú**, **only**, **alone**, **in solitude**, **singly**)

丿 犭 犭 犭 犭 犭 狆 独 独

独 独 独 独 独 独 独 独 独

独	独	独	独	独	独	独	独	独	独
dú	dú	dú	dú	dú	dú	dú	dú	dú	dú
alone	alone	alone	alone	alone	alone	alone	alone	alone	alone
独	独	独	独	独	独	独	独	独	独
dú	dú	dú	dú	dú	dú	dú	dú	dú	dú
alone	alone	alone	alone	alone	alone	alone	alone	alone	alone

独	独	独	独	独	独	独	独
独	独	独	独	独	独	独	独
独	独	独	独	独	独	独	独
独	独	独	独	独	独	独	独
独	独	独	独	独	独	独	独
独	独	独	独	独	独	独	独
独	独	独	独	独	独	独	独
独	独	独	独	独	独	独	独

罗

luó
collect

Notes: Verb

(罗, luó, collect, gather together, display, spread out, sift, net)

(罗, luó, net for catching birds)

(罗, Luó, surname Luó)

(罗, luó, measure word for twelve dozen, a gross)

丨 冂 冂 冚 罒 罗 罗 罗

罗 罗 罗 罗 罗 罗 罗 罗 罗

罗	罗	罗	罗	罗	罗	罗	罗	罗	罗
luó	luó	luó	luó	luó	luó	luó	luó	luó	luó
collect	collect	collect	collect	collect	collect	collect	collect	collect	collect
罗	罗	罗	罗	罗	罗	罗	罗	罗	罗
luó	luó	luó	luó	luó	luó	luó	luó	luó	luó
collect	collect	collect	collect	collect	collect	collect	collect	collect	collect
罗	罗	罗	罗	罗	罗	罗	罗	罗	罗
罗	罗	罗	罗	罗	罗	罗	罗	罗	罗
罗	罗	罗	罗	罗	罗	罗	罗	罗	罗
罗	罗	罗	罗	罗	罗	罗	罗	罗	罗
罗	罗	罗	罗	罗	罗	罗	罗	罗	罗
罗	罗	罗	罗	罗	罗	罗	罗	罗	罗
罗	罗	罗	罗	罗	罗	罗	罗	罗	罗
罗	罗	罗	罗	罗	罗	罗	罗	罗	罗

买

mǎi
buy

Notes: Verb

(买, **mǎi**, **buy**, **purchase**, **hire**)

乛 乛 乛 乛 乛 买 买

买 买 买 买 买 买 买 买 买

买	买	买	买	买	买	买	买	买	买
mǎi	mǎi	mǎi	mǎi	mǎi	mǎi	mǎi	mǎi	mǎi	mǎi
buy	buy	buy	buy	buy	buy	buy	buy	buy	buy
买	买	买	买	买	买	买	买	买	买
mǎi	mǎi	mǎi	mǎi	mǎi	mǎi	mǎi	mǎi	mǎi	mǎi
buy	buy	buy	buy	buy	buy	buy	buy	buy	buy
买	买	买	买	买	买	买	买	买	
买	买	买	买	买	买	买	买	买	
买	买	买	买	买	买	买	买	买	
买	买	买	买	买	买	买	买	买	
买	买	买	买	买	买	买	买	买	
买	买	买	买	买	买	买	买	买	
买	买	买	买	买	买	买	买	买	
买	买	买	买	买	买	买	买	买	

户

Notes: Common Noun

(户, **hù**, **door**, **household**)

(户, **hù**, **household**, **family**)

hù
door

丶　㇒　㇆　户

户 户 户 户 户 户 户 户 户

户	户	户	户	户	户	户	户	户	户
hù	hù	hù	hù	hù	hù	hù	hù	hù	hù
door	door	door	door	door	door	door	door	door	door
户	户	户	户	户	户	户	户	户	户
hù	hù	hù	hù	hù	hù	hù	hù	hù	hù
door	door	door	door	door	door	door	door	door	door
户	户	户	户	户	户	户	户	户	户
户	户	户	户	户	户	户	户	户	户
户	户	户	户	户	户	户	户	户	户
户	户	户	户	户	户	户	户	户	户
户	户	户	户	户	户	户	户	户	户
户	户	户	户	户	户	户	户	户	户
户	户	户	户	户	户	户	户	户	户

护	Notes: Verb (护, **hù**, **protect**, **guard**)
hù	
protect	

一　十　扌　扩　扩　护　护

护 护 护 护 护 护 护 护 护

护	护	护	护	护	护	护	护	护	护
hù	hù	hù	hù	hù	hù	hù	hù	hù	hù
protect	protect	protect	protect	protect	protect	protect	protect	protect	protect
护	护	护	护	护	护	护	护	护	护
hù	hù	hù	hù	hù	hù	hù	hù	hù	hù
protect	protect	protect	protect	protect	protect	protect	protect	protect	protect

喝

hē
drink

Notes: Verb

(喝, **hē**, **drink**)

(喝, **hè**, **shout**)

丨 𠃌 𠃌 叩 叩 叩 叩 吲 喝 喝 喝 喝

喝 喝 喝 喝 喝 喝 喝 喝 喝

喝	喝	喝	喝	喝	喝	喝	喝	喝	喝
hē	hē	hē	hē	hē	hē	hē	hē	hē	hē
drink	drink	drink	drink	drink	drink	drink	drink	drink	drink
喝	喝	喝	喝	喝	喝	喝	喝	喝	喝
hē	hē	hē	hē	hē	hē	hē	hē	hē	hē
drink	drink	drink	drink	drink	drink	drink	drink	drink	drink
喝	喝	喝	喝	喝	喝	喝	喝	喝	喝
喝	喝	喝	喝	喝	喝	喝	喝	喝	喝
喝	喝	喝	喝	喝	喝	喝	喝	喝	喝
喝	喝	喝	喝	喝	喝	喝	喝	喝	喝
喝	喝	喝	喝	喝	喝	喝	喝	喝	喝
喝	喝	喝	喝	喝	喝	喝	喝	喝	喝
喝	喝	喝	喝	喝	喝	喝	喝	喝	喝
喝	喝	喝	喝	喝	喝	喝	喝	喝	喝

朋	Notes: Common Noun (朋, **péng**, friend)
péng	
friend	

丿　几　月　月　朋　朋　朋　朋

朋　朋　朋　朋　朋　朋　朋　朋

朋	朋	朋	朋	朋	朋	朋	朋	朋	朋
péng	péng	péng	péng	péng	péng	péng	péng	péng	péng
friend	friend	friend	friend	friend	friend	friend	friend	friend	friend
朋	朋	朋	朋	朋	朋	朋	朋	朋	朋
péng	péng	péng	péng	péng	péng	péng	péng	péng	péng
friend	friend	friend	friend	friend	friend	friend	friend	friend	friend
朋	朋	朋	朋	朋	朋	朋	朋	朋	朋
朋	朋	朋	朋	朋	朋	朋	朋	朋	朋
朋	朋	朋	朋	朋	朋	朋	朋	朋	朋
朋	朋	朋	朋	朋	朋	朋	朋	朋	朋
朋	朋	朋	朋	朋	朋	朋	朋	朋	朋
朋	朋	朋	朋	朋	朋	朋	朋	朋	朋
朋	朋	朋	朋	朋	朋	朋	朋	朋	朋
朋	朋	朋	朋	朋	朋	朋	朋	朋	朋

供

gōng
supply

Notes: Verb

(供, **gōng**, **supply**, **feed**)

(供, **gòng**, **confess**, **own up to**)

(供, **gòng**, **offer sacrifices**)

丿 亻 仁 什 什 供 供 供

供 供 供 供 供 供 供 供 供

供	供	供	供	供	供	供	供	供	供
gōng	gōng	gōng	gōng	gōng	gōng	gōng	gōng	gōng	gōng
supply	supply	supply	supply	supply	supply	supply	supply	supply	supply
供	供	供	供	供	供	供	供	供	供
gōng	gōng	gōng	gōng	gōng	gōng	gōng	gōng	gōng	gōng
supply	supply	supply	supply	supply	supply	supply	supply	supply	supply
供	供	供	供	供	供	供	供	供	供
供	供	供	供	供	供	供	供	供	供
供	供	供	供	供	供	供	供	供	供
供	供	供	供	供	供	供	供	供	供
供	供	供	供	供	供	供	供	供	供
供	供	供	供	供	供	供	供	供	供
供	供	供	供	供	供	供	供	供	供
供	供	供	供	供	供	供	供	供	供

责	Notes: Common Noun
zé	(责, **zé**, **duty**, **responsibility**)
duty	

一 二 キ 丰 声 青 责 责

责 责 责 责 责 责 责 责 责

责	责	责	责	责	责	责	责	责	责
zé	zé	zé	zé	zé	zé	zé	zé	zé	zé
duty	duty	duty	duty	duty	duty	duty	duty	duty	duty
责	责	责	责	责	责	责	责	责	责
zé	zé	zé	zé	zé	zé	zé	zé	zé	zé
duty	duty	duty	duty	duty	duty	duty	duty	duty	duty
责	责	责	责	责	责	责	责	责	
责	责	责	责	责	责	责	责	责	
责	责	责	责	责	责	责	责	责	
责	责	责	责	责	责	责	责	责	
责	责	责	责	责	责	责	责	责	
责	责	责	责	责	责	责	责	责	
责	责	责	责	责	责	责	责	责	
责	责	责	责	责	责	责	责	责	

项 xiàng items	Notes: Common Noun (项, **xiàng**, **items or things**) (项, **xiàng**, **measure word for items or clauses**) (项, **xiàng**, **back of neck**) (项, **Xiàng**, **surname Xiàng**)

一 丁 工 厂 厅 圹 顶 项 项

项 项 项 项 项 项 项 项 项

项	项	项	项	项	项	项	项	项	项
xiàng items	xiàng items	xiàng items	xiàng items	xiàng items	xiàng items	xiàng items	xiàng items	xiàng items	xiàng items
项	项	项	项	项	项	项	项	项	项
xiàng items	xiàng items	xiàng items	xiàng items	xiàng items	xiàng items	xiàng items	xiàng items	xiàng items	xiàng items

背

bèi
items

Notes: Common Noun

(背, bèi, back, back of a body or object)

(背, bèi, turn one's back, turn away, hide something)

(背, bēi, carry on the back)

(背, bèi, learn by heart, recite from memory)

丨 十 キ 扩 北 北 背 背 背

背 背 背 背 背 背 背 背 背

背	背	背	背	背	背	背	背	背	背
bèi	bèi	bèi	bèi	bèi	bèi	bèi	bèi	bèi	bèi
back	back	back	back	back	back	back	back	back	back
背	背	背	背	背	背	背	背	背	背
bèi	bèi	bèi	bèi	bèi	bèi	bèi	bèi	bèi	bèi
back	back	back	back	back	back	back	back	back	back
背	背	背	背	背	背	背	背	背	背
背	背	背	背	背	背	背	背	背	背
背	背	背	背	背	背	背	背	背	背
背	背	背	背	背	背	背	背	背	背
背	背	背	背	背	背	背	背	背	背
背	背	背	背	背	背	背	背	背	背
背	背	背	背	背	背	背	背	背	背
背	背	背	背	背	背	背	背	背	背

余

yú
me

Notes: Personal Pronoun

(余, **yú**, **I, me**)

(余, **yú**, **surplus, remainder**)

(余, **Yú**, **surname Yú**)

丿 人 𠆢 𠆢 仐 佘 余

余 余 余 余 余 余 余 余 余

余	余	余	余	余	余	余	余	余	余
yú	yú	yú	yú	yú	yú	yú	yú	yú	yú
me	me	me	me	me	me	me	me	me	me
余	余	余	余	余	余	余	余	余	余
yú	yú	yú	yú	yú	yú	yú	yú	yú	yú
me	me	me	me	me	me	me	me	me	me

余	余	余	余	余	余	余	余	余	余
余	余	余	余	余	余	余	余	余	余
余	余	余	余	余	余	余	余	余	余
余	余	余	余	余	余	余	余	余	余
余	余	余	余	余	余	余	余	余	余
余	余	余	余	余	余	余	余	余	余
余	余	余	余	余	余	余	余	余	余
余	余	余	余	余	余	余	余	余	余

希	
	Notes: Common Noun
	(希, xī, hope)
	(希, xī, sparse, scattered)
	(希, xī, watery, thin)
xī	(希, xī, rare, scarce, uncommon)
hope	

ノ ㄨ 二 产 产 希 希

希 希 希 希 希 希 希 希 希

希	希	希	希	希	希	希	希	希	希
xī	xī	xī	xī	xī	xī	xī	xī	xī	xī
hope	hope	hope	hope	hope	hope	hope	hope	hope	hope
希	希	希	希	希	希	希	希	希	希
xī	xī	xī	xī	xī	xī	xī	xī	xī	xī
hope	hope	hope	hope	hope	hope	hope	hope	hope	hope
希	希	希	希	希	希	希	希	希	
希	希	希	希	希	希	希	希	希	
希	希	希	希	希	希	希	希	希	
希	希	希	希	希	希	希	希	希	
希	希	希	希	希	希	希	希	希	
希	希	希	希	希	希	希	希	希	
希	希	希	希	希	希	希	希	希	

卫

Notes: Verb

(卫, wèi, guard, defend)

(卫, Wèi, surname Wèi)

wèi

guard

wèi	wèi	wèi	wèi	wèi	wèi	wèi	wèi	wèi	wèi
guard	guard	guard	guard	guard	guard	guard	guard	guard	guard
wèi	wèi	wèi	wèi	wèi	wèi	wèi	wèi	wèi	wèi
guard	guard	guard	guard	guard	guard	guard	guard	guard	guard

列	Notes: Verb
	(列, liè, line up, arrange)
	(列, liè, list, enter in a list, column)
	(列, liè, various, each and every
liè	(列, liè, measure word for rows, files, ranks)
arrange	

一　厂　歹　歹　列　列

列 列 列 列 列 列 列 列 列

列	列	列	列	列	列	列	列	列	列
liè	liè	liè	liè	liè	liè	liè	liè	liè	liè
arrange	arrange	arrange	arrange	arrange	arrange	arrange	arrange	arrange	arrange
列	列	列	列	列	列	列	列	列	列
liè	liè	liè	liè	liè	liè	liè	liè	liè	liè
arrange	arrange	arrange	arrange	arrange	arrange	arrange	arrange	arrange	arrange

列	列	列	列	列	列	列	列	列	列
列	列	列	列	列	列	列	列	列	列
列	列	列	列	列	列	列	列	列	列
列	列	列	列	列	列	列	列	列	列
列	列	列	列	列	列	列	列	列	列
列	列	列	列	列	列	列	列	列	列
列	列	列	列	列	列	列	列	列	列
列	列	列	列	列	列	列	列	列	列

图	Notes: Common Noun (图, tú, picture, drawing, chart, map) (图, tú, scheme, plan)
tú	
plan	

丨 冂 冂 冈 图 图 图 图

图 图 图 图 图 图 图 图 图

图	图	图	图	图	图	图	图	图	图
tú	tú	tú	tú	tú	tú	tú	tú	tú	tú
plan	plan	plan	plan	plan	plan	plan	plan	plan	plan
图	图	图	图	图	图	图	图	图	图
tú	tú	tú	tú	tú	tú	tú	tú	tú	tú
plan	plan	plan	plan	plan	plan	plan	plan	plan	plan
图	图	图	图	图	图	图	图	图	图
图	图	图	图	图	图	图	图	图	图
图	图	图	图	图	图	图	图	图	图
图	图	图	图	图	图	图	图	图	图
图	图	图	图	图	图	图	图	图	图
图	图	图	图	图	图	图	图	图	图
图	图	图	图	图	图	图	图	图	图

室	Notes: Common Noun (室, shì, room)
shì	
room	

` ´ 宀 宀 宀 宓 宓 宓 室 室

室 室 室 室 室 室 室 室 室

室	室	室	室	室	室	室	室	室	室
shì	shì	shì	shì	shì	shì	shì	shì	shì	shì
room	room	room	room	room	room	room	room	room	room
室	室	室	室	室	室	室	室	室	室
shì	shì	shì	shì	shì	shì	shì	shì	shì	shì
room	room	room	room	room	room	room	room	room	room

室	室	室	室	室	室	室	室	室	
室	室	室	室	室	室	室	室	室	
室	室	室	室	室	室	室	室	室	
室	室	室	室	室	室	室	室	室	
室	室	室	室	室	室	室	室	室	
室	室	室	室	室	室	室	室	室	
室	室	室	室	室	室	室	室	室	
室	室	室	室	室	室	室	室	室	

乱	Notes: Verb
	(乱, **luàn, confuse, mix up**)
	(乱, **luàn, chaotic, disorderly, messy, confused**)
	(乱, **luàn, indiscriminate, random, arbitrary**)
luàn	
confuse	

丿 二 千 千 舌 舌 乱

乱 乱 乱 乱 乱 乱 乱 乱 乱

乱	乱	乱	乱	乱	乱	乱	乱	乱	乱
luàn	luàn	luàn	luàn	luàn	luàn	luàn	luàn	luàn	luàn
confuse	confuse	confuse	confuse	confuse	confuse	confuse	confuse	confuse	confuse
乱	乱	乱	乱	乱	乱	乱	乱	乱	乱
luàn	luàn	luàn	luàn	luàn	luàn	luàn	luàn	luàn	luàn
confuse	confuse	confuse	confuse	confuse	confuse	confuse	confuse	confuse	confuse
乱	乱	乱	乱	乱	乱	乱	乱	乱	乱
乱	乱	乱	乱	乱	乱	乱	乱	乱	乱
乱	乱	乱	乱	乱	乱	乱	乱	乱	乱
乱	乱	乱	乱	乱	乱	乱	乱	乱	乱
乱	乱	乱	乱	乱	乱	乱	乱	乱	乱
乱	乱	乱	乱	乱	乱	乱	乱	乱	乱
乱	乱	乱	乱	乱	乱	乱	乱	乱	乱
乱	乱	乱	乱	乱	乱	乱	乱	乱	乱

刘

Notes: Proper Noun

(刘, **Liú**, surname Liú)

Liú
Liú

丶 亠 ナ 文 刘 刘

刘 刘 刘 刘 刘 刘 刘 刘 刘

刘	刘	刘	刘	刘	刘	刘	刘	刘	刘
Liú	Liú	Liú	Liú	Liú	Liú	Liú	Liú	Liú	Liú
Liú	Liú	Liú	Liú	Liú	Liú	Liú	Liú	Liú	Liú
刘	刘	刘	刘	刘	刘	刘	刘	刘	刘
Liú	Liú	Liú	Liú	Liú	Liú	Liú	Liú	Liú	Liú
Liú	Liú	Liú	Liú	Liú	Liú	Liú	Liú	Liú	Liú

刘	刘	刘	刘	刘	刘	刘	刘	刘	刘
刘	刘	刘	刘	刘	刘	刘	刘	刘	刘
刘	刘	刘	刘	刘	刘	刘	刘	刘	刘
刘	刘	刘	刘	刘	刘	刘	刘	刘	刘
刘	刘	刘	刘	刘	刘	刘	刘	刘	刘
刘	刘	刘	刘	刘	刘	刘	刘	刘	刘
刘	刘	刘	刘	刘	刘	刘	刘	刘	刘
刘	刘	刘	刘	刘	刘	刘	刘	刘	刘

Notes: Common Noun

(爷, yé, father, grandfather)

爷
yé
father

丶 ハ 父 父 爷 爷

爷 爷 爷 爷 爷 爷 爷 爷 爷

爷	爷	爷	爷	爷	爷	爷	爷	爷	爷
yé	yé	yé	yé	yé	yé	yé	yé	yé	yé
father	father	father	father	father	father	father	father	father	father
爷	爷	爷	爷	爷	爷	爷	爷	爷	爷
yé	yé	yé	yé	yé	yé	yé	yé	yé	yé
father	father	father	father	father	father	father	father	father	father

龙

lóng
dragon

Notes: Common Noun

(龙, lóng, dragon)

(龙, Lóng, surname Lóng)

一 ナ 九 龙 龙

龙 龙 龙 龙 龙 龙 龙 龙 龙

龙	龙	龙	龙	龙	龙	龙	龙	龙	龙
lóng	lóng	lóng	lóng	lóng	lóng	lóng	lóng	lóng	lóng
dragon	dragon	dragon	dragon	dragon	dragon	dragon	dragon	dragon	dragon
龙	龙	龙	龙	龙	龙	龙	龙	龙	龙
lóng	lóng	lóng	lóng	lóng	lóng	lóng	lóng	lóng	lóng
dragon	dragon	dragon	dragon	dragon	dragon	dragon	dragon	dragon	dragon

龙	龙	龙	龙	龙	龙	龙	龙	龙	龙
龙	龙	龙	龙	龙	龙	龙	龙	龙	龙
龙	龙	龙	龙	龙	龙	龙	龙	龙	龙
龙	龙	龙	龙	龙	龙	龙	龙	龙	龙
龙	龙	龙	龙	龙	龙	龙	龙	龙	龙
龙	龙	龙	龙	龙	龙	龙	龙	龙	龙
龙	龙	龙	龙	龙	龙	龙	龙	龙	龙

咱

zán
we

Notes: Personal Pronoun

(咱, **zán, we, you and I**)

丨 冂 冂 冋′ 冋′ 叭 咟 咱 咱

咱 咱 咱 咱 咱 咱 咱 咱 咱

咱	咱	咱	咱	咱	咱	咱	咱	咱	咱
zán	zán	zán	zán	zán	zán	zán	zán	zán	zán
we	we	we	we	we	we	we	we	we	we
咱	咱	咱	咱	咱	咱	咱	咱	咱	咱
zán	zán	zán	zán	zán	zán	zán	zán	zán	zán
we	we	we	we	we	we	we	we	we	we
咱	咱	咱	咱	咱	咱	咱	咱	咱	咱
咱	咱	咱	咱	咱	咱	咱	咱	咱	咱
咱	咱	咱	咱	咱	咱	咱	咱	咱	咱
咱	咱	咱	咱	咱	咱	咱	咱	咱	咱
咱	咱	咱	咱	咱	咱	咱	咱	咱	咱
咱	咱	咱	咱	咱	咱	咱	咱	咱	咱
咱	咱	咱	咱	咱	咱	咱	咱	咱	咱
咱	咱	咱	咱	咱	咱	咱	咱	咱	咱

章	Notes: Common Noun (章, **zhāng**, **chapter**, **seal**, **stamp**, **medal**, **badge**, **rules**) (章, **Zhāng**, **surname Zhāng**)
zhāng	
rules	

丶 亠 丷 立 产 产 咅 咅 音 音 章

章 章 章 章 章 章 章 章 章

章	章	章	章	章	章	章	章	章	章
zhāng	zhāng	zhāng	zhāng	zhāng	zhāng	zhāng	zhāng	zhāng	zhāng
rules	rules	rules	rules	rules	rules	rules	rules	rules	rules
章	章	章	章	章	章	章	章	章	章
zhāng	zhāng	zhāng	zhāng	zhāng	zhāng	zhāng	zhāng	zhāng	zhāng
rules	rules	rules	rules	rules	rules	rules	rules	rules	rules
章	章	章	章	章	章	章	章	章	章
章	章	章	章	章	章	章	章	章	章
章	章	章	章	章	章	章	章	章	章
章	章	章	章	章	章	章	章	章	章
章	章	章	章	章	章	章	章	章	章
章	章	章	章	章	章	章	章	章	章
章	章	章	章	章	章	章	章	章	章
章	章	章	章	章	章	章	章	章	章

席

xí
seat

Notes: Common Noun

(席, xí, mat, seat, banquet)

(席, xí, measure word for banquets and talks)

(席, Xí, surname Xí)

丶 亠 广 户 庐 庐 庐 庐 庐 席

席 席 席 席 席 席 席 席 席

席	席	席	席	席	席	席	席	席	席
xí	xí	xí	xí	xí	xí	xí	xí	xí	xí
seat	seat	seat	seat	seat	seat	seat	seat	seat	seat
席	席	席	席	席	席	席	席	席	席
xí	xí	xí	xí	xí	xí	xí	xí	xí	xí
seat	seat	seat	seat	seat	seat	seat	seat	seat	seat
席	席	席	席	席	席	席	席	席	席
席	席	席	席	席	席	席	席	席	席
席	席	席	席	席	席	席	席	席	席
席	席	席	席	席	席	席	席	席	席
席	席	席	席	席	席	席	席	席	席
席	席	席	席	席	席	席	席	席	席
席	席	席	席	席	席	席	席	席	席

席	Notes: Adjective
	(错, **cuò**, **wrong, mistaken, bad, poor, error**)
	(错, **cuò**, **confused, complex, be interlocked**)
	(错, **cuò**, **miss, let slip, evade, dodge**)
cuò	(错, **cuò**, **rub**)
bad	

丿 丿 𠂉 牛 牛 钅 针 钎 铒 错 错 错 错

席 席 席 席 席 席 席 席 席

席	席	席	席	席	席	席	席	席	席
cuò	cuò	cuò	cuò	cuò	cuò	cuò	cuò	cuò	cuò
bad	bad	bad	bad	bad	bad	bad	bad	bad	bad
席	席	席	席	席	席	席	席	席	席
cuò	cuò	cuò	cuò	cuò	cuò	cuò	cuò	cuò	cuò
bad	bad	bad	bad	bad	bad	bad	bad	bad	bad
席	席	席	席	席	席	席	席	席	
席	席	席	席	席	席	席	席	席	
席	席	席	席	席	席	席	席	席	
席	席	席	席	席	席	席	席	席	
席	席	席	席	席	席	席	席	席	
席	席	席	席	席	席	席	席	席	
席	席	席	席	席	席	席	席	席	

兄

Notes: Common Noun

(兄, **xiōng, elder brother**)

xiōng

brother

丨 冂 口 尸 兄

兄 兄 兄 兄 兄 兄 兄 兄 兄

兄	兄	兄	兄	兄	兄	兄	兄	兄	兄
xiōng	xiōng	xiōng	xiōng	xiōng	xiōng	xiōng	xiōng	xiōng	xiōng
brother	brother	brother	brother	brother	brother	brother	brother	brother	brother
兄	兄	兄	兄	兄	兄	兄	兄	兄	兄
xiōng	xiōng	xiōng	xiōng	xiōng	xiōng	xiōng	xiōng	xiōng	xiōng
brother	brother	brother	brother	brother	brother	brother	brother	brother	brother
兄	兄	兄	兄	兄	兄	兄	兄	兄	兄
兄	兄	兄	兄	兄	兄	兄	兄	兄	兄
兄	兄	兄	兄	兄	兄	兄	兄	兄	兄
兄	兄	兄	兄	兄	兄	兄	兄	兄	兄
兄	兄	兄	兄	兄	兄	兄	兄	兄	兄
兄	兄	兄	兄	兄	兄	兄	兄	兄	兄
兄	兄	兄	兄	兄	兄	兄	兄	兄	兄
兄	兄	兄	兄	兄	兄	兄	兄	兄	兄

暗	Notes: Adjective
	(暗, **àn**, **dark**, **dim**, **dull**)
	(暗, **àn**, **secretly**)
àn	
dark	

丨 冂 冂 日 日 日 旷 旷 旷 暗 暗 暗 暗 暗 暗

暗 暗 暗 暗 暗 暗 暗 暗 暗

暗	暗	暗	暗	暗	暗	暗	暗	暗	暗
àn	àn	àn	àn	àn	àn	àn	àn	àn	àn
dark	dark	dark	dark	dark	dark	dark	dark	dark	dark
暗	暗	暗	暗	暗	暗	暗	暗	暗	暗
àn	àn	àn	àn	àn	àn	àn	àn	àn	àn
dark	dark	dark	dark	dark	dark	dark	dark	dark	dark

暗	暗	暗	暗	暗	暗	暗	暗	暗	
暗	暗	暗	暗	暗	暗	暗	暗	暗	
暗	暗	暗	暗	暗	暗	暗	暗	暗	
暗	暗	暗	暗	暗	暗	暗	暗	暗	
暗	暗	暗	暗	暗	暗	暗	暗	暗	
暗	暗	暗	暗	暗	暗	暗	暗	暗	
暗	暗	暗	暗	暗	暗	暗	暗	暗	
暗	暗	暗	暗	暗	暗	暗	暗	暗	

创

Notes: Common Noun

(创, **chuāng**, **wound**)

(创, **chuàng**, **initiate something**)

chuàng

wound

丿 𠂉 𠂊 今 仓 创 创

创 创 创 创 创 创 创 创 创

创	创	创	创	创	创	创	创	创	创
chuàng	chuàng	chuàng	chuàng	chuàng	chuàng	chuàng	chuàng	chuàng	chuàng
wound	wound	wound	wound	wound	wound	wound	wound	wound	wound
创	创	创	创	创	创	创	创	创	创
chuàng	chuàng	chuàng	chuàng	chuàng	chuàng	chuàng	chuàng	chuàng	chuàng
wound	wound	wound	wound	wound	wound	wound	wound	wound	wound

创	创	创	创	创	创	创	创	创	创
创	创	创	创	创	创	创	创	创	创
创	创	创	创	创	创	创	创	创	创
创	创	创	创	创	创	创	创	创	创
创	创	创	创	创	创	创	创	创	创
创	创	创	创	创	创	创	创	创	创
创	创	创	创	创	创	创	创	创	创
创	创	创	创	创	创	创	创	创	创

排	Notes: Verb
	(排, **pái, arrange, line-up, put in order, sequence**)
	(排, **pái, remove with force, discharge, exclude, push open**)
	(排, **pái, raft**)
pái	(排, **pái, -anti**)
wound	

一 十 扌 打 扫 捊 拃 拃 排 排 排

排 排 排 排 排 排 排 排 排

排	排	排	排	排	排	排	排	排	排
pái	pái	pái	pái	pái	pái	pái	pái	pái	pái
wound	wound	wound	wound	wound	wound	wound	wound	wound	wound
排	排	排	排	排	排	排	排	排	排
pái	pái	pái	pái	pái	pái	pái	pái	pái	pái
wound	wound	wound	wound	wound	wound	wound	wound	wound	wound

排	排	排	排	排	排	排	排	排	排
排	排	排	排	排	排	排	排	排	排
排	排	排	排	排	排	排	排	排	排
排	排	排	排	排	排	排	排	排	排
排	排	排	排	排	排	排	排	排	排
排	排	排	排	排	排	排	排	排	排
排	排	排	排	排	排	排	排	排	排
排	排	排	排	排	排	排	排	排	排

春

chūn
spring

Notes: Common Noun

(春, **chūn**, spring

(春, **Chūn**, surname Chūn)

一 二 三 声 夫 夫 春 春 春

春 春 春 春 春 春 春 春 春

春	春	春	春	春	春	春	春	春	春
chūn	chūn	chūn	chūn	chūn	chūn	chūn	chūn	chūn	chūn
spring	spring	spring	spring	spring	spring	spring	spring	spring	spring
春	春	春	春	春	春	春	春	春	春
chūn	chūn	chūn	chūn	chūn	chūn	chūn	chūn	chūn	chūn
spring	spring	spring	spring	spring	spring	spring	spring	spring	spring
春	春	春	春	春	春	春	春	春	春
春	春	春	春	春	春	春	春	春	春
春	春	春	春	春	春	春	春	春	春
春	春	春	春	春	春	春	春	春	春
春	春	春	春	春	春	春	春	春	春
春	春	春	春	春	春	春	春	春	春
春	春	春	春	春	春	春	春	春	春
春	春	春	春	春	春	春	春	春	春

须	
xū must	Notes: Verb (须, xū, **must, have to**) (须, xū, **await, wait till**) (须, Xū, **surname Xū**) (须, xū, **beard, moustache**)

丿 丿 乡 乡 乡 犭 犭 狪 须 须

须 须 须 须 须 须 须 须 须

须	须	须	须	须	须	须	须	须	须
xū	xū	xū	xū	xū	xū	xū	xū	xū	xū
must	must	must	must	must	must	must	must	must	must
须	须	须	须	须	须	须	须	须	须
xū	xū	xū	xū	xū	xū	xū	xū	xū	xū
must	must	must	must	must	must	must	must	must	must
须	须	须	须	须	须	须	须	须	须
须	须	须	须	须	须	须	须	须	须
须	须	须	须	须	须	须	须	须	须
须	须	须	须	须	须	须	须	须	须
须	须	须	须	须	须	须	须	须	须
须	须	须	须	须	须	须	须	须	须
须	须	须	须	须	须	须	须	须	须
须	须	须	须	须	须	须	须	须	须

承

chéng
hold

Notes: Verb

(承, **chéng**, **bear**, **hold**, **carry**)

了 了 子 手 承 承 承 承

承 承 承 承 承 承 承 承 承

承	承	承	承	承	承	承	承	承	承
chéng hold	chéng hold	chéng hold	chéng hold	chéng hold	chéng hold	chéng hold	chéng hold	chéng hold	chéng hold
承	承	承	承	承	承	承	承	承	承
chéng hold	chéng hold	chéng hold	chéng hold	chéng hold	chéng hold	chéng hold	chéng hold	chéng hold	chéng hold
承	承	承	承	承	承	承	承	承	承
承	承	承	承	承	承	承	承	承	承
承	承	承	承	承	承	承	承	承	承
承	承	承	承	承	承	承	承	承	承
承	承	承	承	承	承	承	承	承	承
承	承	承	承	承	承	承	承	承	承
承	承	承	承	承	承	承	承	承	承
承	承	承	承	承	承	承	承	承	承

案

àn
law case

Notes: Verb

(案, àn, law case)

(案, àn, table, desk)

丶 丷 宀 灾 安 安 窀 宰 窀 案

案 案 案 案 案 案 案 案 案

案	案	案	案	案	案	案	案	案	案
àn	àn	àn	àn	àn	àn	àn	àn	àn	àn
law case	law case	law case	law case	law case	law case	law case	law case	law case	law case
案	案	案	案	案	案	案	案	案	案
àn	àn	àn	àn	àn	àn	àn	àn	àn	àn
law case	law case	law case	law case	law case	law case	law case	law case	law case	law case
案	案	案	案	案	案	案	案	案	
案	案	案	案	案	案	案	案	案	
案	案	案	案	案	案	案	案	案	
案	案	案	案	案	案	案	案	案	
案	案	案	案	案	案	案	案	案	
案	案	案	案	案	案	案	案	案	
案	案	案	案	案	案	案	案	案	

忙

máng
busy

Notes: Adjective

(忙, **máng**, **busy**, **fully occupied**)

(忙, **máng**, **hurry**, **hasten**, **make haste**)

丶 丶丶 忄 忄 忙 忙

忙 忙 忙 忙 忙 忙 忙 忙 忙

忙	忙	忙	忙	忙	忙	忙	忙	忙	忙
máng	máng	máng	máng	máng	máng	máng	máng	máng	máng
busy	busy	busy	busy	busy	busy	busy	busy	busy	busy
忙	忙	忙	忙	忙	忙	忙	忙	忙	忙
máng	máng	máng	máng	máng	máng	máng	máng	máng	máng
busy	busy	busy	busy	busy	busy	busy	busy	busy	busy
忙	忙	忙	忙	忙	忙	忙	忙	忙	忙
忙	忙	忙	忙	忙	忙	忙	忙	忙	忙
忙	忙	忙	忙	忙	忙	忙	忙	忙	忙
忙	忙	忙	忙	忙	忙	忙	忙	忙	忙
忙	忙	忙	忙	忙	忙	忙	忙	忙	忙
忙	忙	忙	忙	忙	忙	忙	忙	忙	忙
忙	忙	忙	忙	忙	忙	忙	忙	忙	忙
忙	忙	忙	忙	忙	忙	忙	忙	忙	忙

	Notes: Verb
呼	(呼, **hū**, **shout, exhale, breathe out, exhale**)
	(呼, **hū**, **cry out, call, page**)
hū	(呼, **hū**, **the onset of**)
shout	

丨 冂 口 口ʼ 口ʼ 口ʼ 叩 呼

呼 呼 呼 呼 呼 呼 呼 呼 呼

呼	呼	呼	呼	呼	呼	呼	呼	呼	呼
hū	hū	hū	hū	hū	hū	hū	hū	hū	hū
shout	shout	shout	shout	shout	shout	shout	shout	shout	shout
呼	呼	呼	呼	呼	呼	呼	呼	呼	呼
hū	hū	hū	hū	hū	hū	hū	hū	hū	hū
shout	shout	shout	shout	shout	shout	shout	shout	shout	shout
呼	呼	呼	呼	呼	呼	呼	呼	呼	呼
呼	呼	呼	呼	呼	呼	呼	呼	呼	呼
呼	呼	呼	呼	呼	呼	呼	呼	呼	呼
呼	呼	呼	呼	呼	呼	呼	呼	呼	呼
呼	呼	呼	呼	呼	呼	呼	呼	呼	呼
呼	呼	呼	呼	呼	呼	呼	呼	呼	呼
呼	呼	呼	呼	呼	呼	呼	呼	呼	呼
呼	呼	呼	呼	呼	呼	呼	呼	呼	呼

树

shù
tree

Notes: Common Noun

(树, shù, tree

(树, Shù, surname Shù)

(树, shù, plant, cultivate)

(树, shù, set up, establish, uphold)

一 十 十 木 朷 权 杸 树 树

树 树 树 树 树 树 树 树 树

树	树	树	树	树	树	树	树	树	树
shù	shù	shù	shù	shù	shù	shù	shù	shù	shù
tree	tree	tree	tree	tree	tree	tree	tree	tree	tree
树	树	树	树	树	树	树	树	树	树
shù	shù	shù	shù	shù	shù	shù	shù	shù	shù
tree	tree	tree	tree	tree	tree	tree	tree	tree	tree
树	树	树	树	树	树	树	树	树	树
树	树	树	树	树	树	树	树	树	树
树	树	树	树	树	树	树	树	树	树
树	树	树	树	树	树	树	树	树	树
树	树	树	树	树	树	树	树	树	树
树	树	树	树	树	树	树	树	树	树
树	树	树	树	树	树	树	树	树	树
树	树	树	树	树	树	树	树	树	树

痛

tòng
pain

Notes: Common Noun

(痛, tòng, painful, pain)

丶 亠 广 广 广 疒 疒 疒 疔 疖 痌 痛

痛 痛 痛 痛 痛 痛 痛 痛

痛	痛	痛	痛	痛	痛	痛	痛	痛	痛
tòng	tòng	tòng	tòng	tòng	tòng	tòng	tòng	tòng	tòng
pain	pain	pain	pain	pain	pain	pain	pain	pain	pain
痛	痛	痛	痛	痛	痛	痛	痛	痛	痛
tòng	tòng	tòng	tòng	tòng	tòng	tòng	tòng	tòng	tòng
pain	pain	pain	pain	pain	pain	pain	pain	pain	pain

痛	痛	痛	痛	痛	痛	痛	痛	痛	
痛	痛	痛	痛	痛	痛	痛	痛	痛	
痛	痛	痛	痛	痛	痛	痛	痛	痛	
痛	痛	痛	痛	痛	痛	痛	痛	痛	
痛	痛	痛	痛	痛	痛	痛	痛	痛	
痛	痛	痛	痛	痛	痛	痛	痛	痛	
痛	痛	痛	痛	痛	痛	痛	痛	痛	
痛	痛	痛	痛	痛	痛	痛	痛	痛	

沉

Notes: Verb

(沉, chén, to sink, keep down, lower)

(沉, chén, deep, profound, heavy)

chén
sink

丶 丶 氵 氵 沪 沪 沉

沉 沉 沉 沉 沉 沉 沉 沉 沉

沉	沉	沉	沉	沉	沉	沉	沉	沉	沉
chén sink	chén sink	chén sink	chén sink	chén sink	chén sink	chén sink	chén sink	chén sink	chén sink
沉	沉	沉	沉	沉	沉	沉	沉	沉	沉
chén sink	chén sink	chén sink	chén sink	chén sink	chén sink	chén sink	chén sink	chén sink	chén sink
沉	沉	沉	沉	沉	沉	沉	沉	沉	
沉	沉	沉	沉	沉	沉	沉	沉	沉	
沉	沉	沉	沉	沉	沉	沉	沉	沉	
沉	沉	沉	沉	沉	沉	沉	沉	沉	
沉	沉	沉	沉	沉	沉	沉	沉	沉	
沉	沉	沉	沉	沉	沉	沉	沉	沉	
沉	沉	沉	沉	沉	沉	沉	沉	沉	
沉	沉	沉	沉	沉	沉	沉	沉	沉	

啊	Notes: Grammatical Particle
	(啊, a, a suffix, indicating obviousness or impatience)
	(啊, ā, a suffix indicating elation)
	(啊, á, a suffix indicating doubt or questioning)
	(啊, ǎ, a suffix indicating puzzled surprise)
a	(啊, à, a suffix indicating agreement or approval)
suffix	

丨 丨丨 丨丨 丨丨 啊 啊 啊 啊 啊 啊

啊 啊 啊 啊 啊 啊 啊 啊 啊

啊	啊	啊	啊	啊	啊	啊	啊	啊	啊
a	a	a	a	a	a	a	a	a	a
suffix	suffix	suffix	suffix	suffix	suffix	suffix	suffix	suffix	suffix
啊	啊	啊	啊	啊	啊	啊	啊	啊	啊
a	a	a	a	a	a	a	a	a	a
suffix	suffix	suffix	suffix	suffix	suffix	suffix	suffix	suffix	suffix
啊	啊	啊	啊	啊	啊	啊	啊	啊	
啊	啊	啊	啊	啊	啊	啊	啊	啊	
啊	啊	啊	啊	啊	啊	啊	啊	啊	
啊	啊	啊	啊	啊	啊	啊	啊	啊	
啊	啊	啊	啊	啊	啊	啊	啊	啊	
啊	啊	啊	啊	啊	啊	啊	啊	啊	
啊	啊	啊	啊	啊	啊	啊	啊	啊	
啊	啊	啊	啊	啊	啊	啊	啊	啊	

灵	Notes: Adjective
	(灵, **líng**, **quick witted, clever, sharp**)
	(灵, **líng**, **efficacious, effective**)
	(灵, **líng**, **mysterious, divine**)
líng	(灵, **líng**, **spirit, soul, elf**)
clever	

ㄱ　ㄱ　ㅋ　ㅋ　ㅋ　ㅋ　尹　灵

灵　灵　灵　灵　灵　灵　灵　灵　灵

灵	灵	灵	灵	灵	灵	灵	灵	灵	灵
líng	líng	líng	líng	líng	líng	líng	líng	líng	líng
clever	clever	clever	clever	clever	clever	clever	clever	clever	clever
灵	灵	灵	灵	灵	灵	灵	灵	灵	灵
líng	líng	líng	líng	líng	líng	líng	líng	líng	líng
clever	clever	clever	clever	clever	clever	clever	clever	clever	clever

灵	灵	灵	灵	灵	灵	灵	灵	灵	灵
灵	灵	灵	灵	灵	灵	灵	灵	灵	灵
灵	灵	灵	灵	灵	灵	灵	灵	灵	灵
灵	灵	灵	灵	灵	灵	灵	灵	灵	灵
灵	灵	灵	灵	灵	灵	灵	灵	灵	灵
灵	灵	灵	灵	灵	灵	灵	灵	灵	灵
灵	灵	灵	灵	灵	灵	灵	灵	灵	灵
灵	灵	灵	灵	灵	灵	灵	灵	灵	灵

职	Notes: Common Noun (职, **zhí**, **duty**, **job**, **profession**)
zhí	
duty	

一 丆 丆 耵 耵 耵 耳 职 职 职 职 职

职 职 职 职 职 职 职 职 职

职	职	职	职	职	职	职	职	职	职
zhí	zhí	zhí	zhí	zhí	zhí	zhí	zhí	zhí	zhí
duty	duty	duty	duty	duty	duty	duty	duty	duty	duty
职	职	职	职	职	职	职	职	职	职
zhí	zhí	zhí	zhí	zhí	zhí	zhí	zhí	zhí	zhí
duty	duty	duty	duty	duty	duty	duty	duty	duty	duty
职	职	职	职	职	职	职	职	职	
职	职	职	职	职	职	职	职	职	
职	职	职	职	职	职	职	职	职	
职	职	职	职	职	职	职	职	职	
职	职	职	职	职	职	职	职	职	
职	职	职	职	职	职	职	职	职	
职	职	职	职	职	职	职	职	职	
职	职	职	职	职	职	职	职	职	

Notes: Common Noun

(乡, **xiāng**, **countryside**, **home town**, **township**, **village**, **rural area**)

xiāng

home town

xiāng	xiāng	xiāng	xiāng	xiāng	xiāng	xiāng	xiāng	xiāng	xiāng
home	home	home	home	home	home	home	home	home	home

xiāng	xiāng	xiāng	xiāng	xiāng	xiāng	xiāng	xiāng	xiāng	xiāng
home	home	home	home	home	home	home	home	home	home

细	
xì thin	Notes: Adjective (细, xì, thin, slender) (细, xì, fine, in small particles) (细, xì, thin and soft, exquisite, delicate) (细, xì, careful, meticulous, detailed, minute, trifling)

ノ 幺 幺 纟 纟 纫 细 细

细 细 细 细 细 细 细 细 细

细	细	细	细	细	细	细	细	细	细
xì	xì	xì	xì	xì	xì	xì	xì	xì	xì
thin	thin	thin	thin	thin	thin	thin	thin	thin	thin
细	细	细	细	细	细	细	细	细	细
xì	xì	xì	xì	xì	xì	xì	xì	xì	xì
thin	thin	thin	thin	thin	thin	thin	thin	thin	thin
细	细	细	细	细	细	细	细	细	细
细	细	细	细	细	细	细	细	细	细
细	细	细	细	细	细	细	细	细	细
细	细	细	细	细	细	细	细	细	细
细	细	细	细	细	细	细	细	细	细
细	细	细	细	细	细	细	细	细	细
细	细	细	细	细	细	细	细	细	细
细	细	细	细	细	细	细	细	细	细

诉

sù

tell

Notes: Verb

(诉, sù, tell, relate, inform)

丶 讠 讠 讠 讠 诉 诉

诉 诉 诉 诉 诉 诉 诉 诉 诉

诉	诉	诉	诉	诉	诉	诉	诉	诉	诉
sù	sù	sù	sù	sù	sù	sù	sù	sù	sù
tell	tell	tell	tell	tell	tell	tell	tell	tell	tell
诉	诉	诉	诉	诉	诉	诉	诉	诉	诉
sù	sù	sù	sù	sù	sù	sù	sù	sù	sù
tell	tell	tell	tell	tell	tell	tell	tell	tell	tell
诉	诉	诉	诉	诉	诉	诉	诉	诉	
诉	诉	诉	诉	诉	诉	诉	诉	诉	
诉	诉	诉	诉	诉	诉	诉	诉	诉	
诉	诉	诉	诉	诉	诉	诉	诉	诉	
诉	诉	诉	诉	诉	诉	诉	诉	诉	
诉	诉	诉	诉	诉	诉	诉	诉	诉	
诉	诉	诉	诉	诉	诉	诉	诉	诉	
诉	诉	诉	诉	诉	诉	诉	诉	诉	

態

tài

form

Notes: Common Noun

(態, **tài**, **form**, **appearance**, **state**, **condition**)

一 ナ 大 太 朩 态 态 态

态 态 态 态 态 态 态 态 态

态	态	态	态	态	态	态	态	态	态
tài	tài	tài	tài	tài	tài	tài	tài	tài	tài
form	form	form	form	form	form	form	form	form	form
态	态	态	态	态	态	态	态	态	态
tài	tài	tài	tài	tài	tài	tài	tài	tài	tài
form	form	form	form	form	form	form	form	form	form
态	态	态	态	态	态	态	态		
态	态	态	态	态	态	态	态		
态	态	态	态	态	态	态	态		
态	态	态	态	态	态	态	态		
态	态	态	态	态	态	态	态		
态	态	态	态	态	态	态	态		
态	态	态	态	态	态	态	态		

停

tíng
stop

Notes: Verb

(停, **tíng, stop, pause**)

丿 亻 亻 广 广 广 庐 停 庐 停 停 停

停 停 停 停 停 停 停 停 停

停	停	停	停	停	停	停	停	停	停
tíng	tíng	tíng	tíng	tíng	tíng	tíng	tíng	tíng	tíng
stop	stop	stop	stop	stop	stop	stop	stop	stop	stop
停	停	停	停	停	停	停	停	停	停
tíng	tíng	tíng	tíng	tíng	tíng	tíng	tíng	tíng	tíng
stop	stop	stop	stop	stop	stop	stop	stop	stop	stop
停	停	停	停	停	停	停	停	停	
停	停	停	停	停	停	停	停	停	
停	停	停	停	停	停	停	停	停	
停	停	停	停	停	停	停	停	停	
停	停	停	停	停	停	停	停	停	
停	停	停	停	停	停	停	停	停	
停	停	停	停	停	停	停	停	停	
停	停	停	停	停	停	停	停	停	

印	Notes: Verb
	(印, yìn, print, engrave, mark, trace)
	(印, yìn, seal, stamp, image, chop)
	(印, Yìn, surname Yìn)
yìn	
print	

´ 乚 乛 乛 印

印 印 印 印 印 印 印 印 印

印	印	印	印	印	印	印	印	印	印
yìn	yìn	yìn	yìn	yìn	yìn	yìn	yìn	yìn	yìn
print	print	print	print	print	print	print	print	print	print
印	印	印	印	印	印	印	印	印	印
yìn	yìn	yìn	yìn	yìn	yìn	yìn	yìn	yìn	yìn
print	print	print	print	print	print	print	print	print	print
印	印	印	印	印	印	印	印	印	印
印	印	印	印	印	印	印	印	印	印
印	印	印	印	印	印	印	印	印	印
印	印	印	印	印	印	印	印	印	印
印	印	印	印	印	印	印	印	印	印
印	印	印	印	印	印	印	印	印	印
印	印	印	印	印	印	印	印	印	印

笔		Notes: Common Noun

(笔, bǐ, writing implement, pen)

(笔, bǐ, technique of writing, calligraphy, drawing)

bǐ

pen

丿 ⺮ ⺮ ⺮⺮ ⺮⺮ ⺮⺮ 竺 竺 笁 笔

笔 笔 笔 笔 笔 笔 笔 笔 笔

笔	笔	笔	笔	笔	笔	笔	笔	笔	笔
bǐ	bǐ	bǐ	bǐ	bǐ	bǐ	bǐ	bǐ	bǐ	bǐ
pen	pen	pen	pen	pen	pen	pen	pen	pen	pen
笔	笔	笔	笔	笔	笔	笔	笔	笔	笔
bǐ	bǐ	bǐ	bǐ	bǐ	bǐ	bǐ	bǐ	bǐ	bǐ
pen	pen	pen	pen	pen	pen	pen	pen	pen	pen
笔	笔	笔	笔	笔	笔	笔	笔	笔	笔
笔	笔	笔	笔	笔	笔	笔	笔	笔	笔
笔	笔	笔	笔	笔	笔	笔	笔	笔	笔
笔	笔	笔	笔	笔	笔	笔	笔	笔	笔
笔	笔	笔	笔	笔	笔	笔	笔	笔	笔
笔	笔	笔	笔	笔	笔	笔	笔	笔	笔
笔	笔	笔	笔	笔	笔	笔	笔	笔	笔
笔	笔	笔	笔	笔	笔	笔	笔	笔	笔

夏

xià

summer

Notes: Common Noun

(夏, **xià**, **summer**)

(夏, **Xià**, **surname Xià**)

一 一 厂 亓 万 百 百 頁 夏 夏

夏 夏 夏 夏 夏 夏 夏 夏 夏

夏	夏	夏	夏	夏	夏	夏	夏	夏	夏
xià	xià	xià	xià	xià	xià	xià	xià	xià	xià
summer	summer	summer	summer	summer	summer	summer	summer	summer	summer
夏	夏	夏	夏	夏	夏	夏	夏	夏	夏
xià	xià	xià	xià	xià	xià	xià	xià	xià	xià
summer	summer	summer	summer	summer	summer	summer	summer	summer	summer

夏	夏	夏	夏	夏	夏	夏	夏	夏	
夏	夏	夏	夏	夏	夏	夏	夏	夏	
夏	夏	夏	夏	夏	夏	夏	夏	夏	
夏	夏	夏	夏	夏	夏	夏	夏	夏	
夏	夏	夏	夏	夏	夏	夏	夏	夏	
夏	夏	夏	夏	夏	夏	夏	夏	夏	
夏	夏	夏	夏	夏	夏	夏	夏	夏	
夏	夏	夏	夏	夏	夏	夏	夏	夏	

助	Notes: Verb
	(助, zhù, help, assist, aid)
zhù	
help	

丨 冂 冃 月 目 刖 助

助 助 助 助 助 助 助 助 助

助	助	助	助	助	助	助	助	助	助
zhù	zhù	zhù	zhù	zhù	zhù	zhù	zhù	zhù	zhù
help	help	help	help	help	help	help	help	help	help
助	助	助	助	助	助	助	助	助	助
zhù	zhù	zhù	zhù	zhù	zhù	zhù	zhù	zhù	zhù
help	help	help	help	help	help	help	help	help	help
助	助	助	助	助	助	助	助	助	助
助	助	助	助	助	助	助	助	助	助
助	助	助	助	助	助	助	助	助	助
助	助	助	助	助	助	助	助	助	助
助	助	助	助	助	助	助	助	助	助
助	助	助	助	助	助	助	助	助	助
助	助	助	助	助	助	助	助	助	助

福	Notes: Common Noun
	(福, **fú**, **blessing, good fortune, happiness, luck**)
fú	
luck	

丶 丁 ﾃ 礻 礻 礻 礻 祄 祄 祸 福 福 福

福 福 福 福 福 福 福 福 福

福	福	福	福	福	福	福	福	福	福
fú	fú	fú	fú	fú	fú	fú	fú	fú	fú
luck	luck	luck	luck	luck	luck	luck	luck	luck	luck
福	福	福	福	福	福	福	福	福	福
fú	fú	fú	fú	fú	fú	fú	fú	fú	fú
luck	luck	luck	luck	luck	luck	luck	luck	luck	luck

福	福	福	福	福	福	福	福	福	
福	福	福	福	福	福	福	福	福	
福	福	福	福	福	福	福	福	福	
福	福	福	福	福	福	福	福	福	
福	福	福	福	福	福	福	福	福	
福	福	福	福	福	福	福	福	福	
福	福	福	福	福	福	福	福	福	
福	福	福	福	福	福	福	福	福	

块

kuài
piece

Notes: Grammatical Particle

(块, **kuài**, **measure word for piece**, **lump**, **chunk**)

(块, **kuài**, **piece**, **lump**, **chunk**)

一　十　土　扌　扫　坍　块

块　块　块　块　块　块　块　块　块

块	块	块	块	块	块	块	块	块	块
kuài	kuài	kuài	kuài	kuài	kuài	kuài	kuài	kuài	kuài
piece	piece	piece	piece	piece	piece	piece	piece	piece	piece
块	块	块	块	块	块	块	块	块	块
kuài	kuài	kuài	kuài	kuài	kuài	kuài	kuài	kuài	kuài
piece	piece	piece	piece	piece	piece	piece	piece	piece	piece
块	块	块	块	块	块	块	块	块	块
块	块	块	块	块	块	块	块	块	块
块	块	块	块	块	块	块	块	块	块
块	块	块	块	块	块	块	块	块	块
块	块	块	块	块	块	块	块	块	块
块	块	块	块	块	块	块	块	块	块
块	块	块	块	块	块	块	块	块	块
块	块	块	块	块	块	块	块	块	块

冷	Notes: Adjective
	(冷, **lěng**, **cold**)
	(冷, **lěng**, **frosty in manner**)
	(冷, **lěng**, **unfrequented, deserted, out-of-the-way**)
lěng	(冷, **Lěng**, **surname Lěng**)
cold	

丶 冫 冫 冹 冹 冷 冷

冷 冷 冷 冷 冷 冷 冷 冷 冷

冷	冷	冷	冷	冷	冷	冷	冷	冷	冷
lěng	lěng	lěng	lěng	lěng	lěng	lěng	lěng	lěng	lěng
cold	cold	cold	cold	cold	cold	cold	cold	cold	cold
冷	冷	冷	冷	冷	冷	冷	冷	冷	冷
lěng	lěng	lěng	lěng	lěng	lěng	lěng	lěng	lěng	lěng
cold	cold	cold	cold	cold	cold	cold	cold	cold	cold
冷	冷	冷	冷	冷	冷	冷	冷		
冷	冷	冷	冷	冷	冷	冷	冷		
冷	冷	冷	冷	冷	冷	冷	冷		
冷	冷	冷	冷	冷	冷	冷	冷		
冷	冷	冷	冷	冷	冷	冷	冷		
冷	冷	冷	冷	冷	冷	冷	冷		
冷	冷	冷	冷	冷	冷	冷	冷		
冷	冷	冷	冷	冷	冷	冷	冷		

球		
qiú		
ball		

Notes: Common Noun

(球, qiú, ball)

一 二 丁 王 王 王 刊 玎 玎 球 球 球

球 球 球 球 球 球 球 球 球

球	球	球	球	球	球	球	球	球	球
qiú	qiú	qiú	qiú	qiú	qiú	qiú	qiú	qiú	qiú
ball	ball	ball	ball	ball	ball	ball	ball	ball	ball
球	球	球	球	球	球	球	球	球	球
qiú	qiú	qiú	qiú	qiú	qiú	qiú	qiú	qiú	qiú
ball	ball	ball	ball	ball	ball	ball	ball	ball	ball

球	球	球	球	球	球	球	球	球	球
球	球	球	球	球	球	球	球	球	球
球	球	球	球	球	球	球	球	球	球
球	球	球	球	球	球	球	球	球	球
球	球	球	球	球	球	球	球	球	球
球	球	球	球	球	球	球	球	球	球
球	球	球	球	球	球	球	球	球	球

姑	Notes: Common Noun (姑, gū, father's sister, husband's sister, husband's mother) (姑, gū, nun) (姑, gū, tentatively, for the time being)
gū ball	

く 女 女 妒 妒 姑 姑 姑

姑 姑 姑 姑 姑 姑 姑 姑 姑

姑	姑	姑	姑	姑	姑	姑	姑	姑	姑
gū	gū	gū	gū	gū	gū	gū	gū	gū	gū
ball	ball	ball	ball	ball	ball	ball	ball	ball	ball
姑	姑	姑	姑	姑	姑	姑	姑	姑	姑
gū	gū	gū	gū	gū	gū	gū	gū	gū	gū
ball	ball	ball	ball	ball	ball	ball	ball	ball	ball

划

Notes: Common Noun

(划, **huá, paddle, row**)
(划, **huá, be to one's profit, pay**)
(划, **huà, delimit, differentiate**)
(划, **huà, transfer, assign**)

huá
ball

一 弋 戈 戈 划 划

划 划 划 划 划 划 划 划

划	划	划	划	划	划	划	划	划	划
huá	huá	huá	huá	huá	huá	huá	huá	huá	huá
ball	ball	ball	ball	ball	ball	ball	ball	ball	ball
划	划	划	划	划	划	划	划	划	划
huá	huá	huá	huá	huá	huá	huá	huá	huá	huá
ball	ball	ball	ball	ball	ball	ball	ball	ball	ball
划	划	划	划	划	划	划	划	划	划
划	划	划	划	划	划	划	划	划	划
划	划	划	划	划	划	划	划	划	划
划	划	划	划	划	划	划	划	划	划
划	划	划	划	划	划	划	划	划	划
划	划	划	划	划	划	划	划	划	划
划	划	划	划	划	划	划	划	划	划

划

Notes: Verb

(划, **huà, draw, mark, delete**)

(划, **huà, stroke of Chinese character**)

(划, **huá, scratch, cut the surface of**)

huá

ball

一　七　戈　戈　划　划

划 划 划 划 划 划 划 划 划

划	划	划	划	划	划	划	划	划	划
huá	huá	huá	huá	huá	huá	huá	huá	huá	huá
ball	ball	ball	ball	ball	ball	ball	ball	ball	ball
划	划	划	划	划	划	划	划	划	划
huá	huá	huá	huá	huá	huá	huá	huá	huá	huá
ball	ball	ball	ball	ball	ball	ball	ball	ball	ball

划	划	划	划	划	划	划	划	划	
划	划	划	划	划	划	划	划	划	
划	划	划	划	划	划	划	划	划	
划	划	划	划	划	划	划	划	划	
划	划	划	划	划	划	划	划	划	
划	划	划	划	划	划	划	划	划	
划	划	划	划	划	划	划	划	划	
划	划	划	划	划	划	划	划	划	

既

jì
since

Notes: Adverb

(既, jì, since, already, then, later on)

(既, jì, complete, full)

丁 彐 彐 𣎳 艮 既 既 既 既

既 既 既 既 既 既 既 既 既

既	既	既	既	既	既	既	既	既	既
jì	jì	jì	jì	jì	jì	jì	jì	jì	jì
since	since	since	since	since	since	since	since	since	since

既	既	既	既	既	既	既	既	既	既
jì	jì	jì	jì	jì	jì	jì	jì	jì	jì
since	since	since	since	since	since	since	since	since	since

既	既	既	既	既	既	既	既	既	既
既	既	既	既	既	既	既	既	既	既
既	既	既	既	既	既	既	既	既	既
既	既	既	既	既	既	既	既	既	既
既	既	既	既	既	既	既	既	既	既
既	既	既	既	既	既	既	既	既	既
既	既	既	既	既	既	既	既	既	既
既	既	既	既	既	既	既	既	既	既

质
zhì
nature

Notes: Common Noun

(质, zhì, quality, nature, character, temperament)

一 厂 厂 斤 严 斥 斥 质 质

质 质 质 质 质 质 质 质 质

质	质	质	质	质	质	质	质	质	质
zhì	zhì	zhì	zhì	zhì	zhì	zhì	zhì	zhì	zhì
nature	nature	nature	nature	nature	nature	nature	nature	nature	nature
质	质	质	质	质	质	质	质	质	质
zhì	zhì	zhì	zhì	zhì	zhì	zhì	zhì	zhì	zhì
nature	nature	nature	nature	nature	nature	nature	nature	nature	nature

巴

bā
near

Notes: Verb

(巴, **bā**, **hope for, cling to, be near**)

(巴, **Bā**, **surname Bā**)

(巴, **Bā**, **ancient name for eastern Sichuan**)

フ フ 刊 卫 巴

巴 巴 巴 巴 巴 巴 巴 巴

巴	巴	巴	巴	巴	巴	巴	巴	巴	巴
bā	bā	bā	bā	bā	bā	bā	bā	bā	bā
near	near	near	near	near	near	near	near	near	near
巴	巴	巴	巴	巴	巴	巴	巴	巴	巴
bā	bā	bā	bā	bā	bā	bā	bā	bā	bā
near	near	near	near	near	near	near	near	near	near

致	Notes: Verb
	(致, zhì, send, convey, extend, deliver)
	(致, zhì, return, give up)
	(致, zhì, incur, cause)
zhì	(致, zhì, fine, delicate, meticulous)
send	

一 工 云 亙 至 至 到 致 致 致

致 致 致 致 致 致 致 致 致

致	致	致	致	致	致	致	致	致	致
zhì	zhì	zhì	zhì	zhì	zhì	zhì	zhì	zhì	zhì
send	send	send	send	send	send	send	send	send	send

致	致	致	致	致	致	致	致	致	致
zhì	zhì	zhì	zhì	zhì	zhì	zhì	zhì	zhì	zhì
send	send	send	send	send	send	send	send	send	send

湾

wān
harbour

Notes: Common Noun

(湾, wān, harbour)

(湾, wān, bend in a stream)

丶 丶 氵 氵 广 疒 沛 沛 沵 湾 湾 湾

湾 湾 湾 湾 湾 湾 湾 湾 湾

湾	湾	湾	湾	湾	湾	湾	湾	湾	湾
wān	wān	wān	wān	wān	wān	wān	wān	wān	wān
harbour	harbour	harbour	harbour	harbour	harbour	harbour	harbour	harbour	harbour
湾	湾	湾	湾	湾	湾	湾	湾	湾	湾
wān	wān	wān	wān	wān	wān	wān	wān	wān	wān
harbour	harbour	harbour	harbour	harbour	harbour	harbour	harbour	harbour	harbour

演

yǎn
harbour

Notes: Verb

(演, yǎn, perform, play, act)

(演, yǎn, develop, evolve)

丶 丶 氵 氵 氵 氵 广 宀 宀 宀 宀 宀 宀 演 演

演 演 演 演 演 演 演 演 演

演	演	演	演	演	演	演	演	演	演
yǎn	yǎn	yǎn	yǎn	yǎn	yǎn	yǎn	yǎn	yǎn	yǎn
harbour	harbour	harbour	harbour	harbour	harbour	harbour	harbour	harbour	harbour
演	演	演	演	演	演	演	演	演	演
yǎn	yǎn	yǎn	yǎn	yǎn	yǎn	yǎn	yǎn	yǎn	yǎn
harbour	harbour	harbour	harbour	harbour	harbour	harbour	harbour	harbour	harbour

演	演	演	演	演	演	演	演	演
演	演	演	演	演	演	演	演	演
演	演	演	演	演	演	演	演	演
演	演	演	演	演	演	演	演	演
演	演	演	演	演	演	演	演	演
演	演	演	演	演	演	演	演	演
演	演	演	演	演	演	演	演	演
演	演	演	演	演	演	演	演	演

木	Notes: Common Noun
	(木, mù, tree)
mù	
tree	

一 十 才 木

木 木 木 木 木 木 木 木 木

木	木	木	木	木	木	木	木	木	木
mù	mù	mù	mù	mù	mù	mù	mù	mù	mù
tree	tree	tree	tree	tree	tree	tree	tree	tree	tree
木	木	木	木	木	木	木	木	木	木
mù	mù	mù	mù	mù	mù	mù	mù	mù	mù
tree	tree	tree	tree	tree	tree	tree	tree	tree	tree

韦	Notes: Common Noun
	(韦, **wéi**, **soft leather**)
wéi	(韦, **Wéi**, **surname Wéi**)
leather	

一 二 亏 韦

韦 韦 韦 韦 韦 韦 韦 韦 韦

韦	韦	韦	韦	韦	韦	韦	韦	韦	韦
wéi	wéi	wéi	wéi	wéi	wéi	wéi	wéi	wéi	wéi
leather	leather	leather	leather	leather	leather	leather	leather	leather	leather
韦	韦	韦	韦	韦	韦	韦	韦	韦	韦
wéi	wéi	wéi	wéi	wéi	wéi	wéi	wéi	wéi	wéi
leather	leather	leather	leather	leather	leather	leather	leather	leather	leather
韦	韦	韦	韦	韦	韦	韦	韦	韦	
韦	韦	韦	韦	韦	韦	韦	韦	韦	
韦	韦	韦	韦	韦	韦	韦	韦	韦	
韦	韦	韦	韦	韦	韦	韦	韦	韦	
韦	韦	韦	韦	韦	韦	韦	韦	韦	
韦	韦	韦	韦	韦	韦	韦	韦	韦	
韦	韦	韦	韦	韦	韦	韦	韦	韦	

怪	Notes: Verb
	(怪, guài, blame, at blame)
	(怪, guài, surprising, strange, find something strange)
	(怪, guài, quite, very)
guài	(怪, guài, quite, monster, evil spirit)
blame	

丿 丷 忄 忄 忉 怪 怪 怪

怪 怪 怪 怪 怪 怪 怪 怪 怪

怪	怪	怪	怪	怪	怪	怪	怪	怪	怪
guài	guài	guài	guài	guài	guài	guài	guài	guài	guài
blame	blame	blame	blame	blame	blame	blame	blame	blame	blame
怪	怪	怪	怪	怪	怪	怪	怪	怪	怪
guài	guài	guài	guài	guài	guài	guài	guài	guài	guài
blame	blame	blame	blame	blame	blame	blame	blame	blame	blame
怪	怪	怪	怪	怪	怪	怪	怪	怪	怪
怪	怪	怪	怪	怪	怪	怪	怪	怪	怪
怪	怪	怪	怪	怪	怪	怪	怪	怪	怪
怪	怪	怪	怪	怪	怪	怪	怪	怪	怪
怪	怪	怪	怪	怪	怪	怪	怪	怪	怪
怪	怪	怪	怪	怪	怪	怪	怪	怪	怪
怪	怪	怪	怪	怪	怪	怪	怪	怪	怪
怪	怪	怪	怪	怪	怪	怪	怪	怪	怪

围
wéi
enclose

Notes: Verb

(围, **wéi**, **surround, enclose, around, all around**)

(围, **wéi**, **corral**)

丨 冂 冂 冃 冃 围 围

围 围 围 围 围 围 围 围 围

围	围	围	围	围	围	围	围	围	围
wéi	wéi	wéi	wéi	wéi	wéi	wéi	wéi	wéi	wéi
enclose	enclose	enclose	enclose	enclose	enclose	enclose	enclose	enclose	enclose
围	围	围	围	围	围	围	围	围	围
wéi	wéi	wéi	wéi	wéi	wéi	wéi	wéi	wéi	wéi
enclose	enclose	enclose	enclose	enclose	enclose	enclose	enclose	enclose	enclose

静

jìng
quiet

Notes: Adjective

(靜, **jìng**, **still, quiet, calm**)

一 二 キ 丰 主 青 青 青 青 静 静 静 静 静

静 静 静 静 静 静 静 静 静

静	静	静	静	静	静	静	静	静	静
jìng	jìng	jìng	jìng	jìng	jìng	jìng	jìng	jìng	jìng
quiet	quiet	quiet	quiet	quiet	quiet	quiet	quiet	quiet	quiet
静	静	静	静	静	静	静	静	静	静
jìng	jìng	jìng	jìng	jìng	jìng	jìng	jìng	jìng	jìng
quiet	quiet	quiet	quiet	quiet	quiet	quiet	quiet	quiet	quiet
静	静	静	静	静	静	静	静	静	静
静	静	静	静	静	静	静	静	静	静
静	静	静	静	静	静	静	静	静	静
静	静	静	静	静	静	静	静	静	静
静	静	静	静	静	静	静	静	静	静
静	静	静	静	静	静	静	静	静	静
静	静	静	静	静	静	静	静	静	静
静	静	静	静	静	静	静	静	静	静

旁	Notes: Common Noun
	(旁, **páng**, side)
páng	
side	

丶 亠 产 产 产 产 产 产 㫄 旁 旁

旁 旁 旁 旁 旁 旁 旁 旁 旁

旁	旁	旁	旁	旁	旁	旁	旁	旁	旁
páng	páng	páng	páng	páng	páng	páng	páng	páng	páng
side	side	side	side	side	side	side	side	side	side
旁	旁	旁	旁	旁	旁	旁	旁	旁	旁
páng	páng	páng	páng	páng	páng	páng	páng	páng	páng
side	side	side	side	side	side	side	side	side	side
旁	旁	旁	旁	旁	旁	旁	旁	旁	
旁	旁	旁	旁	旁	旁	旁	旁	旁	
旁	旁	旁	旁	旁	旁	旁	旁	旁	
旁	旁	旁	旁	旁	旁	旁	旁	旁	
旁	旁	旁	旁	旁	旁	旁	旁	旁	
旁	旁	旁	旁	旁	旁	旁	旁	旁	
旁	旁	旁	旁	旁	旁	旁	旁	旁	
旁	旁	旁	旁	旁	旁	旁	旁	旁	

园

yuán

side

Notes: Common Noun

(园, **yuán**, **garden**)

一 冂 冂 同 同 园 园

园 园 园 园 园 园 园 园 园

园	园	园	园	园	园	园	园	园	园
yuán	yuán	yuán	yuán	yuán	yuán	yuán	yuán	yuán	yuán
side	side	side	side	side	side	side	side	side	side
园	园	园	园	园	园	园	园	园	园
yuán	yuán	yuán	yuán	yuán	yuán	yuán	yuán	yuán	yuán
side	side	side	side	side	side	side	side	side	side
园	园	园	园	园	园	园	园	园	园
园	园	园	园	园	园	园	园	园	园
园	园	园	园	园	园	园	园	园	园
园	园	园	园	园	园	园	园	园	园
园	园	园	园	园	园	园	园	园	园
园	园	园	园	园	园	园	园	园	园
园	园	园	园	园	园	园	园	园	园
园	园	园	园	园	园	园	园	园	园

否

fǒu

not

Notes: Common Noun

(否, fǒu, not, negate, deny)

(否, pǐ, bad, inferior)

一 丆 丆 不 不 否 否

否 否 否 否 否 否 否 否 否

否	否	否	否	否	否	否	否	否	否
fǒu	fǒu	fǒu	fǒu	fǒu	fǒu	fǒu	fǒu	fǒu	fǒu
not	not	not	not	not	not	not	not	not	not
否	否	否	否	否	否	否	否	否	否
fǒu	fǒu	fǒu	fǒu	fǒu	fǒu	fǒu	fǒu	fǒu	fǒu
not	not	not	not	not	not	not	not	not	not

否	否	否	否	否	否	否	否	否	
否	否	否	否	否	否	否	否	否	
否	否	否	否	否	否	否	否	否	
否	否	否	否	否	否	否	否	否	
否	否	否	否	否	否	否	否	否	
否	否	否	否	否	否	否	否	否	
否	否	否	否	否	否	否	否	否	
否	否	否	否	否	否	否	否	否	

副

Notes: Common Noun

(副, **fù**, **assistant**, **vice**, **deputy**) as an occupation title.

(副, **fù**, **auxiliary, subsidiary**)

(副, **fù**, **measure word for sets of things or facial expressions**)

(副, **fù**, **tally with, conform to, fit**)

fù
deputy

一 厂 厅 币 币 畐 畐 畐 畐 副 副

副 副 副 副 副 副 副 副 副

副	副	副	副	副	副	副	副	副	副
fù	fù	fù	fù	fù	fù	fù	fù	fù	fù
deputy	deputy	deputy	deputy	deputy	deputy	deputy	deputy	deputy	deputy
副	副	副	副	副	副	副	副	副	副
fù	fù	fù	fù	fù	fù	fù	fù	fù	fù
deputy	deputy	deputy	deputy	deputy	deputy	deputy	deputy	deputy	deputy
副	副	副	副	副	副	副	副	副	副
副	副	副	副	副	副	副	副	副	副
副	副	副	副	副	副	副	副	副	副
副	副	副	副	副	副	副	副	副	副
副	副	副	副	副	副	副	副	副	副
副	副	副	副	副	副	副	副	副	副
副	副	副	副	副	副	副	副	副	副
副	副	副	副	副	副	副	副	副	副

辑

Notes: Verb

(辑, jí, compile, collect, edit)

(辑, jí, peaceful)

(辑, jí, measure word for part, volume, division)

jí
collect

一 厂 厂 厇 厈 咠 咠 咠 畐 副 副

辑 辑 辑 辑 辑 辑 辑 辑 辑

辑	辑	辑	辑	辑	辑	辑	辑	辑	辑
jí	jí	jí	jí	jí	jí	jí	jí	jí	jí
collect	collect	collect	collect	collect	collect	collect	collect	collect	collect
辑	辑	辑	辑	辑	辑	辑	辑	辑	辑
jí	jí	jí	jí	jí	jí	jí	jí	jí	jí
collect	collect	collect	collect	collect	collect	collect	collect	collect	collect

辑	辑	辑	辑	辑	辑	辑	辑	辑	
辑	辑	辑	辑	辑	辑	辑	辑	辑	
辑	辑	辑	辑	辑	辑	辑	辑	辑	
辑	辑	辑	辑	辑	辑	辑	辑	辑	
辑	辑	辑	辑	辑	辑	辑	辑	辑	
辑	辑	辑	辑	辑	辑	辑	辑	辑	
辑	辑	辑	辑	辑	辑	辑	辑	辑	
辑	辑	辑	辑	辑	辑	辑	辑	辑	

采

căi
gather

Notes: Verb

(采, căi, pick, gather, select)

(采, căi, mine)

(采, căi, variegated color)

(采, căi, facial color and expression)

一 ┌ ┌ ┌ 罒 罒 罒 平 乎 采

采 采 采 采 采 采 采 采 采

采	采	采	采	采	采	采	采	采	采
căi	căi	căi	căi	căi	căi	căi	căi	căi	căi
gather	gather	gather	gather	gather	gather	gather	gather	gather	gather
采	采	采	采	采	采	采	采	采	采
căi	căi	căi	căi	căi	căi	căi	căi	căi	căi
gather	gather	gather	gather	gather	gather	gather	gather	gather	gather
采	采	采	采	采	采	采	采	采	采
采	采	采	采	采	采	采	采	采	采
采	采	采	采	采	采	采	采	采	采
采	采	采	采	采	采	采	采	采	采
采	采	采	采	采	采	采	采	采	采
采	采	采	采	采	采	采	采	采	采
采	采	采	采	采	采	采	采	采	采
采	采	采	采	采	采	采	采	采	采

食	Notes: Verb
	(食, shí, eat)
	(食, shí, meal, having to do with food)
	(食, give food to a person)
shí	
eat	

丿 人 人 仒 今 今 仒 食 食

食 食 食 食 食 食 食 食 食

食	食	食	食	食	食	食	食	食	食
shí	shí	shí	shí	shí	shí	shí	shí	shí	shí
eat	eat	eat	eat	eat	eat	eat	eat	eat	eat
食	食	食	食	食	食	食	食	食	食
shí	shí	shí	shí	shí	shí	shí	shí	shí	shí
eat	eat	eat	eat	eat	eat	eat	eat	eat	eat

食	食	食	食	食	食	食	食	食	
食	食	食	食	食	食	食	食		
食	食	食	食	食	食	食	食		
食	食	食	食	食	食	食	食		
食	食	食	食	食	食	食	食		
食	食	食	食	食	食	食	食		
食	食	食	食	食	食	食	食		
食	食	食	食	食	食	食	食		

登

dēng
climb

Notes: Verb

(登, **dēng**, **climb, ascend, climb, mount, step on**)

(登, **dēng**, **publish, record**)

(登, **dēng**, **harvest**)

(登, **dēng**, **pedal**)

丁 丁 丁 丁 丁 癶 癶 癶 癶 癶 癶 登

登 登 登 登 登 登 登 登 登

登	登	登	登	登	登	登	登	登	登
dēng climb	dēng climb	dēng climb	dēng climb	dēng climb	dēng climb	dēng climb	dēng climb	dēng climb	dēng climb
登	登	登	登	登	登	登	登	登	登
dēng climb	dēng climb	dēng climb	dēng climb	dēng climb	dēng climb	dēng climb	dēng climb	dēng climb	dēng climb

够

gòu
enough

Notes: Common Noun

(够, gòu, enough, be or have enough, be sufficient or adequate)

(够, gòu, reach something with one's hand)

(够, gòu, quite)

丿 勹 勹 甸 甸 甸 够 够 够 够 够

够 够 够 够 够 够 够 够 够

够	够	够	够	够	够	够	够	够	够
gòu	gòu	gòu	gòu	gòu	gòu	gòu	gòu	gòu	gòu
enough	enough	enough	enough	enough	enough	enough	enough	enough	enough
够	够	够	够	够	够	够	够	够	够
gòu	gòu	gòu	gòu	gòu	gòu	gòu	gòu	gòu	gòu
enough	enough	enough	enough	enough	enough	enough	enough	enough	enough
够	够	够	够	够	够	够	够	够	
够	够	够	够	够	够	够	够	够	
够	够	够	够	够	够	够	够	够	
够	够	够	够	够	够	够	够	够	
够	够	够	够	够	够	够	够	够	
够	够	够	够	够	够	够	够	够	
够	够	够	够	够	够	够	够	够	

赛

sài
contest

Notes: Common Noun

(赛, sài, contest, game, competition)

(赛, sài, exceed, surpass)

(赛, sài, compete)

丶丷宀宀宁审审审寒寒寒寨赛赛

赛 赛 赛 赛 赛 赛 赛 赛 赛

赛	赛	赛	赛	赛	赛	赛	赛	赛	赛
sài	sài	sài	sài	sài	sài	sài	sài	sài	sài
contest	contest	contest	contest	contest	contest	contest	contest	contest	contest
赛	赛	赛	赛	赛	赛	赛	赛	赛	赛
sài	sài	sài	sài	sài	sài	sài	sài	sài	sài
contest	contest	contest	contest	contest	contest	contest	contest	contest	contest
赛	赛	赛	赛	赛	赛	赛	赛	赛	赛
赛	赛	赛	赛	赛	赛	赛	赛	赛	赛
赛	赛	赛	赛	赛	赛	赛	赛	赛	赛
赛	赛	赛	赛	赛	赛	赛	赛	赛	赛
赛	赛	赛	赛	赛	赛	赛	赛	赛	赛
赛	赛	赛	赛	赛	赛	赛	赛	赛	赛
赛	赛	赛	赛	赛	赛	赛	赛	赛	赛
赛	赛	赛	赛	赛	赛	赛	赛	赛	赛

米	Notes: Common Noun
	(米, mǐ, rice, meter)
	(米, mǐ, shelled or husked grain)
	(米, mǐ, metre)
mǐ	米, Mǐ, surname Mǐ)
rice	

丶　丷　丷　㐅　半　米　米

米 米 米 米 米 米 米 米 米

米	米	米	米	米	米	米	米	米	米
mǐ	mǐ	mǐ	mǐ	mǐ	mǐ	mǐ	mǐ	mǐ	mǐ
rice	rice	rice	rice	rice	rice	rice	rice	rice	rice
米	米	米	米	米	米	米	米	米	米
mǐ	mǐ	mǐ	mǐ	mǐ	mǐ	mǐ	mǐ	mǐ	mǐ
rice	rice	rice	rice	rice	rice	rice	rice	rice	rice
米	米	米	米	米	米	米	米	米	
米	米	米	米	米	米	米	米	米	
米	米	米	米	米	米	米	米	米	
米	米	米	米	米	米	米	米	米	
米	米	米	米	米	米	米	米	米	
米	米	米	米	米	米	米	米	米	
米	米	米	米	米	米	米	米	米	
米	米	米	米	米	米	米	米	米	

假	Notes: Adjective
	(假, **jiǎ**, **false, fake, phony, artificial**)
	(假, **jiǎ**, **conditional, tentative**)
	(假, **jiǎ**, **borrow, avail of**)
jiǎ	(假, **jiǎ**, **holiday, vacation, leave of absence, furlough**)
fake	

ノ 亻 仃 仃 仔 仔 作 作 作 假 假

假 假 假 假 假 假 假 假 假

假	假	假	假	假	假	假	假	假	假
jiǎ	jiǎ	jiǎ	jiǎ	jiǎ	jiǎ	jiǎ	jiǎ	jiǎ	jiǎ
fake	fake	fake	fake	fake	fake	fake	fake	fake	fake
假	假	假	假	假	假	假	假	假	假
jiǎ	jiǎ	jiǎ	jiǎ	jiǎ	jiǎ	jiǎ	jiǎ	jiǎ	jiǎ
fake	fake	fake	fake	fake	fake	fake	fake	fake	fake
假	假	假	假	假	假	假	假	假	假
假	假	假	假	假	假	假	假	假	假
假	假	假	假	假	假	假	假	假	假
假	假	假	假	假	假	假	假	假	假
假	假	假	假	假	假	假	假	假	假
假	假	假	假	假	假	假	假	假	假
假	假	假	假	假	假	假	假	假	假
假	假	假	假	假	假	假	假	假	假

较

jiào
quite

Notes: Adjective

(较, **jiào**, **relatively**, **rather**, **quite**, **more**)

(较, **jiào**, **compare**)

(较, **jiào**, **dispute**)

(较, **jiào**, **clearly**, **obviously**)

一 七 车 车 车' 车广 车广 车交 车交 较

较 较 较 较 较 较 较 较 较

较	较	较	较	较	较	较	较	较	较
jiào	jiào	jiào	jiào	jiào	jiào	jiào	jiào	jiào	jiào
quite	quite	quite	quite	quite	quite	quite	quite	quite	quite
较	较	较	较	较	较	较	较	较	较
jiào	jiào	jiào	jiào	jiào	jiào	jiào	jiào	jiào	jiào
quite	quite	quite	quite	quite	quite	quite	quite	quite	quite
较	较	较	较	较	较	较	较	较	
较	较	较	较	较	较	较	较	较	
较	较	较	较	较	较	较	较	较	
较	较	较	较	较	较	较	较	较	
较	较	较	较	较	较	较	较	较	
较	较	较	较	较	较	较	较	较	
较	较	较	较	较	较	较	较	较	

姐

Notes: Common Noun

(姐, **jiě**, **older sister**)

(姐, **jiě**, **young woman**)

jiě

sister

く 丿 女 刘 奶 妒 如 姐

姐 姐 姐 姐 姐 姐 姐 姐 姐

姐	姐	姐	姐	姐	姐	姐	姐	姐	姐
jiě	jiě	jiě	jiě	jiě	jiě	jiě	jiě	jiě	jiě
sister	sister	sister	sister	sister	sister	sister	sister	sister	sister
姐	姐	姐	姐	姐	姐	姐	姐	姐	姐
jiě	jiě	jiě	jiě	jiě	jiě	jiě	jiě	jiě	jiě
sister	sister	sister	sister	sister	sister	sister	sister	sister	sister
姐	姐	姐	姐	姐	姐	姐	姐	姐	姐
姐	姐	姐	姐	姐	姐	姐	姐	姐	姐
姐	姐	姐	姐	姐	姐	姐	姐	姐	姐
姐	姐	姐	姐	姐	姐	姐	姐	姐	姐
姐	姐	姐	姐	姐	姐	姐	姐	姐	姐
姐	姐	姐	姐	姐	姐	姐	姐	姐	姐
姐	姐	姐	姐	姐	姐	姐	姐	姐	姐
姐	姐	姐	姐	姐	姐	姐	姐	姐	姐

楼

lóu
floors

Notes: Common Noun

(楼, lóu, story, building, storied building, floors)

(楼, Lóu, surname Lóu)

一 十 才 木 木 术 术 术 楼 楼 楼 楼 楼

楼 楼 楼 楼 楼 楼 楼 楼 楼

楼	楼	楼	楼	楼	楼	楼	楼	楼	楼
lóu	lóu	lóu	lóu	lóu	lóu	lóu	lóu	lóu	lóu
floors	floors	floors	floors	floors	floors	floors	floors	floors	floors
楼	楼	楼	楼	楼	楼	楼	楼	楼	楼
lóu	lóu	lóu	lóu	lóu	lóu	lóu	lóu	lóu	lóu
floors	floors	floors	floors	floors	floors	floors	floors	floors	floors
楼	楼	楼	楼	楼	楼	楼	楼	楼	
楼	楼	楼	楼	楼	楼	楼	楼	楼	
楼	楼	楼	楼	楼	楼	楼	楼	楼	
楼	楼	楼	楼	楼	楼	楼	楼	楼	
楼	楼	楼	楼	楼	楼	楼	楼	楼	
楼	楼	楼	楼	楼	楼	楼	楼	楼	
楼	楼	楼	楼	楼	楼	楼	楼	楼	
楼	楼	楼	楼	楼	楼	楼	楼	楼	

获

huò
obtain

Notes: Verb

(获, **huò**, **get**, **obtain**, **capture**, **catch**)

(获, **huò**, **obtain**, **win**)

(获, **huò**, **reap**, **harvest**, **gather in**)

一 十 艹 艹 艹 艹 芢 茫 获 获

获 获 获 获 获 获 获 获 获

获	获	获	获	获	获	获	获	获	获
huò	huò	huò	huò	huò	huò	huò	huò	huò	huò
obtain	obtain	obtain	obtain	obtain	obtain	obtain	obtain	obtain	obtain
获	获	获	获	获	获	获	获	获	获
huò	huò	huò	huò	huò	huò	huò	huò	huò	huò
obtain	obtain	obtain	obtain	obtain	obtain	obtain	obtain	obtain	obtain
获	获	获	获	获	获	获	获	获	获
获	获	获	获	获	获	获	获	获	获
获	获	获	获	获	获	获	获	获	获
获	获	获	获	获	获	获	获	获	获
获	获	获	获	获	获	获	获	获	获
获	获	获	获	获	获	获	获	获	获
获	获	获	获	获	获	获	获	获	获

孙 sūn g-child	Notes: Common Noun (孙, **sūn**, **grandchild, generations below that of grandchild**) (孙, **sūn**, **second growth of**) (孙, **Sūn**, **surname Sūn**)

ㄱ 了 孑 孖 孙 孙

孙 孙 孙 孙 孙 孙 孙 孙 孙

孙	孙	孙	孙	孙	孙	孙	孙	孙	孙
sūn	sūn	sūn	sūn	sūn	sūn	sūn	sūn	sūn	sūn
g-child	g-child	g-child	g-child	g-child	g-child	g-child	g-child	g-child	g-child
孙	孙	孙	孙	孙	孙	孙	孙	孙	孙
sūn	sūn	sūn	sūn	sūn	sūn	sūn	sūn	sūn	sūn
g-child	g-child	g-child	g-child	g-child	g-child	g-child	g-child	g-child	g-child

孙	孙	孙	孙	孙	孙	孙	孙	孙	
孙	孙	孙	孙	孙	孙	孙	孙	孙	
孙	孙	孙	孙	孙	孙	孙	孙	孙	
孙	孙	孙	孙	孙	孙	孙	孙	孙	
孙	孙	孙	孙	孙	孙	孙	孙	孙	
孙	孙	孙	孙	孙	孙	孙	孙	孙	
孙	孙	孙	孙	孙	孙	孙	孙	孙	
孙	孙	孙	孙	孙	孙	孙	孙	孙	

宣

Notes: Verb

(宣, xuān, declare, proclaim)

(宣, xuān, drain off liquids)

(宣, Xuān, surname Xuān)

xuān
declare

丶 丷 宀 宀 宀 宁 宫 宣 宣

宣 宣 宣 宣 宣 宣 宣 宣 宣

宣	宣	宣	宣	宣	宣	宣	宣	宣	宣
xuān	xuān	xuān	xuān	xuān	xuān	xuān	xuān	xuān	xuān
declare	declare	declare	declare	declare	declare	declare	declare	declare	declare
宣	宣	宣	宣	宣	宣	宣	宣	宣	宣
xuān	xuān	xuān	xuān	xuān	xuān	xuān	xuān	xuān	xuān
declare	declare	declare	declare	declare	declare	declare	declare	declare	declare

宣	宣	宣	宣	宣	宣	宣	宣	宣	宣
宣	宣	宣	宣	宣	宣	宣	宣	宣	宣
宣	宣	宣	宣	宣	宣	宣	宣	宣	宣
宣	宣	宣	宣	宣	宣	宣	宣	宣	宣
宣	宣	宣	宣	宣	宣	宣	宣	宣	宣
宣	宣	宣	宣	宣	宣	宣	宣	宣	宣
宣	宣	宣	宣	宣	宣	宣	宣	宣	宣
宣	宣	宣	宣	宣	宣	宣	宣	宣	宣

穿	Notes: Verb
	(穿, chuān, wear, put on, be dressed)
	(穿, chuān, penetrate, pierce, pass through, cross)
chuān	
wear	

丶 丷 宀 宀 穴 穴 空 穿 穿

穿 穿 穿 穿 穿 穿 穿 穿 穿

穿	穿	穿	穿	穿	穿	穿	穿	穿	穿
chuān	chuān	chuān	chuān	chuān	chuān	chuān	chuān	chuān	chuān
wear	wear	wear	wear	wear	wear	wear	wear	wear	wear
穿	穿	穿	穿	穿	穿	穿	穿	穿	穿
chuān	chuān	chuān	chuān	chuān	chuān	chuān	chuān	chuān	chuān
wear	wear	wear	wear	wear	wear	wear	wear	wear	wear
穿	穿	穿	穿	穿	穿	穿	穿	穿	
穿	穿	穿	穿	穿	穿	穿	穿	穿	
穿	穿	穿	穿	穿	穿	穿	穿	穿	
穿	穿	穿	穿	穿	穿	穿	穿	穿	
穿	穿	穿	穿	穿	穿	穿	穿	穿	
穿	穿	穿	穿	穿	穿	穿	穿	穿	
穿	穿	穿	穿	穿	穿	穿	穿	穿	
穿	穿	穿	穿	穿	穿	穿	穿	穿	

诗

shī
poem

Notes: Common Noun

(诗, shī, poem, poetry, verse, poem, hymn)

丶 讠 讠 计 诗 诗 诗 诗

诗 诗 诗 诗 诗 诗 诗 诗 诗

诗	诗	诗	诗	诗	诗	诗	诗	诗	诗
shī	shī	shī	shī	shī	shī	shī	shī	shī	shī
poem	poem	poem	poem	poem	poem	poem	poem	poem	poem
诗	诗	诗	诗	诗	诗	诗	诗	诗	诗
shī	shī	shī	shī	shī	shī	shī	shī	shī	shī
poem	poem	poem	poem	poem	poem	poem	poem	poem	poem

诗	诗	诗	诗	诗	诗	诗	诗	诗	诗
诗	诗	诗	诗	诗	诗	诗	诗	诗	诗
诗	诗	诗	诗	诗	诗	诗	诗	诗	诗
诗	诗	诗	诗	诗	诗	诗	诗	诗	诗
诗	诗	诗	诗	诗	诗	诗	诗	诗	诗
诗	诗	诗	诗	诗	诗	诗	诗	诗	诗
诗	诗	诗	诗	诗	诗	诗	诗	诗	诗
诗	诗	诗	诗	诗	诗	诗	诗	诗	诗

歌

Notes: Common Noun

(歌, gē, song)

gē

song

一 厂 万 万 可 哥 哥 哥 哥 哥 歌 歌 歌 歌

歌 歌 歌 歌 歌 歌 歌 歌 歌

歌	歌	歌	歌	歌	歌	歌	歌	歌	歌
gē	gē	gē	gē	gē	gē	gē	gē	gē	gē
song	song	song	song	song	song	song	song	song	song
歌	歌	歌	歌	歌	歌	歌	歌	歌	歌
gē	gē	gē	gē	gē	gē	gē	gē	gē	gē
song	song	song	song	song	song	song	song	song	song
歌	歌	歌	歌	歌	歌	歌	歌	歌	
歌	歌	歌	歌	歌	歌	歌	歌	歌	
歌	歌	歌	歌	歌	歌	歌	歌	歌	
歌	歌	歌	歌	歌	歌	歌	歌	歌	
歌	歌	歌	歌	歌	歌	歌	歌	歌	
歌	歌	歌	歌	歌	歌	歌	歌	歌	
歌	歌	歌	歌	歌	歌	歌	歌	歌	

速

sù

quick

Notes: Adjective

(速, sù, fast, rapid, quick, speedy, speed)

一 厂 厂 戸 百 申 東 束 束 涑 速

速 速 速 速 速 速 速 速 速

速	速	速	速	速	速	速	速	速	速
sù	sù	sù	sù	sù	sù	sù	sù	sù	sù
quick	quick	quick	quick	quick	quick	quick	quick	quick	quick
速	速	速	速	速	速	速	速	速	速
sù	sù	sù	sù	sù	sù	sù	sù	sù	sù
quick	quick	quick	quick	quick	quick	quick	quick	quick	quick
速	速	速	速	速	速	速	速	速	速
速	速	速	速	速	速	速	速	速	速
速	速	速	速	速	速	速	速	速	速
速	速	速	速	速	速	速	速	速	速
速	速	速	速	速	速	速	速	速	速
速	速	速	速	速	速	速	速	速	速
速	速	速	速	速	速	速	速	速	速
速	速	速	速	速	速	速	速	速	速

忽

hū
neglect

Notes: Verb

(忽, hū, **disregard**, **neglect**, **overlook**)

(忽, hū, **disdain**)

(忽, hū, **suddenly**)

丿 勹 勺 勿 勿 忽 忽 忽

忽 忽 忽 忽 忽 忽 忽 忽

忽	忽	忽	忽	忽	忽	忽	忽	忽	忽
hū	hū	hū	hū	hū	hū	hū	hū	hū	hū
neglect	neglect	neglect	neglect	neglect	neglect	neglect	neglect	neglect	neglect
忽	忽	忽	忽	忽	忽	忽	忽	忽	忽
hū	hū	hū	hū	hū	hū	hū	hū	hū	hū
neglect	neglect	neglect	neglect	neglect	neglect	neglect	neglect	neglect	neglect
忽	忽	忽	忽	忽	忽	忽	忽	忽	
忽	忽	忽	忽	忽	忽	忽	忽	忽	
忽	忽	忽	忽	忽	忽	忽	忽	忽	
忽	忽	忽	忽	忽	忽	忽	忽	忽	
忽	忽	忽	忽	忽	忽	忽	忽	忽	
忽	忽	忽	忽	忽	忽	忽	忽	忽	
忽	忽	忽	忽	忽	忽	忽	忽	忽	
忽	忽	忽	忽	忽	忽	忽	忽	忽	

堂

táng
hall

Notes: Common Noun

(堂, táng, hall, room used for a purpose, court of law)

(堂, táng, name of a shop, shop sign)

(堂, táng, of the same clan, cousins of the same surname)

(堂, táng, dignified)

(堂, táng, measure word for furniture, classes)

⺍ ⺍ ⺍ ⺍ ⺍ ⺍ ⺍ ⺍ 堂 堂 堂

堂 堂 堂 堂 堂 堂 堂 堂 堂

堂	堂	堂	堂	堂	堂	堂	堂	堂	堂
táng	táng	táng	táng	táng	táng	táng	táng	táng	táng
hall	hall	hall	hall	hall	hall	hall	hall	hall	hall

堂	堂	堂	堂	堂	堂	堂	堂	堂	堂
táng	táng	táng	táng	táng	táng	táng	táng	táng	táng
hall	hall	hall	hall	hall	hall	hall	hall	hall	hall

敌

dí
enemy

Notes: Common Noun

(敌, dí, enemy, foe)

(敌, match, equal)

丿 丷 千 千 舌 舌 舌 甜 敌 敌

敌 敌 敌 敌 敌 敌 敌 敌 敌

敌	敌	敌	敌	敌	敌	敌	敌	敌	敌
dí	dí	dí	dí	dí	dí	dí	dí	dí	dí
enemy	enemy	enemy	enemy	enemy	enemy	enemy	enemy	enemy	enemy

敌	敌	敌	敌	敌	敌	敌	敌	敌	敌
dí	dí	dí	dí	dí	dí	dí	dí	dí	dí
enemy	enemy	enemy	enemy	enemy	enemy	enemy	enemy	enemy	enemy

敌	敌	敌	敌	敌	敌	敌	敌	敌	敌
敌	敌	敌	敌	敌	敌	敌	敌	敌	
敌	敌	敌	敌	敌	敌	敌	敌	敌	
敌	敌	敌	敌	敌	敌	敌	敌	敌	
敌	敌	敌	敌	敌	敌	敌	敌	敌	
敌	敌	敌	敌	敌	敌	敌	敌	敌	
敌	敌	敌	敌	敌	敌	敌	敌	敌	
敌	敌	敌	敌	敌	敌	敌	敌	敌	

试	Notes: Verb
	(试, shì, to try, test, examine)
	(试, shì, test, examination)

shì

test

丶 讠 讠 讠 讠 讠 试 试

试 试 试 试 试 试 试 试 试

试	试	试	试	试	试	试	试	试	试
shì	shì	shì	shì	shì	shì	shì	shì	shì	shì
test	test	test	test	test	test	test	test	test	test
试	试	试	试	试	试	试	试	试	试
shì	shì	shì	shì	shì	shì	shì	shì	shì	shì
test	test	test	test	test	test	test	test	test	test
试	试	试	试	试	试	试	试	试	试
试	试	试	试	试	试	试	试	试	试
试	试	试	试	试	试	试	试	试	试
试	试	试	试	试	试	试	试	试	试
试	试	试	试	试	试	试	试	试	试
试	试	试	试	试	试	试	试	试	试
试	试	试	试	试	试	试	试	试	试
试	试	试	试	试	试	试	试	试	试

谢	Notes: Verb
	(谢, xiè, thank)
	(谢, xiè, wither of flowers or leaves)
	(谢, Xiè, surname Xiè)
xiè	
thank	

丶 讠 讠 讠 讠 讠 讠 讠 讠 讠 谢 谢

谢 谢 谢 谢 谢 谢 谢 谢 谢

谢	谢	谢	谢	谢	谢	谢	谢	谢	谢
xiè	xiè	xiè	xiè	xiè	xiè	xiè	xiè	xiè	xiè
thank	thank	thank	thank	thank	thank	thank	thank	thank	thank
谢	谢	谢	谢	谢	谢	谢	谢	谢	谢
xiè	xiè	xiè	xiè	xiè	xiè	xiè	xiè	xiè	xiè
thank	thank	thank	thank	thank	thank	thank	thank	thank	thank
谢	谢	谢	谢	谢	谢	谢	谢	谢	谢
谢	谢	谢	谢	谢	谢	谢	谢	谢	谢
谢	谢	谢	谢	谢	谢	谢	谢	谢	谢
谢	谢	谢	谢	谢	谢	谢	谢	谢	谢
谢	谢	谢	谢	谢	谢	谢	谢	谢	谢
谢	谢	谢	谢	谢	谢	谢	谢	谢	谢
谢	谢	谢	谢	谢	谢	谢	谢	谢	谢
谢	谢	谢	谢	谢	谢	谢	谢	谢	谢

央	Notes: Verb
	(央, **yāng**, **to end, finish**)
	(央, **yāng**, **center**)
	(央, **yāng**, **entreat**)
yāng	
finish	

丨 冂 冋 央 央

央 央 央 央 央 央 央 央 央

央	央	央	央	央	央	央	央	央	央
yāng	yāng	yāng	yāng	yāng	yāng	yāng	yāng	yāng	yāng
finish	finish	finish	finish	finish	finish	finish	finish	finish	finish
央	央	央	央	央	央	央	央	央	央
yāng	yāng	yāng	yāng	yāng	yāng	yāng	yāng	yāng	yāng
finish	finish	finish	finish	finish	finish	finish	finish	finish	finish
央	央	央	央	央	央	央	央	央	央
央	央	央	央	央	央	央	央	央	央
央	央	央	央	央	央	央	央	央	央
央	央	央	央	央	央	央	央	央	央
央	央	央	央	央	央	央	央	央	央
央	央	央	央	央	央	央	央	央	央
央	央	央	央	央	央	央	央	央	央
央	央	央	央	央	央	央	央	央	央

怀

huái
cherish

Notes: Verb

(怀, huái, cherish, value)
(怀, huái, bosom)
(怀, huái, heart, state of mind)
(怀, huái, conceive a child)
(怀, Huái, surname Huái)

丶　丷　忄　忄　忙　忄　怀

怀 怀 怀 怀 怀 怀 怀 怀 怀

怀	怀	怀	怀	怀	怀	怀	怀	怀	怀
huái	huái	huái	huái	huái	huái	huái	huái	huái	huái
cherish	cherish	cherish	cherish	cherish	cherish	cherish	cherish	cherish	cherish
怀	怀	怀	怀	怀	怀	怀	怀	怀	怀
huái	huái	huái	huái	huái	huái	huái	huái	huái	huái
cherish	cherish	cherish	cherish	cherish	cherish	cherish	cherish	cherish	cherish

怀	怀	怀	怀	怀	怀	怀	怀	怀	
怀	怀	怀	怀	怀	怀	怀	怀	怀	
怀	怀	怀	怀	怀	怀	怀	怀	怀	
怀	怀	怀	怀	怀	怀	怀	怀	怀	
怀	怀	怀	怀	怀	怀	怀	怀	怀	
怀	怀	怀	怀	怀	怀	怀	怀	怀	
怀	怀	怀	怀	怀	怀	怀	怀	怀	
怀	怀	怀	怀	怀	怀	怀	怀		

顾

gù
visit

Notes: Verb

(顾, **gù**, **visit, call on, turn around and look at**)

(顾, **gù**, **attend to, look after, take into consideration**)

(顾, **gù**, **advisor, consultant**)

(顾, **gù**, **contrarily, instead, however, but, indeed, really**)

(顾, **Gù**, **surname Gù**)

顾 顾 顾 顾 顾 顾 顾 顾 顾

顾	顾	顾	顾	顾	顾	顾	顾	顾	顾
gù	gù	gù	gù	gù	gù	gù	gù	gù	gù
visit	visit	visit	visit	visit	visit	visit	visit	visit	visit
顾	顾	顾	顾	顾	顾	顾	顾	顾	顾
gù	gù	gù	gù	gù	gù	gù	gù	gù	gù
visit	visit	visit	visit	visit	visit	visit	visit	visit	visit

验	Notes: Verb
	(验, **yàn, examine, check, test**)
yàn	(验, **yàn, prove effective, intended effect, desired result**)
check	

丁 马 马 马 马 马 马 马 马 马

验 验 验 验 验 验 验 验 验

验	验	验	验	验	验	验	验	验	验
yàn	yàn	yàn	yàn	yàn	yàn	yàn	yàn	yàn	yàn
check	check	check	check	check	check	check	check	check	check
验	验	验	验	验	验	验	验	验	验
yàn	yàn	yàn	yàn	yàn	yàn	yàn	yàn	yàn	yàn
check	check	check	check	check	check	check	check	check	check
验	验	验	验	验	验	验	验	验	
验	验	验	验	验	验	验	验	验	
验	验	验	验	验	验	验	验	验	
验	验	验	验	验	验	验	验	验	
验	验	验	验	验	验	验	验	验	
验	验	验	验	验	验	验	验	验	
验	验	验	验	验	验	验	验	验	
验	验	验	验	验	验	验	验	验	

营	Notes: Verb
	(营, yíng, operate, run, manage)
	(营, yíng, camp, barracks)
	(营, yíng, battalion)
yíng	(营, yíng, nourish)
manage	

一 十 卄 艹 芦 芦 茔 营 营 营 营

营 营 营 营 营 营 营 营 营

营	营	营	营	营	营	营	营	营	营
yíng	yíng	yíng	yíng	yíng	yíng	yíng	yíng	yíng	yíng
manage	manage	manage	manage	manage	manage	manage	manage	manage	manage
营	营	营	营	营	营	营	营	营	营
yíng	yíng	yíng	yíng	yíng	yíng	yíng	yíng	yíng	yíng
manage	manage	manage	manage	manage	manage	manage	manage	manage	manage
营	营	营	营	营	营	营	营	营	营
营	营	营	营	营	营	营	营	营	营
营	营	营	营	营	营	营	营	营	营
营	营	营	营	营	营	营	营	营	营
营	营	营	营	营	营	营	营	营	营
营	营	营	营	营	营	营	营	营	营
营	营	营	营	营	营	营	营	营	营

止	Notes: Verb
yíng	(止, zhǐ, stop, halt, arrive at)
stop	(止, zhǐ, suppress, prohibit)

(止, zhǐ, stop, halt, arrive at)
(止, zhǐ, suppress, prohibit)
(止, zhǐ, stay, detain)
(止, zhǐ, until now, only, merely)
(止, zhǐ, bearing, demeanor)

丨 卜 𠂆 止

止 止 止 止 止 止 止 止 止

止	止	止	止	止	止	止	止	止	止
yíng	yíng	yíng	yíng	yíng	yíng	yíng	yíng	yíng	yíng
stop	stop	stop	stop	stop	stop	stop	stop	stop	stop
止	止	止	止	止	止	止	止	止	止
yíng	yíng	yíng	yíng	yíng	yíng	yíng	yíng	yíng	yíng
stop	stop	stop	stop	stop	stop	stop	stop	stop	stop

姓

Notes: Common Noun

(姓, **xìng**, **surname**, **family**, **clan name**)

xìng

surname

乚 乀 乜 乜 乜 乜 姓 姓

姓 姓 姓 姓 姓 姓 姓 姓 姓

姓	姓	姓	姓	姓	姓	姓	姓	姓	姓
xìng	xìng	xìng	xìng	xìng	xìng	xìng	xìng	xìng	xìng
surname	surname	surname	surname	surname	surname	surname	surname	surname	surname
姓	姓	姓	姓	姓	姓	姓	姓	姓	姓
xìng	xìng	xìng	xìng	xìng	xìng	xìng	xìng	xìng	xìng
surname	surname	surname	surname	surname	surname	surname	surname	surname	surname

姓	姓	姓	姓	姓	姓	姓	姓	姓	姓
姓	姓	姓	姓	姓	姓	姓	姓	姓	姓
姓	姓	姓	姓	姓	姓	姓	姓	姓	姓
姓	姓	姓	姓	姓	姓	姓	姓	姓	姓
姓	姓	姓	姓	姓	姓	姓	姓	姓	姓
姓	姓	姓	姓	姓	姓	姓	姓	姓	姓
姓	姓	姓	姓	姓	姓	姓	姓	姓	姓

养

yǎng
raise

Notes: Verb

(养, yǎng, raise, nourish, maintain)

(养, yǎng, support, provide for)

(养, yǎng, give birth to)

(养, yǎng, form, cultivate)

(养, yǎng, rest, recuperate)

丶 丷 ⺊ 兰 关 兰 关 养 养

养 养 养 养 养 养 养 养

养	养	养	养	养	养	养	养	养	养
yǎng	yǎng	yǎng	yǎng	yǎng	yǎng	yǎng	yǎng	yǎng	yǎng
raise	raise	raise	raise	raise	raise	raise	raise	raise	raise
养	养	养	养	养	养	养	养	养	养
yǎng	yǎng	yǎng	yǎng	yǎng	yǎng	yǎng	yǎng	yǎng	yǎng
raise	raise	raise	raise	raise	raise	raise	raise	raise	raise

丽

lì
beautiful

Notes: Adjective

(丽, lì, beautiful)

一 厂 丌 厅 乕 丽 丽 丽

丽 丽 丽 丽 丽 丽 丽 丽

丽	丽	丽	丽	丽	丽	丽	丽	丽	丽
lì	lì	lì	lì	lì	lì	lì	lì	lì	lì
beautiful	beautiful	beautiful	beautiful	beautiful	beautiful	beautiful	beautiful	beautiful	beautiful
丽	丽	丽	丽	丽	丽	丽	丽	丽	丽
lì	lì	lì	lì	lì	lì	lì	lì	lì	lì
beautiful	beautiful	beautiful	beautiful	beautiful	beautiful	beautiful	beautiful	beautiful	beautiful

属

shǔ

join

Notes: Verb

(属, zhǔ, enjoin, join, together, belong to, fix one's attention)

(属, shǔ, category, genus, family member, dependent)

(属, shǔ, born in a specific year of the Chinese calendar)

(属, shǔ, be subordinate to)

コ ⊐ 尸 尸 尸 尸 尸 尸 尻 属 属 属

属 属 属 属 属 属 属 属 属

属	属	属	属	属	属	属	属	属	属
shǔ	shǔ	shǔ	shǔ	shǔ	shǔ	shǔ	shǔ	shǔ	shǔ
join	join	join	join	join	join	join	join	join	join
属	属	属	属	属	属	属	属	属	属
shǔ	shǔ	shǔ	shǔ	shǔ	shǔ	shǔ	shǔ	shǔ	shǔ
join	join	join	join	join	join	join	join	join	join

属	属	属	属	属	属	属	属	属	
属	属	属	属	属	属	属	属	属	
属	属	属	属	属	属	属	属	属	
属	属	属	属	属	属	属	属	属	
属	属	属	属	属	属	属	属	属	
属	属	属	属	属	属	属	属	属	
属	属	属	属	属	属	属	属	属	
属	属	属	属	属	属	属	属	属	

景

jǐng
view

Notes: Common Noun

(景, jǐng, view, scene, scenery)

(景, jǐng, situation, condition)

(景, jǐng, admire, esteem)

(景, jǐng, great, grand)

(景, Jǐng, surname Jǐng)

丨 冂 冃 日 旦 旦 旦 昌 昌 景 景 景 景

景 景 景 景 景 景 景 景 景

景	景	景	景	景	景	景	景	景	景
jǐng	jǐng	jǐng	jǐng	jǐng	jǐng	jǐng	jǐng	jǐng	jǐng
view	view	view	view	view	view	view	view	view	view
景	景	景	景	景	景	景	景	景	景
jǐng	jǐng	jǐng	jǐng	jǐng	jǐng	jǐng	jǐng	jǐng	jǐng
view	view	view	view	view	view	view	view	view	view
景	景	景	景	景	景	景	景	景	景
景	景	景	景	景	景	景	景	景	景
景	景	景	景	景	景	景	景	景	景
景	景	景	景	景	景	景	景	景	景
景	景	景	景	景	景	景	景	景	景
景	景	景	景	景	景	景	景	景	景
景	景	景	景	景	景	景	景	景	景
景	景	景	景	景	景	景	景	景	景

郭	Notes: Common Noun
	(郭, guō, outer wall of city, surrounding area of a city)
	(郭, Guō, surname Guō)
guō	
wall	

丶 亠 广 产 产 亨 亨 享 郭 郭

郭 郭 郭 郭 郭 郭 郭 郭 郭

郭	郭	郭	郭	郭	郭	郭	郭	郭	郭
guō	guō	guō	guō	guō	guō	guō	guō	guō	guō
wall	wall	wall	wall	wall	wall	wall	wall	wall	wall
郭	郭	郭	郭	郭	郭	郭	郭	郭	郭
guō	guō	guō	guō	guō	guō	guō	guō	guō	guō
wall	wall	wall	wall	wall	wall	wall	wall	wall	wall

郭	郭	郭	郭	郭	郭	郭	郭	郭	
郭	郭	郭	郭	郭	郭	郭	郭	郭	
郭	郭	郭	郭	郭	郭	郭	郭	郭	
郭	郭	郭	郭	郭	郭	郭	郭	郭	
郭	郭	郭	郭	郭	郭	郭	郭	郭	
郭	郭	郭	郭	郭	郭	郭	郭	郭	
郭	郭	郭	郭	郭	郭	郭	郭	郭	

	Notes: Verb
依	(依, yī, depend on, comply with, according to, agree, consent)
yī	(依, yī, according to, judging by)
wall	

丿 亻 亻 仁 仨 佐 依 依

依 依 依 依 依 依 依 依 依

依	依	依	依	依	依	依	依	依	依
yī	yī	yī	yī	yī	yī	yī	yī	yī	yī
consent	consent	consent	consent	consent	consent	consent	consent	consent	consent
依	依	依	依	依	依	依	依	依	依
yī	yī	yī	yī	yī	yī	yī	yī	yī	yī
consent	consent	consent	consent	consent	consent	consent	consent	consent	consent

依	依	依	依	依	依	依	依	依	依
依	依	依	依	依	依	依	依	依	依
依	依	依	依	依	依	依	依	依	依
依	依	依	依	依	依	依	依	依	依
依	依	依	依	依	依	依	依	依	依
依	依	依	依	依	依	依	依	依	依
依	依	依	依	依	依	依	依	依	依
依	依	依	依	依	依	依	依	依	依

威
wēi
wall

Notes: Common Noun

(威, wēi , might, power)

一 厂 厂 反 反 反 威 威 威

威 威 威 威 威 威 威 威 威

威	威	威	威	威	威	威	威	威	威
wēi	wēi	wēi	wēi	wēi	wēi	wēi	wēi	wēi	wēi
consent	consent	consent	consent	consent	consent	consent	consent	consent	consent
威	威	威	威	威	威	威	威	威	威
wēi	wēi	wēi	wēi	wēi	wēi	wēi	wēi	wēi	wēi
consent	consent	consent	consent	consent	consent	consent	consent	consent	consent
威	威	威	威	威	威	威	威	威	
威	威	威	威	威	威	威	威	威	
威	威	威	威	威	威	威	威	威	
威	威	威	威	威	威	威	威	威	
威	威	威	威	威	威	威	威	威	
威	威	威	威	威	威	威	威	威	
威	威	威	威	威	威	威	威	威	
威	威	威	威	威	威	威	威	威	

按	Notes: Verb
	(按, àn, restrain)
	(按, àn, press, push down)
	(按, àn, leave aside, shelve)
	(按, àn, keep one's hand on, check, refer to)
àn	(按, àn, note, notation)
restrain	

一 扌 扌 扌 扩 扩 扩 按 按 按

按 按 按 按 按 按 按 按 按

按	按	按	按	按	按	按	按	按	按
àn	àn	àn	àn	àn	àn	àn	àn	àn	àn
restrain	restrain	restrain	restrain	restrain	restrain	restrain	restrain	restrain	restrain
按	按	按	按	按	按	按	按	按	按
àn	àn	àn	àn	àn	àn	àn	àn	àn	àn
restrain	restrain	restrain	restrain	restrain	restrain	restrain	restrain	restrain	restrain

按	按	按	按	按	按	按	按	按	按
按	按	按	按	按	按	按	按	按	按
按	按	按	按	按	按	按	按	按	按
按	按	按	按	按	按	按	按	按	按
按	按	按	按	按	按	按	按	按	按
按	按	按	按	按	按	按	按	按	按
按	按	按	按	按	按	按	按	按	按
按	按	按	按	按	按	按	按	按	按

恶	Notes: Verb
	(恶, wù, loathe, hate)
	(恶, è, evil, fierce)
wù	
loathe	

一 丁 丌 丌 亓 亚 亚 恶 恶 恶

恶 恶 恶 恶 恶 恶 恶 恶 恶

恶	恶	恶	恶	恶	恶	恶	恶	恶	恶
wù	wù	wù	wù	wù	wù	wù	wù	wù	wù
loathe	loathe	loathe	loathe	loathe	loathe	loathe	loathe	loathe	loathe
恶	恶	恶	恶	恶	恶	恶	恶	恶	恶
wù	wù	wù	wù	wù	wù	wù	wù	wù	wù
loathe	loathe	loathe	loathe	loathe	loathe	loathe	loathe	loathe	loathe
恶	恶	恶	恶	恶	恶	恶	恶		
恶	恶	恶	恶	恶	恶	恶	恶		
恶	恶	恶	恶	恶	恶	恶	恶		
恶	恶	恶	恶	恶	恶	恶	恶		
恶	恶	恶	恶	恶	恶	恶	恶		
恶	恶	恶	恶	恶	恶	恶	恶		
恶	恶	恶	恶	恶	恶	恶	恶		
恶	恶	恶	恶	恶	恶	恶	恶		

慢

màn
slow

Notes: Adjective

(慢, **màn**, **slow**)

(慢, **màn**, **supercilious**, **rude**)

(慢, **màn**, **rude**)

丶 丶 忄 忄 忄 忄 忄 忄 悍 悍 悍 悍 慢 慢

慢 慢 慢 慢 慢 慢 慢 慢 慢

慢	慢	慢	慢	慢	慢	慢	慢	慢	慢
màn	màn	màn	màn	màn	màn	màn	màn	màn	màn
slow	slow	slow	slow	slow	slow	slow	slow	slow	slow
慢	慢	慢	慢	慢	慢	慢	慢	慢	慢
màn	màn	màn	màn	màn	màn	màn	màn	màn	màn
slow	slow	slow	slow	slow	slow	slow	slow	slow	slow

慢	慢	慢	慢	慢	慢	慢	慢	慢	
慢	慢	慢	慢	慢	慢	慢	慢	慢	
慢	慢	慢	慢	慢	慢	慢	慢	慢	
慢	慢	慢	慢	慢	慢	慢	慢	慢	
慢	慢	慢	慢	慢	慢	慢	慢	慢	
慢	慢	慢	慢	慢	慢	慢	慢	慢	
慢	慢	慢	慢	慢	慢	慢	慢	慢	
慢	慢	慢	慢	慢	慢	慢	慢	慢	

座

zuò

sit

Notes: Verb

(座, **zuò sit down, ride on**)

(座, **zuò, seat, place, stand, pedestal, base**)

(座, **zuò, measure word for mountains, bridges**)

(座, **zuò, fare in a hired vehicle**)

(座, **zuò, customer in a restaurant**)

丶 宀 广 广 广 庐 庥 座 座 座

座 座 座 座 座 座 座 座 座

座	座	座	座	座	座	座	座	座	座
zuò	zuò	zuò	zuò	zuò	zuò	zuò	zuò	zuò	zuò
sit	sit	sit	sit	sit	sit	sit	sit	sit	sit
座	座	座	座	座	座	座	座	座	座
zuò	zuò	zuò	zuò	zuò	zuò	zuò	zuò	zuò	zuò
sit	sit	sit	sit	sit	sit	sit	sit	sit	sit

座	座	座	座	座	座	座	座	座	
座	座	座	座	座	座	座	座	座	
座	座	座	座	座	座	座	座	座	
座	座	座	座	座	座	座	座	座	
座	座	座	座	座	座	座	座	座	
座	座	座	座	座	座	座	座	座	
座	座	座	座	座	座	座	座	座	
座	座	座	座	座	座	座	座	座	

罪

zuì
crime

Notes: Common Noun

(罪, **zuì, crime, guilt, sin**)

(罪, **zuì, fault, blame, misconduct**)

(罪, **zuì, suffering, pain, hardship**)

(罪, **zuì, put the blame on, blame**)

丨 冂 冂 罒 罒 罪 罪 罪 罪 罪 罪 罪

罪 罪 罪 罪 罪 罪 罪 罪 罪

罪	罪	罪	罪	罪	罪	罪	罪	罪	罪
zuì	zuì	zuì	zuì	zuì	zuì	zuì	zuì	zuì	zuì
crime	crime	crime	crime	crime	crime	crime	crime	crime	crime
罪	罪	罪	罪	罪	罪	罪	罪	罪	罪
zuì	zuì	zuì	zuì	zuì	zuì	zuì	zuì	zuì	zuì
crime	crime	crime	crime	crime	crime	crime	crime	crime	crime

维

Notes: Verb

(维, wéi, join)

(维, wéi, maintain, save from damage)

wéi

join

⼃ ⼃ ⼃ ⼃ 纟 纠 纤 纩 纴 纵 维 维

维 维 维 维 维 维 维 维 维

维	维	维	维	维	维	维	维	维	维
wéi join	wéi join	wéi join	wéi join	wéi join	wéi join	wéi join	wéi join	wéi join	wéi join
维	维	维	维	维	维	维	维	维	维
wéi join	wéi join	wéi join	wéi join	wéi join	wéi join	wéi join	wéi join	wéi join	wéi join

维	维	维	维	维	维	维	维	维	维
维	维	维	维	维	维	维	维	维	维
维	维	维	维	维	维	维	维	维	维
维	维	维	维	维	维	维	维	维	维
维	维	维	维	维	维	维	维	维	维
维	维	维	维	维	维	维	维	维	维
维	维	维	维	维	维	维	维	维	维
维	维	维	维	维	维	维	维	维	维

渐

Notes: Adjective

(渐, **jiàn**, **gradually, by degrees**)

(渐, **jiān**, **dip or soak in liquid**)

jiàn
gradually

丶　丶　氵　广　汽　汽　汽　汽　渐　渐　渐

渐　渐　渐　渐　渐　渐　渐　渐　渐

渐	渐	渐	渐	渐	渐	渐	渐	渐	渐
jiàn	jiàn	jiàn	jiàn	jiàn	jiàn	jiàn	jiàn	jiàn	jiàn
gradually	gradually	gradually	gradually	gradually	gradually	gradually	gradually	gradually	gradually
渐	渐	渐	渐	渐	渐	渐	渐	渐	渐
jiàn	jiàn	jiàn	jiàn	jiàn	jiàn	jiàn	jiàn	jiàn	jiàn
gradually	gradually	gradually	gradually	gradually	gradually	gradually	gradually	gradually	gradually
渐	渐	渐	渐	渐	渐	渐	渐	渐	
渐	渐	渐	渐	渐	渐	渐	渐	渐	
渐	渐	渐	渐	渐	渐	渐	渐	渐	
渐	渐	渐	渐	渐	渐	渐	渐	渐	
渐	渐	渐	渐	渐	渐	渐	渐	渐	
渐	渐	渐	渐	渐	渐	渐	渐	渐	
渐	渐	渐	渐	渐	渐	渐	渐	渐	
渐	渐	渐	渐	渐	渐	渐	渐	渐	

胜

shèng
succeed

Notes: Verb

(胜, **shèng, win a victory, succeed, to defeat**)

(胜, **shèng, surpass, excel, superb, distinctive, triumphant**)

(胜, **shèng, scenic view**)

丿 刀 刀 月 肜 肛 肸 胖 胜

胜 胜 胜 胜 胜 胜 胜 胜 胜

胜	胜	胜	胜	胜	胜	胜	胜	胜	胜
shèng	shèng	shèng	shèng	shèng	shèng	shèng	shèng	shèng	shèng
succeed	succeed	succeed	succeed	succeed	succeed	succeed	succeed	succeed	succeed
胜	胜	胜	胜	胜	胜	胜	胜	胜	胜
shèng	shèng	shèng	shèng	shèng	shèng	shèng	shèng	shèng	shèng
succeed	succeed	succeed	succeed	succeed	succeed	succeed	succeed	succeed	succeed
胜	胜	胜	胜	胜	胜	胜	胜		
胜	胜	胜	胜	胜	胜	胜	胜	胜	
胜	胜	胜	胜	胜	胜	胜	胜	胜	
胜	胜	胜	胜	胜	胜	胜	胜	胜	
胜	胜	胜	胜	胜	胜	胜	胜	胜	
胜	胜	胜	胜	胜	胜	胜	胜	胜	
胜	胜	胜	胜	胜	胜	胜	胜	胜	

藏

cáng
conceal

Notes: Verb

(藏, cáng, store, conceal, hide)

(藏, zàng, storage place)

(藏, zàng, Buddist or Daoist scripture, sutra, canon)

(藏, Zàng, abbreviation for Xizang or Tibet)

一 十 卅 芦 芦 芦 芦 芹 芹 莽 莽 莽 菥 藏 藏 藏

藏 藏 藏 藏 藏 藏 藏 藏 藏

藏	藏	藏	藏	藏	藏	藏	藏	藏	藏
cáng	cáng	cáng	cáng	cáng	cáng	cáng	cáng	cáng	cáng
conceal	conceal	conceal	conceal	conceal	conceal	conceal	conceal	conceal	conceal
藏	藏	藏	藏	藏	藏	藏	藏	藏	藏
cáng	cáng	cáng	cáng	cáng	cáng	cáng	cáng	cáng	cáng
conceal	conceal	conceal	conceal	conceal	conceal	conceal	conceal	conceal	conceal
藏	藏	藏	藏	藏	藏	藏	藏	藏	藏
藏	藏	藏	藏	藏	藏	藏	藏	藏	藏
藏	藏	藏	藏	藏	藏	藏	藏	藏	藏
藏	藏	藏	藏	藏	藏	藏	藏	藏	藏
藏	藏	藏	藏	藏	藏	藏	藏	藏	藏
藏	藏	藏	藏	藏	藏	藏	藏	藏	藏
藏	藏	藏	藏	藏	藏	藏	藏	藏	藏

Kangxi Radicals

Introduction

The functional building blocks, the alphabet as such, of the written Chinese language known as (汉字, **Hànzì**, **Hanzi**) are the 214 Kangxi Radicals. A Radical is a visual representation, a written image that represents a thought or meaning but variable phonetic information. It may not help to pronounce or verbally ***put forth*** the spoken character but rather may give the character obvious flavour or meaning, or it may not. The Radical can be used alone or in combination to assemble a character.

All characters have one spoken syllable; hence, they are ***monosyllabic***. The character list dates from the year 1615. They were compiled in a dictionary called (字汇, **Zìhuì**, **Zihui**). This allowed for collection, indexing and compilation of characters in an organized fashion. In 1716, a dictionary, the (康熙字典, **Kāngxī Zìdiǎn**, **Kangxi dictionary**) was created organizing the characters using the Radicals as organizational section headers. This dictionary was commissioned by Emperor Kangxi (**1654-1722**) of China's Qing Dynasty. This dictionary has 47,035 characters. Chinese dictionaries are organized not phonetically, but by the Radical then the number of additional strokes in each character. Since then no new Radicals or characters have been added but many words have been.

Modern words are created by creating descriptive character strings. ***Cell phone*** for example is an obvious modern word and is described by ancient characters. The characters are (电, **diàn**, **lightening**) and (话, **huà**, **talk**) forming (电话, **diànhuà**, **lightening talk**) roughly, ***electric talk***. This makes utilization for a ***foreigner*** difficult, as he has to reference a lexicon of unfamiliarity. To get to the train station you must ask for the (火车站, **huǒchēzhàn**, **fire cart stand**).

Learning to write Chinese characters is best achieved by mastering the fundamental graphic components, the Kangxi Radicals. Then you can learn which strokes and Radicals are used in particular characters and how they are combined. This allows for efficient memorization and production of Hanzi. This is much easier than learning to write each character as a sequence of memorized strokes. For example, one can remember how to write (義 **yì**, **right conduct**) by knowing that it consists of the character for (羊, **yáng**, **sheep**) above (我, **wǒ**, **me**).

There are a total of some 50,000 Chinese characters. A far smaller number, some 4,000 to 6,000, are in daily use. All characters no matter how complex can be decomposed into radicals and constituent strokes.

A character may have typically one to three Radicals in its composition. Some of the Radicals are pictographic and visually project meaning. (女, **nǚ**, **female**) has a crossed leg, booty sticking out the back look and is easy to remember as it has visually anchoring clues. The picture however does not give any suggestion to pronunciation and this is what differs from a roman type alphabet. It can stand alone as a Radical forming a character, (女, **nǚ**, **female**), or can be part of a multi-Radical character. The character for (好, **hǎo**, **good**) is the Radical (女, **nǚ**, **female**) plus the Radical for (子, **zǐ**, **child**). However, it is not pronounced **nǚzǐ**. Neither Radical gives phonetic clues. You can draw inference that it is good for a female to have a child. Hence, the character makes some sense visually and adds flavour to the interpretation. However, (女, **nǚ**, **female**) is used as part of many characters that do not have a feminine flavour.

(要, **yào**, **want**) combines the Radical for (西, **xī**, **west**), with the Radical of (女, **nǚ**, **female**) under it. Neither (西, **xī**, **west**), nor (女, **nǚ**, **female**), lend phonetic clues or meaning to the character (要, **yāo**, **want**) If you want to make up a little story about a Chinese man looking *west* and he *want* to find a *female*, more power to you if it helps you remember. However, remember, you will have about 50,000 little stories to make up to remember all the characters.

Radicals and Their Variants

In writing Hanzi, many Radicals are distorted or changed in form in order to fit into a character with other Radicals or characters. They may be narrowed, shortened, or may have different shapes entirely. Changes in shape, rather than simple distortion, may result in a reduction in the number of strokes used to write it. In some cases, these written forms may have several variants. The actual shape of the component when it is used in a character can depend on its placement with respect to the other elements in the character.

Although there are 214 Radicals, some of them have numerous variants that are only generally recognizable once the parent Radical is compared to it. Some variants are very common and some are very obscure. As with all facets of learning Hanyu and Hanzi, it is best to build on the most commonly occurring components and then to add the less common variants. In this book variants are marked with a (**V**), simplified Radicals with an (**S**) and Traditional Radicals with a (**T**).

The tables in this book list the most common variants. Given the huge historic number of characters, you may never see many of the variants in common usage.

Examples

1) (刀, **dāo**, **knife**) can be represented in its full form with the Radical in these positions, appearing on the top, bottom, left and right within a character.

切 刖 分 办 刕 召 刍

A common variant is (刂, **dāo**, **knife**).

刖 刂 刖 刊 㓚 切 刌

A less common variant is (刁, **dāo**, **knife**).

叨 书 汈 艻

2) (人, **rén**, **person**) can be represented in its full form with the Radical in these positions.

大 仈 亾 坐 从 以 贝 因 仄

(亻 , **rén**, **standing person**) appears on the left side of characters.

仈 亿 他 你 仨 仔 仟 仕 仜

(𠆢, **rén**, **person**) become can also appear on the top of characters.

仌 全 弇 会 仝 亼 仓 个

3) (**R#61**, 心, **xīn**, **heart**) the character, is the same as Radical.

必 志 忘 忠 忎 忒 发 㣺 灯

For characters with (**#61'**, 忄 , **xīn**, **standing heart**) the Radical always appears on the left side of the character.

快 怖 怪 悟 忆 忛 忏 忓 㤆

4) (手, **shǒu, hand**) appears in varied positions, top, bottom, left and right.

手 拜 擎 拿 犇 扐 杼

(扌, **shǒu, hand**) appears on the left side of characters.

扎 打 拖 打 扐 扑 扒

(才, **shǒu, hand**)

团 财 材 闭 財 鼐

(手, **shǒu, hand**)

看 拜 掰

(𠂇, **shǒu, hand**)

在 存

(𠂇, **shǒu, hand**)

发

5) (水, **shuǐ, water**) occurs on the top, bottom, left and right of characters.

水 汆 沓 燃 永 汞 氹 氶

(氵, **shuǐ, standing water**) appears on the left of characters. An alternate name for this Radical is (三点水, **sān diǎn shuǐ, three dot water**)

氵 汀 汁 汔 汈 清

(氺, **shuǐ, water**) is a less common variant. There are very few Radicals forming characters with this Radical. Examples: (**录, lǜ, to record**), (**忝, tiǎn, to shame**)

In learning (汉字, **Hànzì**, **Hanzi**) it is imperative to compare the precise meaning of the individual characters to the pinyin to the literal translation. This learning strategy will allow you to see how the Radicals flavour the characters and how the characters are compiled to make sentences. A methodical learning of the Radicals is essential to learn the language. What seems tedious at first and counterproductive to learning will give you the most important tools to (汉字, **Hànzì**, **Hanzi**). A close analogy would be to try to learn English without knowing the alphabet. After you grind away at learning the Radicals, the language will suddenly open up to you. You will no longer need to remember 13 strokes for (想, **xiǎng**, **think**, **desire**) to write the character but only need to remember the individual Radicals that compose it, (木, **mù**, **tree**) *beside* (目, **mù**, **eye**) *over* (心, **xīn**, **heart**) *equal* (想, **xiǎng**, **think**).

This reduces your memory load from 13 to 3 visual images. Again, if you want to make up a little memory aid story about a ***tree*** with an ***eye*** on the top standing on a ***heart*** equal ***think*** that only leaves 49,998 more little stories. However, if you can remember the Hanzi character for (相, **xiāng**, **mutually**), you only need to remember two visual images. ***Mutually*** or ***each other*** over ***heart*** equals ***think***.

It is not a matter of this language being complicated or not, it is only ***how complicated*** you want to make it. However, 2 billion people cannot be wrong. To further complicate the story, each Radical has a name, a category and an assigned number. In addition, the Radical name may be different and more complex than the character name when the Radical stands alone as a character.

Convention dictates that the (汉字, **Hànzì**, **Hanzi**) characters roughly fit into a square. This leads the Radicals to morph to fit the space allowed. They may elongate, widen, deepen or narrow to fit the space. Some Radicals even change in form from the right side to the left side to the top to bottom of a character. Throughout this book are examples of Radicals in characters and they are represented by the various physical mutations as they change position in a character.

There will come a time when you have no choice but to buy a very large amount of paper, I would recommend a case of 10 reams, a box of soft tipped fine marker pens, a cushion for your butt, and start to start copying out the Radicals, writing their name in pinyin, their assigned number, chanting the phonetic and the semantic translation.

Learning Hanzi is more akin to art class than English class. The amount of practice you will need will depend on your innate ability and the complexity of the character. The Radicals are conveniently indexed by order of increasing complexity. You can build on the initial simple Radicals and strokes, and progress through the list. Please look forward to the Work Book and find characters you can overwrite with a plastic sheet or velum paper. There is no other way. This is the way that billions of Chinese students have done it over thousands of years. This is not like learning French, German, Italian or Spanish, with an alphabet with which you are familiar. This is more like learning to draw thousands of pictures and remembering their names, meaning, pronunciation and intonation.

The workbook is a workbook to learn stroke order and to write Hanzi. The characters are not chosen for their general utility. I have tried to find a progressive selection of characters that will build your writing skills. You will not find any two references that give the exact same stroke orders for the Kangxi Radicals. The goal is to make a visual representation and get the meaning of the character communicated. Hanzi is an art form. This must not be forgotten as the Western world rushes to digitalize and standardize the stroke order of characters and Radicals.

Once you arrive in China you will see scripts on signboards that the native Chinese struggle to interpret. Just as we print and write our language, there is a free form artistic *grass script* that will defy your most imaginative interpretation. Also there remains much Traditional Hanzi on old signs and in villages.

The correct stroke choice is that which you have to draw to reproduce or create a character. It varies from font to font and author to author. Further ahead in this book is a detailed chapter on the various strokes of Hanzi. As an example, there are many sources that say the 1st stroke for (月, **yuè**, **moon**) is (撇, **Piě**, ノ). **Piě** stroke is a near 45 degree angle right to left descending stroke. The correct stroke has little curvature. It is obvious on inspection that the first stroke in 月 is not entirely curved but is (竖撇, **Shù Piě**, **SP**, 丿). **SP** is vertical line with a finishing curve to the left.

There are countless examples of these variations. There is no *solution*. Once written with a brush and ink, Hanzi is an artistic expression. If the message of the character is preserved, it is difficult to assign *right* or *wrong* to an individual's efforts.

As another example, here are some of the various expressions of the Radical #45 (**R #45**, 屮, **chè**, **sprout**). 屮, 屮, 屮, 屮. Each example of this character in different fonts introduces questions as to which named strokes are most appropriate. But, the visual meaning is preserved. Although there are tens of thousands of characters, the meaning is readily preserved in these examples even though the strokes are not standardized.

List of the 214 Kangxi Radicals

The following is a list of all 214 Kangxi Radicals categorized under the number of strokes along with some examples of characters containing these Radicals. The accompanying numbers are the officially assigned numbers. Further on in this book are the rules of writing the Radicals. Stroke order, stroke direction and stroke choice become very important. Common variants of each character are displayed such as (**R#64**, 手, **shǒu**, **hand**) and (**R#64'**, 扌, **standing hand**, **shǒu**). Some of the Radicals have both Traditional (**T**) and Simplified (**S**) forms. The written official Chinese language, (汉字, **Hànzì**, **Hanzi**), when broken down to its constituent components, is a combination of the Radicals plus or minus additional strokes.

Knowing how to draw each character stroke and Radical ultimately simplifies learning to write characters. The characters no longer look like a confusing collection of lines but become a small collection of Radicals. There is no way to master this other than repetitive copying and recitation of the name with the correct tone. If you do not do this, you will find that your ability to learn (汉字, **Hànzì**, **Hanzi**) will dead-end when you reach the limits of your usual memory for volume and complexity. It is easy to remember how to draw characters with up to four or five strokes. Beyond that, you need a systematic approach. There is no need to belabour learning theory in this book.

However, the volume and complexity of learning to write (汉字, **Hànzì**, **Hanzi**) and (汉语, **Hànyǔ**, **Hanyu**) is such that you need to recruit every learning tool possible. Native English speakers are not used to a non-phonetic based language with no recognizable alphabet. There are few clues to recognize previously unseen words or characters. You will need lots of paper, many pens and lots of time and patience. Once you can draw every Radical, you can draw every character.

There are numerous variants of many of the Radicals. This book attempts to compile the most common Radicals used in the PRC. These Radicals are shared to a degree by China, Japan and Korea and are often referred to as the CJK Radicals.

There are several defined sets of organized Radicals ranging in number from 187 to 540 Radicals, plus their variants. There is no **correct** collection. Traditional Chinese sets and Radicals are predictably quantitatively greater in number and complexity than Simplified Radicals. The Radical set chosen for this book is the Chinese Japanese Korean (**CJK**) Radicals from the Kangxi dictionary published in 1716. The original set was of course all Traditional Chinese Radicals and characters.

This set uses the original number of Radicals with simplified variants substituted. I have also added the historic Traditional Radicals in the work sheets for comparison. China currently uses a simplified set with 187 Radicals. Although China created and embraced simplification, there is still Traditional Chinese Radicals and characters throughout China. I was once entrenched in not learning any Traditional characters. This changed when I came across very old historic sites with poems, stories and explanations set into stone, bronze and pottery.

China will set the stage for Asia for usage of Simplified characters and spoken Standard Mandarin as the Lingua Franca of Asia. I encourage you to concentrate on Simplified Radicals but to gradually assimilate some Traditional Radicals and characters.

1 Stroke

- 1. 一 (one) (yī) - 丁 七 丈 三

- 2. 丨 (line) (gǔn) - 中 丰 串 十

- 3. 丶 (dot) (zhǔ) - 丸 丹 主 丼

- 4. 丿 (slash) (piě) - 乂 乃 久 乎

- 5. 乙 (second) (yǐ) - 乞 乾 挖 乿

- 5'. 乚 (second) (yǐ) - 也 乳 亂 说

- 6. 亅 (hook) (jué) - 了 予 亅 乎

2 Strokes

- 7. 二 (two) (èr) - 于 五 井 些

- 8. 亠 (lid) (tóu) - 亡 交 亥 京

- 9. 人 (human) (rén) - 今 介 从 令

- 9'. 亻 (standing human) (rén) - 仁 仕 他 休

- 10. 儿 (legs) (ér) - 兄 兆 先 光

- 11. 入 (enter) (rù) - 氽 粂 痊 拴

- 12. 八 (eight) (bā) - 公 共 兵 具

- 13. 冂 (down box) (jiǒng) - 冉 再 同 囧

- 14. 冖 (cover) (mì) - 冗 冠 冢 冥

- 15. 冫 (ice) (bīng) - 冰 冶 冷 凍

- 16. 几 (table) (jī) - 凡 凭 凰 凳

- 17. 凵 (open box) (qǔ) - 凶 凸 凹 出

- 18. 刀 (knife) (dāo) - 刃 分 切 券

- 18'. 刂 (standing knife) (dāo) - 刈 刊 刑 列
- 19. 力 (power) (lì) - 功 劣 努 励
- 20. 勹 (wrap) (bāo) - 勺 匀 勾 包
- 21. 匕 (spoon) (bǐ) - 北 匙 老 能
- 22. 匚 (right open box) (fāng) - 匠 匡 匣 匪
- 23. 匸 (hiding enclosure) (xǐ) - 匹 医 匼 匿
- 24. 十 (ten) (shí) - 千 午 南 博
- 25. 卜 (divination) (bǔ) - 卞 占 卡 卦
- 26. 卩 (seal) (jié) - 卯 印 危 却
- 27. 厂 (cliff) (hàn) - 厄 厘 厚 原
- 28. 厶 (private) (sī) - 厷 去 叀 参
- 29. 又 (again) (yòu) - 叉 友 双 受

3 Strokes

- 30. 口 (mouth) (kǒu) - 史 名 君 吟
- 31. 囗 (enclosure) (wéi) - 囚 因 困 国
- 32. 土 (earth) (tǔ) - 地 均 坊 城
- 33. 士 (scholar) (shì) - 壬 壻 喜 声
- 34. 夂 (go) (zhǐ) - 夆 夅 逢 缝
- 35. 夊 (go slowly) (suī) - 夎 复 夑 夏
- 36. 夕 (evening) (xī) - 外 名 多 夜
- 37. 大 (big) (dà) - 天 太 夫 契
- 38. 女 (woman) (nǚ) - 好 妊 妹 姓

- 39. 子 (child) (zǐ) - 孔 字 孝 孟

- 40. 宀 (roof) (mián) - 宅 字 宗 官

- 41. 寸 (inch) (cùn) - 寺 封 射 时

- 42. 小 (small) (xiǎo) - 少 尖 尔 尚

- 43. 尢 (lame) (wāng) - 允 尤 尬 尪

- 44. 尸 (corpse) (shī) - 尺 尻 尾 局

- 45. 屮 (sprout) (chè) - 屯 纯 出 沌

- 46. 山 (mountain) (shān) - 屹 岳 峰 屹

- 47. 川 (river) (chuān) - 州 训 顺 酬

- 48. 工 (work) (gōng) - 左 巧 巫 差

- 49. 己 已 巳 (oneself) (jǐ) - 巴 卮 巷 巽

- 50. 巾 (turban) (jīn) - 市 布 帆 怖

- 51. 干 (dry) (gān) - 平 开 并 平

- 52. 幺 (tiny) (yāo) - 幻 幼 幻 幼

- 53. 广 (dotted cliff) (yǎn) - 床 底 店 府

- 54. 廴 (long stride) (yǐn) - 延 廷 建 廻

- 55. 廾 (two hands) (gǒng) - 弁 异 弃 弄

- 56. 弋 (shoot) (yì) - 式 式 弍 式

- 57. 弓 (bow) (gōng) - 引 弟 弦 弱

- 58. 彑 (snout) (jì) - 互 象 彘 彝

- 58. 彐 (snout) (jì) - 事 当 档 铛

- 59. 彡 (bristle) (shān) - 形 彦 彩 彬

- 60. 彳 (step) (chì) - 役 往 待 律

4 Strokes

- 61. 心 (heart) (xīn) - 必 志 忘 忠

- 61'. 忄 (standing heart) (xīn) - 忙 快 怖 怪

- 62. 戈 (halberd) (gē) - 戊 戎 成 我

- 63. 戶 (door) (hù) - 房 所 扁 扇

- 64. 手 (hand) (shǒu) - 拜 拳 掌 掔

- 64'. 扌 (standing hand) (shǒu) - 打 批 技 抱

- 65. 支 (branch) (zhī) - 竧 敲 邊 技

- 66. 攴 攵 (rap) (pū) - 改 放 政 故

- 67. 文 (script) (wén) - 孝 斌 斐 斑

- 68. 斗 (dipper) (dǒu) - 料 斛 斜 斟

- 69. 斤 (axe) (jīn) - 斥 斧 斬 新

- 70. 方 (square) (fāng) - 於 施 旁 旅

- 71. 旡 (not) (wú) - 既 旤 慨 暨

- 71. 无 (not) (wú) - 芜 庑 抚 芜

- 72. 日 (sun) (rì) - 旦 旱 明 星

- 73. 曰 (say) (yuē) - 晉 曷 書 曹

- 74. 月 (moon) (yuè) - 朏 朖 期 朦

- 75. 木 (tree) (mù) - 末 本 杉 林

- 76. 欠 (yawn) (qiàn) - 次 欣 欲 歌

- 77. 止 (stop) (zhǐ) - 此 步 武 歪

- 78. 歹 (death) (dǎi) - 死 殉 殊 殘
- 78. 歺 (death) (dǎi)- 妃 餐 璨 瀄
- 79. 殳 (weapon) (shū) - 段 殷 殺 殿
- 80. 毋 (do not) (wú) - 毒 每 盎 冊
- 80. 母 (do not) (wú) - 每 毑 毒 毐
- 81. 比 (compare) (bǐ) - 毕 毖 毘 毚
- 82. 毛 (fur) (máo) - 毫 毬 毯 毳
- 83. 氏 (clan) (shì) - 氏 民 氐 氓
- 84. 气 (steam) (qì) - 氛 氤 氣 氫
- 85. 水 (water) (shuǐ) - 汞 泉 淼 漿
- 85'. 氵 (standing water) (shuǐ) - 河 泣 洋 海
- 85". 氺 (water) (shuǐ) - 求 泰 滕 录
- 86. 火 (fire) (huǒ) - 灼 炊 炎 炒
- 86'. 灬 (fire) (huǒ) - 烈 烹 焦 然
- 87. 爪 (claw) (zhuǎ) - 爬 笊 抓 枛
- 87. 爫 (claw) (zhuǎ) - 采 爭 爯 爰
- 88. 父 (father) (fù) - 爸 爹 爺 交
- 89. 爻 (double crosses) (yáo) - 爼 爾 希 网
- 90. 爿 (bed) (qiáng) - 牀 牁 牂 牒
- 90. 丬 (bed) (qiáng) - 将 状 壮 妆
- 91. 片 (slice) (piàn) - 版 牋 牌 牒
- 92. 牙 (fang) (yá) - 牚 穿 呀 芽

- 93. 牛 (cow) (niú) - 牧 物 牲 犀

- 94. 犬 (dog) (quǎn) - 狀 猋 猒 獸

- 94'. 犭 (standing dog) - 犯 狂 狗 狩

5 Strokes

- 95. 玄 (profound) (xuán) - 玅 兹 率 旒

- 96. 玉 (jade) (yù) - 瑩 瑬 璧 璧

- 96'. 王 (jade) (yù) - 珍 珠 現 球

- 97. 瓜 (melon) (guā) - 胍 瓞 瓠 瓢

- 98. 瓦 (earthenware) (wǎ) - 瓮 瓷 甄 甌

- 99. 甘 (sweet) (gān) - 甙 甚 甜 甝

- 100. 生 (life) (shēng) - 甡 產 甥 甦

- 101. 用 (use) (yòng) - 甩 甫 甬 甯

- 102. 田 (field) (tián) - 男 界 留 畦

- 103. 疋 (bolt of cloth) (pǐ) - 疌 疏 疏 疑

- 104. 疒 (sickness) (chuáng) - 疼 疾 病 痴

- 105. 癶 (dotted tent) (bō) - 举 癸 發 登

- 106. 白 (white) (bái) - 的 皆 皇 皎

- 107. 皮 (skin) (pí) - 皰 皴 皸 皺

- 108. 皿 (dish) (mǐn) - 盂 盆 盒 盛

- 109. 目 (eye) (mù) - 盲 看 眺 眼

- 110. 矛 (halberd) (máo) - 矜 矜 矞 矠

- 111. 矢 (arrow) (shǐ) - 矣 知 矩 短

- 112. 石 (stone) (shí) - 砂 砥 砲 硬
- 113. 示 (spirit) (shì) - 崇 票 祭 禁
- 113'. 礻 (standing spirit) (shì) - 礼 社 祈 祝
- 114. 内 (track) (róu) - 禹 禺 离 禽
- 115. 禾 (grain) (hé) - 秋 税 稔 稻
- 116. 穴 (cave) (xué) - 究 空 穿 突
- 117. 立 (stand) (lì) - 站 竝 章 竣

6 Strokes

- 118. 竹 (bamboo) (zhú) - 竿 笏 算 箱
- 119. 米 (rice) (mǐ) - 粒 粗 粟 精
- 120. 糸 (silk) (mì) - 系 紊 素 索
- 120'. 纟 (standing silk) (mì) - 紅 納 紙 細
- 121. 缶 (jar) (fǒu) - 缸 缺 罅 罐
- 122. 网 (net) (wǎng) - 罨
- 122'. 罒 (net) (wǎng) - 罠 罪 置 罰
- 123. 羊 (sheep) (yáng) - 着 美 群 羯
- 124. 羽 (feather) (yǔ) - 翁 翌 習 翔
- 125. 老 (old) (lǎo) - 耄 耆 耋 姥
- 125'. 耂 (old) (lǎo) - 考 者 耇
- 126. 而 (and) (ér) - 耍 耏 耐 耑
- 127. 耒 (plow) (lěi) - 耕 耗 耘 耙
- 128. 耳 (ear) (ěr) - 耽 聰 聲 聽

- 129. 聿 (brush) (yù) - 殏 肄 肅 肇
- 130. 肉 (meat) (ròu) - 胬 胾 腐 臠
- 130. 月 (standing meat) (ròu) - 肌 肝 肥 肱
- 131. 臣 (minister) (chén) - 臤 臥 𢘐 臧
- 132. 自 (self) (zì) - 臫 臬 臭 臲
- 133. 至 (arrive) (zhì) - 致 桎 輊 臻
- 134. 臼 (mortar) (jiù) - 臾 舁 舂 與
- 135. 舌 (tongue) (shé) - 舍 舐 舒 舔
- 136. 舛 (oppose) (chuǎn) - 舜 舞 桀 嶙
- 137. 舟 (boat) (zhōu) - 航 舫 般 船
- 138. 艮 (stopping) (gèn) - 艱 很 恨 狠
- 139. 色 (color) (sè) - 艴 艳 艷 绝
- 140. 艸 (grass) (cǎo) - 芔 芻 芔 芔
- 140'. 艹 (grass) (cǎo) – 花 茶 草 菓 槊
- 141. 虍 (tiger) (hǔ) – 虎 虐 處 號
- 142. 虫 (insect) (chóng) – 蛇 蛙 蜜 蝶
- 143. 血 (blood) (xiě) – 衄 衃 衆 衉
- 144. 行 (walk enclosure) (xíng) – 衕 術 街 衝
- 145. 衣 (clothes) (yī) – 表 衰 袋 裔
- 145'. 衤 (standing clothes) (yī) – 袂 袖 裸 裾
- 146. 襾 覀 西 (west) (yà) – 西 覂 覃 覊

- 146. 覀 (west) (yà) – 覃 覆 覇 覈

- 146. 西 (west) (yà) – 洒 牺 晒 栖

   7 Strokes

- 147. 见 (see) (jiàn) – 现 觉 观 视

- 148. 角 (horn) (jiǎo) – 觜 确 嘴 触

- 149. 言 (speech) (yán) – 罟 誓 馨 警

- 149'. 讠 (standing speech) (yán) – 证 记 认 训

- 150. 谷 (valley) (gǔ) – 容 裕 浴 峪

- 151. 豆 (bean) (dòu) – 豈 豉 豌 短

- 152. 豕 (pig) (shǐ) – 豚 象 豢 家

- 153. 豸 (badger) (zhì) – 豹 豺 貂 貌

- 154. 贝 (shell) (bèi) – 员 则 责 负

- 155. 赤 (red) (chì) – 赦 赧 赫 郝

- 156. 走 (run) (zǒu) – 赴 起 超 越

- 157. 足 (foot) (zú) – 距 跨 跪 路

- 158. 身 (body) (shēn) – 躬 躯 躺 射

- 159. 车 (car) (chē) – 军 转 连 较

- 160. 辛 (bitter) (xīn) – 辜 辟 辣 新

- 161. 辰 (morning) (chén) – 辱 晨 唇 震

- 162. 辵 (walk) (chuò) – 辵 起 趏 趱

- 162'. 辶 (walk) (chuò) – 近 返 述 道

- 163. 邑 (city) (yì) – 扈 挹 悒 邕

- 163'. 阝 (city) (yì) – 那 邦 邸 郁

- 164. 酉 (wine) (yǒu) – 酋 配 酒 酸

- 165. 采 (distinguish) (biàn) – 釉 釋 悉 奧

- 166. 里 (village) (lǐ) – 重 野 量 理

8 Strokes

- 167. 金 (metal) (jīn) – 釜 鏖 鏨 鑾

- 167'. 釒 (standing metal) (jīn) – 銀 銅 鋼 錫

- 167'. 钅 (standing metal) (jīn) – 钱 错 银 铁

- 168. 长 (long) (cháng) – 长 张 涨 帐

- 169. 门 (gate) (mén) – 间 们 闷 扪

- 170. 阜 (mound) (fù) – 阜 埠 頎 焯

- 170'. 阝 (standing mound) (fù) – 防 降 陰 階

- 171. 隶 (slave) (lì) – 逮 隸 康 逮

- 172. 隹 (small bird) (zhuī) – 隻 隼 雀 雄

- 173. 雨 (rain) (yǔ) – 雪 雲 零 雷

- 174. 青 靑 (blue) (qīng) – 靖 靘 靚 靛

- 175. 非 (wrong) (fēi) – 辈 靠 靡 悲

9 Strokes

- 176. 面 (face) (miàn) – 靤 靦 靨 靨

- 177. 革 (leather) (gé) – 勒 靴 鞋 鞍

- 178. 韦 (tanned leather) (wéi) – 韧 韨 韓 韙

- 179. 韭 (leek) (jiǔ) – 韭 韰 韱 韲

- 180. 音 (sound) (yīn) – 韴 韶 韸 響
- 181. 页 (face) (yè) – 项 顶 顺 顸
- 182. 风 (wind) (fēng) – 疯 枫 讽 砜
- 183. 飞 (fly) (fēi) – 飞 鼣 霏 鱻
- 184. 食 (eat) (shí) – 養 餐 餮 饕
- 184'. 饣 (standing eat) (shí) – 饰 蚀 饵 钚
- 185. 首 (head) (shǒu) – 馗 馘 道 湝
- 186. 香 (fragrant) (xiāng) – 馛 馞 馥 馨

10 Strokes

- 187. 马 (horse) (mǎ) – 吗 妈 骂 玛
- 188. 骨 (bone) (gǔ) – 骰 骸 髀 髓
- 189. 高 (tall) (gāo) – 亢 韒 觓 髞
- 190. 髟 (hair) (biāo) – 髦 髮 髯 鬆
- 191. 鬥 (fight) (dòu) – 鬧 鬮 鬩 鬪
- 192. 鬯 (sacrificial wine) (chàng) – 鬱 鬵 鬷 秬
- 193. 鬲 (cauldron) (lì) – 鬵 鬴 鬶 鬷
- 194. 鬼 (ghost) (guǐ) – 魁 魂 魃 魅

11 Strokes

- 195. 鱼 (fish) (yú) – 渔 鲜 鲁 鱀
- 196. 鸟 (bird) (niǎo) – 茑 袅 岛 鸡
- 197. 卤 (alkaline) (lǔ) – 龄 龄 鹹 鹾
- 198. 鹿 (deer) (lù) – 麋 麒 麓 麗

- 199. 麦 (wheat) (mài) – 唛 麸 麺 陵
- 200. 麻 (hemp) (má) – 摩魔 蘼 磨

12 Strokes

- 201. 黄 (yellow) (huáng) – 黆 黇 黉 黋
- 202. 黍 (millet) (shǔ) – 黎 黏 黐 漆
- 203. 黑 (black) (hēi) – 嘿 潶 黔 熏
- 204. 黹 (needlework) (zhǐ) – 黺 黻 黼 黻

13 Strokes

- 205. 黾 (amphibian) (mǐn) – 黿 鼆 鼇 鼈
- 206. 鼎 (tripod) (dǐng) – 鼏 鼐 鼑 鼒
- 207. 鼓 (drum) (gǔ) – 鼕 鼗 鼖 鼛
- 208. 鼠 (rat) (shǔ) – 鼦 鼨 鼬 鼯

14 Strokes

- 209. 鼻 (nose) (bí) – 濞 劓 齈 鼾
- 210. 齐 (uniformly) (qí) – 剂 济 挤 侪

15 Strokes

- *211*. 齿 (tooth) (chǐ) - 啮 龀 龅 龈

16 Strokes

- 212. 龙 (dragon) (lóng) – 笼 拢 陇 珑
- 213. 龟 (tortoise) (guī) – 阄 龟

17 Strokes

- 214 龠 (flute) (yuè) – 龡 龢 龣 龥

Written Variants

Orthography

The nature of Chinese characters makes it very easy to produce an allograph for any character. There have been many efforts at orthographical standardization throughout history. The widespread usage of the characters in different nations that do not see *eye to eye* has prevented any one system from becoming universally adopted. Consequently, the standard stroke order of any given character in Chinese usage may differ subtly from its standard shape in Japanese or Korean usage, even where no simplification has taken place. With inherent individuality in hand writing, there is significant difference between individuals. Even type fonts create a great number of variations.

Usually each Hanzi character takes up the same amount of space due to their block-like square nature. This is more true for electronic fonts than free hand writing. Some introductory books typically practice writing with a grid as a guide. In addition to strictness for the space that a character takes up, Hanzi characters are written with very precise rules. The three most important rules are the strokes employed, stroke placement, and the order in which they are written, stroke order. Most words can be written with just one stroke order. Some words also have variant stroke orders. This may occasionally result in different stroke counts. Certain characters are also written with different stroke orders in different countries.

Common Typefaces

There are two common typeface groups. These typefaces are based on the regular script for Chinese characters, which are akin to serif and sans serif fonts in the West.

The popular set for body text is a family of serif fonts called Song typeface (宋体), also known as Minchō (明朝) in Japan, and Ming typeface (明體) in Taiwan and Hong Kong. This typeface is similar to Western serif fonts such as Times New Roman in both appearance and function. These two fonts give strong clues to named stroke and stroke direction.

The other common group of fonts are called the black typeface, (黑体) in Chinese, and Gothic typeface. This group is characterized by straight lines of even thickness for each stroke, akin to sans-serif styles such as Arial and Helvetica in Western typography. This group of fonts, first introduced on newspaper headlines, is commonly used on headings, websites, signs and billboards.

The sans-serif style fonts take away the esthetic beauty and clues to stroke and stroke order. The lines of even thickness give the beginner writer little visual clue to stroke technique. Microsoft operating systems have numerous Asian fonts that are esthetically appealing and many more can be purchased online. I encourage you to learn to type in pinyin and convert to Hanzi and to use a font that shows the esthetic beauty and stroke clues.

If I was to pick one font that encompasses the spirit of the artistic nature of Hanzi, I would chose (楷体, **Kai Ti**). This is embedded in the Microsoft Office 2007 Word program. This font makes clear the artistic nature and defined strokes of each character. It retains a flavour of hand printed script.

Below are examples of the characters for (汉字, **Hànzì**, **Hanzi**) written with different type faces and type fonts. You can see how the top six fonts preserve the shape and definition of the individual strokes while the bottom four do not.

汉字	**Sim Sun**
汉字	**Kai Ti**
汉字	**MS Mincho**
汉字	**P Ming Li U**
汉字	**DF Kai-SB**
汉字	**Sim Hei**
汉字	**MS YaHei**
汉字	**Arial Unicode MS**
汉字	**MS Jheng Hei**

Stroke Order

(筆順, **bǐshùn**, **stroke order**) refers to the way in which Hanzi characters are written. A stroke is a movement of the writing instrument. In modern times, this is most commonly a pen, pencil or writing brush. Historically, a (毛笔, **máobǐ**, **hair-brush**) was held vertically in the right hand and dipped in ink and the strokes were made. *Stroke Order* can refer both to the numerical order in which the strokes of a given character are written and to the direction in which the writing instrument must move in producing a particular stroke.

A common misconception is that Chinese characters were originally engraved into wood. In fact, Chinese characters are believed to have originally been brush-written on perishable materials such as bamboo or on wood slats. These would then be bound together like Venetian blinds and rolled for storage. Examples of such books have been found dating to the late Zhou dynasty. (周朝, **Zhōu Cháo, 1122 BC to 256 BC**)

History has shown that it would take over a thousand years for uniform, defined forms for each character to appear. Now, as then, each character comprises a number of strokes, which must be written in a prescribed order.

The number of strokes per character for most characters is usually between one and thirty. However, the number of strokes in some obscure characters may reach as many as seventy strokes. In the twentieth century, simplification of Hanzi characters took place in mainland China. This greatly reduced the number of strokes in some characters. The basic rules of stroke order, however, remained the same.

Basic and Compound Strokes

There are six basic strokes, eight classic strokes and an overall total of about 55 distinct named strokes recognized in Chinese characters. Many of these are compound strokes, that is, sequential single strokes comprising more than one movement of the writing instrument. There are also variants of some strokes that can be named. In addition, with the advent of electronic fonts and digitalization of the written Chinese language, each named font type has its own variation of the written characters.

All of the simple strokes have more than one name in Chinese literature. This book uses the most current and common names. Many of the compound strokes have no agreed-upon name. They are thus named by an acronym compilation of their strokes. Digitalization of the fonts has taken much of the shape and *character* out of the strokes.

Each single stroke includes all the motions necessary to produce a given part of a character before lifting the writing instrument from the writing surface. Thus, a single setting down of the brush may use more than one *stroke* and may produce complex lines.

永

The character above for *eternity* has eight strokes, two of which, the second and third, are compound strokes. These are considered the eight *classic strokes*. All of the six *basic strokes* are used in this character.

Development of Stroke Order Rules

This is an outline of the character (永, **yǒng**, **forever**) This character, meaning *eternity*, contains 8 stroke shapes in 5 sequential strokes, 3 basic and 2 compound strokes, and is often used for practice by beginning calligraphers.

The rules for stroke order facilitate vertical character writing, to maximize ease of writing and reading and to further aid in producing uniform characters. A person who has learned the rules of stroke order can infer the stroke order of most characters. This eases the process of learning to write.

Many experienced writers may ignore or forget the normalized stroke order characters, or develop idiosyncratic ways of writing.

The author encourages using the exact stroke order as prescribed by rules. This eases and hastens learning. It also produces a more visually appealing character.

The Eight Principles of Yong (永字八法, yǒngzì bā fǎ, Yong character 8 rules) often uses the single character (永, **yǒng**, eternity) meaning *eternity*, to teach the eight most basic strokes. These rules will be presented graphically starting on page 289. I encourage you to photocopy the page 366 and get a brush and some ink and get to it. This is what billions of Chinese have done over thousands of years.

Modern Stroke Order

The Chinese government began to reform the Hanzi character set in 1956. They also reformed the number of strokes and the stroke order of some characters. An obvious notable innovation of this reformed stroke order was the conception of a horizontal writing stroke order. This facilitates horizontal writing. The history of written Chinese had included right to left, top to bottom and now left to right.

Basic Rules of Stroke Order

(左, **zuǒ, left**)   (左-右, **zuǒ-yòu, left to right**)

(右, **yòu, right**)   (上-下, **shàng-xià, upper- lower**)

(上, **shàng, upper**)   (字, **zì, character**)

(中, **zhōng, middle**)   (筆順, **bǐshùn, stroke order**)

(下, **xià, lower**)   (文, **wén, language**)

1. Left to Right on Horizontal Strokes 一

The first character to learn is the number one, (一, **yī, one**), which is written with a single horizontal line. This character has one simple stroke, which is written from left (左, **zuǒ, left**) to right (右, **yòu, right**). The name of the horizontal character stroke is (横, **héng, H, horizontal character stroke**). Throughout this book, it will be abbreviated as **H**.

2. Left to Right and Top to Bottom on Multiple Horizontal Strokes 二

As a rule, characters are written from the top to the bottom, (上, **shàng, upper**) to (下, **xià, lower**). If the components of the character are horizontally stacked and the lowermost is towards the left (左, **zuǒ**, **left**), yet under the upper strokes, the top to bottom priority is preserved.

The character for *two* has two strokes. (二, **èr**, **two**) In this case, both are written from (左, **zuǒ**, **left**) to (右, **yòu**, **right**) hence **héng**, **héng** or **H**, **H**. The top stroke is written first, hence (上, **shàng**, **upper**) to (下, **xià**, **lower**). The character for three has three strokes, (三, **sān**, **three**), hence, **héng**, **héng**, **héng**, or **H**, **H**, **H**. Hence each stroke is written from left to right, 左-右, starting of course with the uppermost stroke, (上, **shàng**, **upper**), then next (中, **zhōng**, **middle**), then the lower most stroke (下, **xià**, **under**). The structures thus take the form of the first three examples below.

1st   一   **1st**   二   **1st**   三
              2nd   **2nd**
                                3rd

The Chinese character for *person*, (人, **rén**, **person**), has two strokes. The first stroke is the compound accelerating curve downward to the left (弯撇, **Wān Piě**, **downwards left double curved stroke**). The second stroke is the down swooping stroke on the right side thickening at the base (捺, **nà**, **downwards-right curved stroke**). This preserves the stroke order of (上-下, **shàng-xià**, **upper-lower**) and the (左-右, **zuǒ-yòu**, **left to right**) stroke order.

This rule applies also to characters that are formed more complexly. Take for example, (相, **xiāng**, **each other**). The polymorphic character can be divided into two separate characters. (木, **mù**, **tree**) and (目, **mù**, **eye**). The leftmost side of the character, (木, **mù**, **tree**) is written first. The right side (目, **mù**, **eye**) is written second.

1st 2nd

There are some exceptions to this rule, mainly occurring when the right side of a character has an underscore originating from the left character. Take for example the character (这, **zhè**, **this**) In this case, the right side is written first, followed by the left side, and finally the lower underscore stroke. This can be further seen in the characters, (迷, **mí**, **bewilder**) and (过, **guò**, **to live**). In a multi component character such as (谜, **mí**, **riddle**), there are three components. The left component is first, the right component (米, **mǐ**, **rice**) is second and the middle component (**R#162'**, 辶, **chuò**, **walk**) underlining the right component goes last. When there are upper and lower components, the upper components are written first, then the lower components, as in (旦, **dàn**, **dawn**) which is composed of the character for *day* or *sun*,(日, **rì**, **day**) plus (˙, **yī**, **one**).

3. Top to Bottom on Single Vertical Strokes 丨

The general rule for single vertical strokes is that they are written from top to bottom. The name of the stroke is (竖, **shù**, **vertical down character stroke**).

4. Left to Right and Top to Bottom in Multiple Vertical Strokes. 川

In a simple character such as (川, **chuān**, **river**), the rules of stroke are readily apparent in the top to bottom and left to right order. Again, the rules are preserved, all three strokes are written top to bottom. The name of the first vertical character stroke is (竖撇, 丿, **shùpiě**, **SP**, **vertical down stroke left curve**). Hence, the order is **shùpiě, shù, shù** or **SP, S, S**. The left side vertical down stroke has a short left curve finish on it (撇, ノ, **piě, downwards-left curved character stroke**).The stroke order is thus numerically,

1st 2nd 3rd

There is not a fixed consensus on compound stroke naming. The names I will use will be functional and may not agree with other sources but will adequately describe the stroke.

(儿, **ér, son**) is another example. This is formed from two compound strokes, (竖撇, ノ, **shùpiě, SP, vertical stroke left curve**) then the right side stroke is   (竖折弯鉤, 乚, **shùzhéwāngōu, SZWG, vertical down stroke, break, hook**).

5. **Top Left Side Vertical Stroke meets Top Left Side Horizontal Stroke**.

There is not a simple unifying rule to clarify what happens on the top left part of a character or Radical. Ultimately one needs to simply memorize the Radicals that deal with this. The first category of the Radicals that fit into this designation can be divided into groups that have similar patterns. The first group are Radicals in which **S** and **HZ** meet together.

｜　冂

For these closed box Radicals the stroke order is the same. The left side **S** is always first. This is observed in (口, **kǒu, mouth**), (囗, **wéi, enclosure**), (日, **rì, sun**), (曰, **yuē, speak**), (田, **tián, field**), (目, **mù, eye**) and (**R#108** 皿, **mǐn, dish**). All other characters that contain these Radicals within another Radical or character follow the initial stroke order **S-HZ**.

The second category of Radicals that fit into this designation are the Radicals in which **S** and **HZG** meet. For (**R#13**, 冂, **jiǒng**, **down box**) the stroke order is **S-HZG**.

丨 冂

However, for (**R#26**, 卩, **jié seal**) the stroke order becomes **HZG-S**. You can see that it is the scale that differs, for **R#26**, **S** is proportionately longer.

乛 卩

The third category are Radicals in which **SP / WP** and **HZWG** meet. For the Radical (**R#16**, 几, **jī**, **table**) the stroke order is **SP-HZWG**.

丿 几

The fourth category are Radicals in which **WP** and **HZG** meet or intersect. For (**R#18**, 刀, **dāo**, **knife**) the stroke order is **HZG-WP**. This stroke order is also preserved for (**R#19**, 力, **lì**, **power**) in which the stroke order is also **HZG-WP**.

乛 刀 and 乛 力

The fifth category of Radicals are those in which **SZ** and **H** meet. For both Radical (**R#22**, 匚, **fāng**, **right open box**) and (**R#23**, 匸, **xǐ**, **hiding enclosure**) the stroke order is **H-SZ** or **H-SW**. For Radical (**R#131**, 臣, **chén**, **minister**) **H** is written first, the other strokes are written and **SZ** is written last. This follows a pattern in which characters based on **R#22** and **R#23** have **H** written first.

The sixth category are Radicals in which **SP** and **HZG** meet. The lone representative in this category is Radical (**R#74**, 月, **yuè**, **moon**). The stroke order is **SP-HZG**.

The seventh category are Radicals in which **SP** and **HZ** meet. The lone representative is Radical (**R#44**, 尸, **shī**, **corpse**). The stroke order is **HZ-(x)-SP**.

The eighth category are Radicals and characters in which **SZ** and **HZG** meet. The lone Radical in this category is Radical (**R#80**, 毋 /母, **wú**, **do not**). The stroke order is **SZ-HZG**.

The ninth category are characters and Radicals in which **H** and **S** meet. Radical (**R#99**, 甘, **gān**, **sweet**) and (**R#128**, 耳, **ěr**, **ear**) represent this category. The stroke order for both is **H-S**. A variant of **H-S** is (年, nián, year).

and

The tenth category are characters and Radicals in which **ST** and **HZ** meet. The representative Radical is (**R#138**, 艮, **gèn**, **stopping**). In this Radical **HZ** comes before **ST**.

コ ヨ ヨ 𦣞

The eleventh category are characters and Radicals in which **SP** and **HG** meet. Radical (**R#107**, 皮, **pí**, **skin**) is the lone member of this category. The stroke order is **HG-SP**.

フ 厂 ナ 皮 皮

The twelfth category are Radicals in which **H** and **SP** meet. This is seen in Radicals (**R#27**, 厂, **hàn**, **cliff**) and (**R#104**, 疒, **chuáng**, **sickness**). In both of these Radicals **H** precedes **SP**.

一 厂 and 丶 亠 广 疒 疒

6. Horizontal before Vertical 十

When **S** and **H** strokes cross, horizontal strokes are written before vertical strokes. The character for (十, **shí**, **ten**), has two strokes. The left to right horizontal stroke (横, **héng**, **H**, **horizontal stroke**) is written first. The top to bottom vertical stroke (竖, **shù**, **S**, **vertical down stroke**) is written second. Hence, the stroke order is **héng-shù** or **H-S**.

7. Bottom Horizontal Stroke Last 王

In situations where a horizontal stroke is on the bottom of a character and it is not crossed by the vertical stroke, but intersects with it, the vertical stroke is drawn before the last horizontal **H** stroke. Example, (王, **wáng**, **king**), the stroke order is **héng**, **héng**, **shù**, **héng** or **H, H, S, H**. This allows for a neater finish in which the horizontal stroke can neatly intersect the vertical line. This dates from the use of a hair brush and ink in which the descending hand would obscure the neat intersection of a horizontal line being drawn first. Further examples are (土, **tǔ**, **earth**), (工, **gōng**, **work**) and (主, **zhǔ**, **master**)

8. Vertical Cutting Strokes Last 中

Vertical strokes that cut through a character are written after the horizontal strokes that they cut through, as in (中, **zhōng**, **centre**). This rule applies when the vertical line starts above the top horizontal line and finishes below the bottom horizontal line. (中, **zhōng**, **center**) is such an example. The box is completed and then the vertical line is drawn through it.

9. Horizontal Cutting Strokes Last 母

Horizontal strokes that cut through a character are written last, as in 母 and 海. The usual strokes to cut through are **H** and **T**. Example (母, **mǔ**, **female**)

10. Right to Left down Sloping before Left to Right down Sloping 文

Right-to-left diagonals (ノ) are written before left-to-right diagonals (㇏) such as in (文, **wén**, **language**), (这, **zhè**, **this**) and (友, **yǒu**, **friend**). The crossing strokes are typically **P**, **N** or **CD**.

11. Centre Verticals before Left and Right Strokes. 永

In characters that show a left to right symmetry with a central dividing vertical stroke, the central stroke is written first. Vertical centre strokes are written before vertical or diagonal outside strokes, left outside strokes are written before right outside strokes (水, **shùǐ**, **water**), (永, **yǒng**, **eternity**), (小, **xiǎo**, **small**).

12. Box Rules, Left Vertical First, Outside before Inside 回

All closed boxes are constructed the same. The left vertical edge is drawn first with the vertical downward stroke **S**. The top horizontal and right vertical strokes are written in one continuous stroke using (**HZ**, **héngzhé**). This is the left to right horizontal stroke with a down dropping vertical stroke. The box is left open at this time if it has contents inside. All inside contents are then finished. The bottom horizontal left to right box-closing stroke **H** is written last. If there is a box within a box, the inner box is closed first. Example, (回, **huí**, **turn around**). An easy order to remember is ***make three sided down box***, ***fill box***, ***close box***.

This rule applies also to top enclosing characters that have no bottom stroke, such as 同 and 月. The outer structure is finished first, then the inside contents are added.

13. Bottom Enclosure Last (R#17, qǔ, 凵, Open Box)

Bottom box enclosures, (**R#17**, **qǔ**, 凵, **open box**) are always written last. The contents of the box are written first. Then the box encloses the contents. Examples are (画, **huà**, **draw**), (涵, **hán**, **contain**), (凶, **xiōng**, **fierce**). The box is made in two strokes, **SZ-S**. This follows the rule of underlining strokes being placed last.

14. Down Box Rules 冂

(**R#13**, **jiǒng**, 冂, **down box**) is made with **S-HZG**. If there is a Radical, stroke or character over top of (**R#13**, **jiǒng**, 冂, **down box**), as in (再, **zài**, **again**), it is made first. Next, (**R#13**, **jiǒng**, 冂, **down box**) is formed. Strokes dropping from above and entering the box, in this situation, **S**, are made after the open Down Box is formed. Strokes inside the box are made after the box is formed, (同, **tóng**, **same**).

15. Ride Side Open Box Rules 匚, 匚

(**R#22**, **fāng**, 匚, **right open box**) as a Radical, is formed with the strokes **H-SZ**. However, the stroke order is **H** plus whatever is under **H**, then **SZ** when a character is made. This follows the general rule of underlining and enclosing strokes occurring last. (匠, **jiàng**, **craftsman**) (匡, **kuāng**, **correct**) (匣, **xiá**, **box**).

(**R#23**, **xǐ**, 匚, **hiding enclosure**) as a Radical, is formed with the strokes **H-SW**. Again, any Radical or character is made under **H** then the enclosing-underlining stroke **SW** occurs last. This follows the general rule of underlining and enclosing strokes occurring last. (匹, **pī**, **mate**) (医, **yī**, **to treat**)

16. Bottom Underlining Strokes Last 这

Bottom underlining strokes are always written last. If the left hand Radical of a character has a bottom underlining stroke, it is written last. Examples are Radical

(**R#162'**, 辶, **chuò**, **walk**) and (这, **zhè**, **this**). This construction can even occur in the middle of a character composed of three radicals side by side. (谜, **mí**, **riddle**).

谜

17. Dots and Minor Strokes Last 戈

Minor strokes are usually written last, as the small *dot* (点, **diǎn**, **dot**) in the following. (玉, **yù**, **jade**) In a character such as (国, **guó**, **country**), the **Box Rules** are preserved and the (玉, **yù**, **jade**) character is finished first then the box is closed. It must be remembered that **R#8**, (亠, **tóu**, **lid**) is a Radical and as it occurs at the top of a character (点, **diǎn**, **dot**) comes first.

18. 提, **Tí**, Stroke Rule ㇀

(提, **Tí**, ㇀) when it crosses another stroke is drawn after the stroke it crosses. Examples are (孑, **jié**, **alone**), (扌, **shǒu**, **hand**), (我, **wǒ**, **me**)

19. Not Withstanding Rule

There are apparent exceptions to many rules. However the apparent exceptions are often misinterpretations through choice of fonts or characters that have so many strokes that in a small sized font you cannot see the definition of the individual strokes. (**R#67**, 文, **wén**, **script**) appear to offend rule #**17**, **Dots and Minor Strokes Last**. It does follow the rule however of completion of radicals within a character and the first stroke (点, **diǎn**, **dot**) is part of the Radical (**R#8**, 亠, **tóu**, **lid**).

R#97, 瓜, **guā**, **melon** may appear to have a stroke selection of **H-P** or **H-WP** for the first two strokes. However, the first two strokes are not the **Radical R#27**, 厂, **hàn**, **cliff** but rather **PP-WP**. Despite trying four different fonts, 瓜 瓜 瓜 瓜, the proper strokes cannot be seen until you increase the size of the character.

瓜

(**R#26**, 卩, **jié**, **seal**) is another example of an apparent exception. On casual inspection it may look like **HZ-H-S**. The stroke order is in fact **HZG-S**. If one was to follow rule # **14. Down Box Rules**, it would be easy to assume that **S** is the first stroke. Again, font selection demonstrates the correct strokes. 卩 卩 卩 卩 In fact, some fonts make it look like Radical (**R# 13**, 冂, **jiǒng**, **down box**) 卩 卩 卩.

Hanzi characters are built up from basic strokes. The simplest characters have only one stroke while the more complex ones can have more than 60 strokes. You will find in the workbook below some Hanzi characters and the most common basic strokes in Hanzi. The strokes must be written in the right order and in the right direction. It is important to follow those rules. If you always write a character the same way you will develop a memorized pattern for how to write it. The character will also look much more symmetrical and be reproducible if you follow the rules. Proportions are very important so you have to have it in mind when you write.

Often a stroke can be altered to look more aesthetically pleasing in a character. If you look at the character for (学, **xué**, **study**), you find a character with a group of two (点, **diǎn**, **dot**) strokes on top and one **DP**. The two to the left are written angled from left to right while the last one is written angled from right to left. This is made to make the character more visually appealing.

学 学 学 学 学 学 学

The same occurs if you have many (横, 一, **héng**, **H**, **horizontal stroke**) in a character such as in the character (三, **sān**, **three**). In this example it is three **héng** and they are all different sizes.

However, in characters such as (士, **shì**, **scholar**) and (土, **tǔ**, **dirt**) the proportion of stroke length does have meaning. The upper (横, 一, **héng**, **H**,) stroke of (士, **shì**, **scholar**) is longer that the base **héng**. In the character (土, **tǔ**, **dirt**), the top most **héng** is shorter and this is what defines the difference between the two characters.

Certain strokes such as (折, **zhé**, **break**) and (钩, **gōu**, **left down hook**) never occur alone, but are components in compound strokes. Thus, they are not in themselves individual strokes. (折, **zhé**, **break**) is often described as a right angle turn but it often is not as in (也, **yě**, **also**) which has the compound character stroke (横折鈎, **Héng Zhé Gōu**, 乛) also seen as right-angled as in (刀, **Dāo**, **knife**). Other named components give ***character*** to names strokes by modifying their curvature or slope.

The Six Single Strokes

横, **Héng**, **H**, **Horizontal**, 一, is a horizontal or near horizontal stroke. It is drawn from the left to the right. As you can see with the character (三, **sān**, **three**) and angled in (七, **qī**, **seven**).

竖, **Shù**, **S**, **Line**, 丨, is a vertical or near vertical top to bottom stroke. You can clearly see this is the character (中, **zhōng**, **middle**). However, in the character (五, **wǔ**, **five**) it is it is leaning to the right.

提, **Tí**, **T**, **Flick**, ⁄, is a left to right *flick* stroke at an upward and variable angle. It is drawn from the left to the right. As you can see in the example (玫, **méi**, **rose**) it rises slightly from the left to the right.

捺, **Nà**, **N**, **Press Down**, ╲, is a left to right falling arc stroke at a 45 degree angle. It has a small concavity. In many electronic fonts it appears as a line and loses the brush stroke character.

撇, **Piě**, **P**, **Slash**, 丿, is a right to left falling slash stroke at a 45 degree angle. It has a small concavity. In many electronic fonts it appears as a line and loses the brush stroke character.

点, **Diǎn**, **D**, **Dot**, ╲, is a *dot* falling from the left to the right with a convexity. In many electronic fonts it appears as a line with no tear drop like character.

Stroke Variations and Additives

丿亅 鉤, **Gōu**, **G** , **Hook**, ⟶ 亅, is a *hook* that is added to 6 other strokes to create the compound strokes; **HG, SG, PG, WG, XG, BXG**. It is not a named stroke by its self.

乛 折, **Zhé**, **Z**, **Break**, 乛 indicates a right angle or near angle change in direction. It is not a stroke but is used to describe the transition from (横, 一, **Héng**, **H**) to (横折, **Héng Zhé**, **HZ**, 乛).

乚 折, **Zhé**, **Z**, **Break**, 乚 indicates a right angle or near angle change in direction. It is not a stroke but is used as a descriptive to describe the transition from (竖, **Shù**, **S**) to (竖折, **Shù Zhé**, **SZ**).

丿 短撇, **Duǎn Piě**, **DP**, **Short Slash**, 丿 is a short variant of 撇, **Piě**. In this book, in a character with multiple variants of the stroke (撇, **Piě**, 丿), the shorter will be called **DP**.

一 平撇, **Píng Piě**, **PP**, **Flat Slash**, is a flattened stroke seen on the top of characters. It is a flattened version of 撇, **Piě**. It can be mistaken for (横, **Héng**) with some fonts.

丶 右点, **Yòu Diǎn**, **YD**, **Right Dot**, is the most common variation of (点, **Diǎn**, **Dot**). It is not commonly referred to as (右点, **Yòu Diǎn**) but simply as (点, **Diǎn**, **Dot**).

左点, **Zuǒ Diǎn**, **ZD**, **Left Dot**, is a right to left falling concave dot. It is a mirror image inverse reflection of the right handed (右点, **Yòu Diǎn**, **right dot**).

长点, **Cháng Diǎn**, **CD**, **Long Dot** is the long dot seen as a long convex arc. It occurs in characters such as (这, **zhè**, **this**). As characters are scaled up **D** loses its dot shape and becomes **CD**

扁斜, **Biǎn Xié**, **BX**, is a curve flattening trait seen in one stroke (扁斜鉤, **Biǎn Xié Gōu**, ⌣). (扁, **biǎn**, **flat**) and (斜, **xié**, **slanting**) combine to form this trait.

直提, **Zhí Tí**, **ZT** is an upright version of (提, **Tí**).

点提, **Diǎn Tí**, **DT**, retains brush stroke character and is an alternative 提, **Tí**. It is formed by making (右点, **Yòu Diǎn**, **right dot**) then an uprising **T**.

短撇长点, **Duǎn Piě Cháng Diǎn**, **DPCD** is the same character stroke as (撇点, **Piě Diǎn**, **PD**). This alternate name is offered to provide a better sense of proportion.

弯, **Wān**, **W**, is a right to left falling slightly concave stroke.

Compound Strokes

竖鉤, **Shù Gōu**, **SG**, 亅 is a vertical down stroke with a hook to the left.

點捺, **Diǎn Nà**, **DN** is seen only in the character (入, **rù**, **to enter**) and its derivatives. It can be mistaken for (提捺, **Tí Nà**).

平捺, **Píng Nà**, **PN** is a left to right flattened falling stroke. It is a flattened version of 捺, Nà. It is seen as the underlining stroke in characters as above.

提捺, **Tí Nà**, **TN** can be confused with 点捺, **Diǎn Nà** as in (入, **rù**, **enter**).

提平捺, **Tí Píng Nà**, **TPN** occurs as an under stroke as demonstrated. 心

横折, **Héng Zhé**, **HZ** is a right angle or near right angle turn from (横, **Héng**, **H**, **Horizontal**)

フ

横撇, **Héng Piě**, **HP** exists as a compound stroke and can be confused with **H-P**.

→

横鉤, **Héng Gōu**, **HG** is often seen at the top of a character as **Diǎn - Héng Gōu**, ⌐.

乚

竖折, **Shù Zhé**, **SZ** has a right angle turn and can be confused with 竖弯, **Shù Wān** which has a curved transition versus a right angle transition.

乚

竖弯, **Shù Wān**, **SW** has a smooth turn and can be mistaken for (竖折, **Shù Zhé**, **SZ**).

レ

竖提, **Shù Tí**, **ST**. The (提, **Tí**, **T**, **Flick**, ⁄) component can be proportionally different lengths compared to (竖, **Shù**, **S**, **Line**, │) component.

丿

竖折, **Shù Piě**, **SP** is a vertical down stroke with a 45 degree tail to the left.

丿

弯撇, **Wān Piě**, **WP** differs from (竖撇, **Shù Piě**) in the non-vertical initial stroke. Characters described as (撇, **Piě**, **P**) often are in fact (弯撇, **Wān Piě**, **WP**).

撇折, **Piě Zhé**, **PZ**, the (折, **Zhé**, **Z**) stroke is horizontal and longer than the stroke (提, **Tí**, **T**) in (竖提, **Shù Tí**, **ST**). ㄥ vs ㇄.

撇點, **Piě Diǎn**, **PD**

撇鉤, **Piě Gōu**, **PG** is a very rare stroke.

弯鉤, **Wān Gōu**, **WG** is characterized by the top portion of the stroke being to the left of the apex of the curve that occurs in the vertical plane.

斜鉤, **Xié Gōu**, **XG**

扁斜鉤, **Biǎn Xié Gōu**, **BXG** is the flattened character stroke (斜鉤, **Xié Gōu**, **XG**) as seen in (心, **xīn**, **heart**) versus the stroke in (心, **xīn**, **heart**).

竖弯左, **Shù Wān Zuǒ**, **SWZ** differs from the compound stroke (竖折, **Shù Piě**, **SP**) in that the tail is not as acutely deviating from the vertical.

竖折折,**Shù Zhé Zhé**, **SZZ**

竖折撇, **Shù Zhé Piě**, **SZP**

竖折鉤, **Shù Zhé Gōu**, **SZG**

竖折弯鉤, **Shù Zhé Wān Gōu**, **SZWG** is a brush stroke variant of (竖折鉤, **Shù Zhé Gōu**, **SZG**).

横撇弯, **Héng Piě Wān**, **HPW**

横折折,**Héng Zhé Zhé**, **HZZ**

横折弯, **Héng Zhé Wān**, **HZW** differs from the compound stroke (横折折, **Héng Zhé Zhé**, **HZZ**) in that the transition from vertical to horizontal is curved versus a right angle.

横折提, **Héng Zhé Tí**, **HZT**

横折鉤, **Héng Zhé Gōu**, **HZG**

横折弯鉤, **Héng Zhé Wān Gōu**, **HZWG** is a brush stroke variant of (横折鉤, **Héng Zhé Gōu**, **HZG**).

横斜鉤, **Héng Xié Gōu**, **HXG**

横折折折, **Héng Zhé Zhé Zhé**, **HZZZ**

横折折撇, **Héng Zhé Zhé Piě**, **HZZP**

横折折弯鉤, **Héng Zhé Zhé Wān Gōu**, **HZZWG** is a variant of (**R#5**, 乙, **yǐ**, **second**).

了 横撇弯鈎, **Héng Piě Wān Gōu, HPWG**

勹 竖折折鈎, **Shù Zhé Zhé Gōu, SZZG**

勹 竖折折弯鈎, **Shù Zhé Zhé Wān Gōu, SZZWG** is a brush stroke variant of (竖折折鈎, **Shù Zhé Zhé Gōu, SZZG**).

乙 横撇折弯鈎, **Héng Piě Zhé Wān Gōu, HPZWG** as a Radical is (**R#5**, 乙, **yǐ, second**). This stroke is often called **HZWG**.

了 横折折弯鈎, **Héng Zhé Zhé Wān Gōu, HZZWG**

○ 圈, **Quān, Q** is an extraordinarily rare stroke.

Exercise for Individual Strokes

This is the introduction to practical stroke and character writing in this book. Using the templates provided you can directly trace over the strokes. Alternately you can photocopy or use a clear acetate sheet and a wipe-off marker. Equally important is to recite the pinyin word and tone. In the appendix you will find a section on pronunciation and tone.

Pick groups of five to ten sheets to practice by doing one character on each sheet and then going to the next. If you simply write over an entire page while watching television you may find that you flip the page over and do not remember any of it.

Once you have mastered the simple strokes and stroke additives, then it is time to move on to compound strokes. Try and stick to logical groups of strokes rather than randomly picking appealing strokes. For example, learn all the compound strokes that start with (横, **héng**, **H**, **horizontal**, 一) then move on to all the compound strokes with (竖, **shù**, **S**, **vertical line**, 丨).

The first 15 work sheets are the most important as the entire written language is built upon compounding and compiling these most basic units. Like all learning, set reasonable objectives. As your skills develop, you will see that more complex characters require balancing the proportions of different radicals to make the result esthetically pleasing.

Radicals are compilations of one or more strokes. The higher you go through the numbered Radical list the more the Radical is a composite of previous Radicals and additional strokes.

横

héng

H

Notes:

(横, héng, H, horizontal, 一)

héng	héng	héng	héng	héng	héng	héng	héng	héng	héng
H	H	H	H	H	H	H	H	H	H

héng	héng	héng	héng	héng	héng	héng	héng	héng	héng
H	H	H	H	H	H	H	H	H	H

竖

Notes:

(竖, shù, S, vertical line, 丨)

shù

S

shù	shù	shù	shù	shù	shù	shù	shù	shù	shù
S	S	S	S	S	S	S	S	S	S

shù	shù	shù	shù	shù	shù	shù	shù	shù	shù
S	S	S	S	S	S	S	S	S	S

提

tí

T

Notes:

(提, tí, T, flick, ✓)

tí	tí	tí	tí	tí	tí	tí	tí	tí	tí
T	T	T	T	T	T	T	T	T	T

tí	tí	tí	tí	tí	tí	tí	tí	tí	tí
T	T	T	T	T	T	T	T	T	T

315

撇

piě

P

Notes:

(撇, **piě**, **P**, slash, ノ)

piě	piě	piě	piě	piě	piě	piě	piě	piě	piě
P	P	P	P	P	P	P	P	P	P

piě	piě	piě	piě	piě	piě	piě	piě	piě	piě
P	P	P	P	P	P	P	P	P	P

316

捺

nà
N

Notes:

(捺, nà, N, press down, ㇏)

| nà | nà | nà | nà | nà | nà | nà | nà | nà | nà |
| N | N | N | N | N | N | N | N | N | N |

| nà | nà | nà | nà | nà | nà | nà | nà | nà | nà |
| N | N | N | N | N | N | N | N | N | N |

点

Notes:

(点, **diǎn**, **D**, dot, 丶)

diǎn

D

diǎn	diǎn	diǎn	diǎn	diǎn	diǎn	diǎn	diǎn	diǎn	diǎn
D	D	D	D	D	D	D	D	D	D
diǎn	diǎn	diǎn	diǎn	diǎn	diǎn	diǎn	diǎn	diǎn	diǎn
D	D	D	D	D	D	D	D	D	D

鉤

gōu

G

Notes:

(鉤, **gōu**, **G**, hook) is added as an accessory to other strokes.

↲	↲	↲	↲	↲	↲	↲	↲	↲	↲
gōu	gōu	gōu	gōu	gōu	gōu	gōu	gōu	gōu	gōu
G	G	G	G	G	G	G	G	G	G
↲	↲	↲	↲	↲	↲	↲	↲	↲	↲
gōu	gōu	gōu	gōu	gōu	gōu	gōu	gōu	gōu	gōu
G	G	G	G	G	G	G	G	G	G
↲	↲	↲	↲	↲	↲	↲	↲	↲	↲
↲	↲	↲	↲	↲	↲	↲	↲	↲	↲
↲	↲	↲	↲	↲	↲	↲	↲	↲	↲
↲	↲	↲	↲	↲	↲	↲	↲	↲	↲
↲	↲	↲	↲	↲	↲	↲	↲	↲	↲
↲	↲	↲	↲	↲	↲	↲	↲	↲	↲
↲	↲	↲	↲	↲	↲	↲	↲	↲	↲
↲	↲	↲	↲	↲	↲	↲	↲	↲	↲
↲	↲	↲	↲	↲	↲	↲	↲	↲	↲
↲	↲	↲	↲	↲	↲	↲	↲	↲	↲

折

zhé

Z

Notes:

(折, **Zhé**, **Z**, **break**, ㄱㄴ) indicates a right angle or near right angle change in direction. It is not a stroke but is used as a descriptive to describe the transition from one linear stroke to another.

zhé	zhé	zhé	zhé	zhé	zhé	zhé	zhé	zhé	zhé
Z	Z	Z	Z	Z	Z	Z	Z	Z	Z

zhé	zhé	zhé	zhé	zhé	zhé	zhé	zhé	zhé	zhé
Z	Z	Z	Z	Z	Z	Z	Z	Z	Z

短	撇
duǎn	piě
D	P

Notes:

(短撇, **duǎn piě**, **DP**) The difference between this stroke and (撇, **piě**, **P**, **slash**, ノ) is only in scale proportionate to the character. In this book **DP** will be marked when it is ½ or less of the character height or unmatched to **N**.

ノ ノ ノ ノ ノ ノ ノ ノ ノ ノ

ノ	ノ	ノ	ノ	ノ	ノ	ノ	ノ	ノ	ノ
DP	DP	DP	DP	DP	DP	DP	DP	DP	DP

ノ	ノ	ノ	ノ	ノ	ノ	ノ	ノ	ノ	ノ
DP	DP	DP	DP	DP	DP	DP	DP	DP	DP

平	撇
píng	piě
P	P

Notes:

(平撇, **píng piě**, **PP**, **flat slash**) is a flattened version of (撇, **piě**) seen on the top of characters. It can be mistaken for (横, **héng**, **H**) with some fonts.

PP	PP	PP	PP	PP	PP	PP	PP	PP	PP

PP	PP	PP	PP	PP	PP	PP	PP	PP	PP

右	点
yòu	diǎn
Y	D

Notes:

(右点, **yòu diǎn**, **right dot**, **YD**) is the most common variation of (点, **diǎn**, **dot**). It is not commonly referred to as (右点, **yòu diǎn**) but simply as (点, **diǎn**, **D**).

`	`	`	`	`	`	`	`	`	`
YD	YD	YD	YD	YD	YD	YD	YD	YD	YD
`	`	`	`	`	`	`	`	`	`
YD	YD	YD	YD	YD	YD	YD	YD	YD	YD

左	点
zuǒ	diǎn
Z	D

Notes:

(左点, **zuǒ diǎn**, **left dot**, **ZD**) is a right to left falling concave dot.

✔	✔	✔	✔	✔	✔	✔	✔	✔	✔
ZD	ZD	ZD	ZD	ZD	ZD	ZD	ZD	ZD	ZD
✔	✔	✔	✔	✔	✔	✔	✔	✔	✔
ZD	ZD	ZD	ZD	ZD	ZD	ZD	ZD	ZD	ZD

324

长	点
cháng	diǎn
C	D

Notes:

(长点, **cháng diǎn**, **long dot, CD**) is a elongated version of the (右点, **yòu diǎn**, **right dot, D**)

CD	CD	CD	CD	CD	CD	CD	CD	CD	CD

CD	CD	CD	CD	CD	CD	CD	CD	CD	CD

325

直	提
zhí	**tí**
Z	**T**

Notes:

(直提, **zhí tí**, **ZT**) is an upright version of the stroke (提, **Tí**, **T**).

✓	✓	✓	✓	✓	✓	✓	✓	✓	✓
ZT	**ZT**	**ZT**	**ZT**	**ZT**	**ZT**	**ZT**	**ZT**	**ZT**	**ZT**
✓	✓	✓	✓	✓	✓	✓	✓	✓	✓
ZT	**ZT**	**ZT**	**ZT**	**ZT**	**ZT**	**ZT**	**ZT**	**ZT**	**ZT**

点	提
diǎn	**tí**
D	**T**

Notes:

(点提, **diǎn tí**, **DT**) retains brush stroke character and is an alternate (提, **Tí**).

DT	DT	DT	DT	DT	DT	DT	DT	DT	DT

DT	DT	DT	DT	DT	DT	DT	DT	DT	DT

短	撇	长	点	Notes:
duǎn	piě	cháng	diǎn	see page 100
D	P	C	D	

ㄑ ㄑ ㄑ ㄑ ㄑ ㄑ ㄑ ㄑ

ㄑ	ㄑ	ㄑ	ㄑ	ㄑ	ㄑ	ㄑ	ㄑ	ㄑ	ㄑ
DPCD	DPCD	DPCD	DPCD	DPCD	DPCD	DPCD	DPCD	DPCD	DPCD

ㄑ	ㄑ	ㄑ	ㄑ	ㄑ	ㄑ	ㄑ	ㄑ	ㄑ	ㄑ
DPCD	DPCD	DPCD	DPCD	DPCD	DPCD	DPCD	DPCD	DPCD	DPCD

ㄑ	ㄑ	ㄑ	ㄑ	ㄑ	ㄑ	ㄑ	ㄑ		
ㄑ	ㄑ	ㄑ	ㄑ	ㄑ	ㄑ	ㄑ	ㄑ		
ㄑ	ㄑ	ㄑ	ㄑ	ㄑ	ㄑ	ㄑ	ㄑ		
ㄑ	ㄑ	ㄑ	ㄑ	ㄑ	ㄑ	ㄑ	ㄑ		
ㄑ	ㄑ	ㄑ	ㄑ	ㄑ	ㄑ	ㄑ	ㄑ		
ㄑ	ㄑ	ㄑ	ㄑ	ㄑ	ㄑ	ㄑ	ㄑ		
ㄑ	ㄑ	ㄑ	ㄑ	ㄑ	ㄑ	ㄑ	ㄑ		
ㄑ	ㄑ	ㄑ	ㄑ	ㄑ	ㄑ	ㄑ	ㄑ		
ㄑ	ㄑ	ㄑ	ㄑ	ㄑ	ㄑ	ㄑ	ㄑ		

竪	鉤
shù	gōu
S	G

Notes:

(竪鉤, shù gōu, SG, ⅃)

⅃ ⅃ ⅃ ⅃ ⅃ ⅃ ⅃ ⅃ ⅃

⅃	⅃	⅃	⅃	⅃	⅃	⅃	⅃	⅃	⅃
SG	SG	SG	SG	SG	SG	SG	SG	SG	SG
⅃	⅃	⅃	⅃	⅃	⅃	⅃	⅃	⅃	⅃
SG	SG	SG	SG	SG	SG	SG	SG	SG	SG
⅃	⅃	⅃	⅃	⅃	⅃	⅃	⅃	⅃	⅃
⅃	⅃	⅃	⅃	⅃	⅃				
⅃	⅃	⅃	⅃	⅃					
⅃	⅃	⅃	⅃						
⅃	⅃	⅃							
⅃	⅃	⅃							
⅃	⅃	⅃							

竖	撇	Notes:
shù	**piě**	(竖撇, **shù piě**, **SP**, 丿) has an initial vertical
S	**P**	component to the stroke.

丿 丿 丿 丿 丿 丿 丿 丿 丿

丿	丿	丿	丿	丿	丿	丿	丿	丿	丿
SP	SP	SP	SP	SP	SP	SP	SP	SP	SP

丿	丿	丿	丿	丿	丿	丿	丿	丿	丿
SP	SP	SP	SP	SP	SP	SP	SP	SP	SP

平	捺
píng	nà
P	N

Notes:

(平捺, **píng nà**, **PN**) is a left to right flattened falling stroke. It is a flattened version of (捺, **nà**). It is seen as the underlining stroke in characters.

PN	PN	PN	PN	PN	PN	PN	PN	PN	PN

PN	PN	PN	PN	PN	PN	PN	PN	PN	PN

提	捺	Notes:
tí	nà	(提捺, **Tí Nà**, **TN**) is a rare stroke.
T	N	

TN	TN	TN	TN	TN	TN	TN	TN	TN	TN

TN	TN	TN	TN	TN	TN	TN	TN	TN	TN

提	平	捺
tí	píng	nà
T	P	N

Notes:

(提平捺, **Tí Píng Nà, TPN**) occurs as an under stroke as demonstrated. 心

TPN	TPN	TPN	TPN	TPN	TPN	TPN	TPN	TPN	TPN
TPN	TPN	TPN	TPN	TPN	TPN	TPN	TPN	TPN	TPN

点	捺
diǎn	nà
D	N

Notes:

(點捺, **diǎn nà**, **DN**) is a very rare stroke.

㇇	㇇	㇇	㇇	㇇	㇇	㇇	㇇	㇇

㇇	㇇	㇇	㇇	㇇	㇇	㇇	㇇	㇇	㇇
TN	TN	TN	TN	TN	TN	TN	TN	TN	TN
㇇	㇇	㇇	㇇	㇇	㇇	㇇	㇇	㇇	㇇
TN	TN	TN	TN	TN	TN	TN	TN	TN	TN

横	折
héng	zhé
H	Z

Notes:

(横折, **Héng Zhé**, **HZ** is a right angle or near right angle turn from (横, **Héng**, **H**, **Horizontal**)

HZ	HZ	HZ	HZ	HZ	HZ	HZ	HZ	HZ	HZ

HZ	HZ	HZ	HZ	HZ	HZ	HZ	HZ	HZ	HZ

横 撇

héng	piě
H	P

Notes:

(横撇, Héng Piě, HP)

フ フ フ フ フ フ フ フ フ フ

フ	フ	フ	フ	フ	フ	フ	フ	フ	フ
HP	HP	HP	HP	HP	HP	HP	HP	HP	HP

フ	フ	フ	フ	フ	フ	フ	フ	フ	フ
HP	HP	HP	HP	HP	HP	HP	HP	HP	HP

フ	フ	フ	フ	フ	フ	フ	フ	フ	フ
フ	フ	フ	フ	フ	フ	フ	フ	フ	フ
フ	フ	フ	フ	フ	フ	フ	フ	フ	フ
フ	フ	フ	フ	フ	フ	フ	フ	フ	フ
フ	フ	フ	フ	フ	フ	フ	フ	フ	フ
フ	フ	フ	フ	フ	フ	フ	フ	フ	フ
フ	フ	フ	フ	フ	フ	フ	フ	フ	フ
フ	フ	フ	フ	フ	フ	フ	フ	フ	フ
フ	フ	フ	フ	フ	フ	フ	フ	フ	フ

横	鈎
héng	gōu
H	G

Notes:

(**橫鈎**, **Héng Gōu**, **HG**) is often seen at the top of a character as **Diǎn - Héng Gōu**, ⁀.

→ → → → → → → → →

→	→	→	→	→	→	→	→	→	→
HG	HG	HG	HG	HG	HG	HG	HG	HG	HG

→	→	→	→	→	→	→	→	→	→
HG	HG	HG	HG	HG	HG	HG	HG	HG	HG

→	→	→	→	→	→	→	→	→	→
→	→	→	→	→	→	→	→	→	→
→	→	→	→	→	→	→	→	→	→
→	→	→	→	→	→	→	→	→	→
→	→	→	→	→	→	→	→	→	→
→	→	→	→	→	→	→	→	→	→
→	→	→	→	→	→	→	→	→	→
→	→	→	→	→	→	→	→	→	→
→	→	→	→	→	→	→	→	→	→

竖	折
shù	zhé
S	Z

Notes:

(竖折, **Shù Zhé**, **SZ**) has a right angle turn and can be confused with 竖弯, **Shù Wān** which has a curved transition versus a right angle transition.

L L L L L L L L L L

L	L	L	L	L	L	L	L	L	L
SZ	SZ	SZ	SZ	SZ	SZ	SZ	SZ	SZ	SZ
L	L	L	L	L	L	L	L	L	L
SZ	SZ	SZ	SZ	SZ	SZ	SZ	SZ	SZ	SZ
L	L	L	L	L	L	L	L		
L	L	L	L	L	L	L	L		
L	L	L	L	L	L	L	L		
L	L	L	L	L	L	L	L		
L	L	L	L	L	L	L	L		
L	L	L	L	L	L	L	L		
L	L	L	L	L	L	L	L		
L	L	L	L	L	L	L	L		

竖	弯
shù	**wān**
S	**W**

Notes:

(竖弯, **shù wān**, **SW**) has a curved transition from the vertical stroke versus **SZ** which is a right angle.

L	L	L	L	L	L	L	L	L	L
SW	SW	SW	SW	SW	SW	SW	SW	SW	SW
L	L	L	L	L	L	L	L	L	L
SW	SW	SW	SW	SW	SW	SW	SW	SW	SW

		Notes:
竖	提	(竖提, **Shù Tí**, ST)
shù	**tí**	
S	**T**	

㇄ ㇄ ㇄ ㇄ ㇄ ㇄ ㇄ ㇄ ㇄ ㇄

㇄	㇄	㇄	㇄	㇄	㇄	㇄	㇄	㇄	㇄
ST	ST	ST	ST	ST	ST	ST	ST	ST	ST
㇄	㇄	㇄	㇄	㇄	㇄	㇄	㇄	㇄	㇄
ST	ST	ST	ST	ST	ST	ST	ST	ST	ST

撇	折
piě	zhé
P	Z

Notes:

(撇折, Piě Zhé, PZ)

乚 乚 乚 乚 乚 乚 乚 乚 乚 乚 乚

乚	乚	乚	乚	乚	乚	乚	乚	乚	乚
PZ	PZ	PZ	PZ	PZ	PZ	PZ	PZ	PZ	PZ

乚	乚	乚	乚	乚	乚	乚	乚	乚	乚
PZ	PZ	PZ	PZ	PZ	PZ	PZ	PZ	PZ	PZ

乚	乚	乚	乚	乚	乚	乚	乚	乚	乚
乚	乚	乚	乚	乚	乚	乚	乚	乚	乚
乚	乚	乚	乚	乚	乚	乚	乚	乚	乚
乚	乚	乚	乚	乚	乚	乚	乚	乚	乚
乚	乚	乚	乚	乚	乚	乚	乚	乚	乚
乚	乚	乚	乚	乚	乚	乚	乚	乚	乚
乚	乚	乚	乚	乚	乚	乚	乚	乚	乚
乚	乚	乚	乚	乚	乚	乚	乚	乚	乚

撇	点
piě	diǎn
P	D

Notes:

(撇點, Piě Diǎn, PD)

ㄑ ㄑ ㄑ ㄑ ㄑ ㄑ ㄑ ㄑ ㄑ ㄑ

ㄑ	ㄑ	ㄑ	ㄑ	ㄑ	ㄑ	ㄑ	ㄑ	ㄑ	ㄑ
PD	PD	PD	PD	PD	PD	PD	PD	PD	PD

ㄑ	ㄑ	ㄑ	ㄑ	ㄑ	ㄑ	ㄑ	ㄑ	ㄑ	ㄑ
PD	PD	PD	PD	PD	PD	PD	PD	PD	PD

撇	鉤
piě	gōu
P	G

Notes:

(撇鉤, **Piě Gōu**, **PG**) is a very rare stroke.

弯	鈎	Notes:
wān	**gōu**	(弯鈎, **Wān Gōu**, **WG**) is characterized by the top portion of the stroke being to the left of the apex of the curve that occurs in the vertical plane.
W	**G**	

)))))))))

)	)	)	)	)	)	)	)	)	)
WG	WG	WG	WG	WG	WG	WG	WG	WG	WG

)	)	)	)	)	)	)	)	)	)
WG	WG	WG	WG	WG	WG	WG	WG	WG	WG

)	)	)	)						
)	)	)	)						
)	)	)	)						
)	)	)	)						
)	)	)	)						
)	)	)	)						
)	)	)	)						
)	)	)	)						
)	)	)	)						

弯	撇	Notes:
wān	**piě**	(弯撇, **wān piě**, **WP**) differs from a similar stroke (竖撇, **shù piě**, **SP**, 丿) in that the initial stroke is non vertical. They are both used interchangeably in many characters without changing meaning.
W	**P**	

丿丿丿丿丿丿丿丿丿丿丿丿丿丿丿丿丿

丿	丿	丿	丿	丿	丿	丿	丿	丿	丿
WP	WP	WP	WP	WP	WP	WP	WP	WP	WP

丿	丿	丿	丿	丿	丿	丿	丿	丿	丿
WP	WP	WP	WP	WP	WP	WP	WP	WP	WP

斜 鉤

xié	gōu
X	G

XG	XG	XG	XG	XG	XG	XG	XG	XG	XG
XG	XG	XG	XG	XG	XG	XG	XG	XG	XG

Notes:

(斜鉤, Xié Gōu, XG)

扁	斜	鉤
biǎn	xié	gōu
B	X	G

Notes:

(扁斜鉤, biǎn xié gōu, ㇃) is seen in (心, xīn, heart).

BXG	BXG	BXG	BXG	BXG	BXG	BXG	BXG	BXG	BXG

BXG	BXG	BXG	BXG	BXG	BXG	BXG	BXG	BXG	BXG

竖	弯	左
shù	wān	zuǒ
S	W	Z

Notes:

(竖弯左, **Shù Wān Zuǒ**) differs from (竖折, **Shù Piě**, **SP**) in that the tail is not as bent from the vertical.

SWZ	SWZ	SWZ	SWZ	SWZ	SWZ	SWZ	SWZ	SWZ	SWZ

SWZ	SWZ	SWZ	SWZ	SWZ	SWZ	SWZ	SWZ	SWZ	SWZ

竖	折	折
shù	zhé	zhé
S	Z	Z

Notes:

(竖折折,Shù Zhé Zhé, SZZ)

SZZ	SZZ	SZZ	SZZ	SZZ	SZZ	SZZ	SZZ	SZZ	SZZ
SZZ	SZZ	SZZ	SZZ	SZZ	SZZ	SZZ	SZZ	SZZ	SZZ

竖	折	撇	Notes:
shù	zhé	piě	(竖折撇, **Shù Zhé Piě, SZP**)
S	Z	P	

ㄥㄥㄥㄥㄥㄥㄥㄥㄥㄥㄥㄥ

ㄥ	ㄥ	ㄥ	ㄥ	ㄥ	ㄥ	ㄥ	ㄥ	ㄥ	ㄥ
SZP	SZP	SZP	SZP	SZP	SZP	SZP	SZP	SZP	SZP
ㄥ	ㄥ	ㄥ	ㄥ	ㄥ	ㄥ	ㄥ	ㄥ	ㄥ	ㄥ
SZP	SZP	SZP	SZP	SZP	SZP	SZP	SZP	SZP	SZP

竖　折　鈎

(竖折鈎, Shù Zhé Gōu, SZG)

Notes:

shù	zhé	gōu
S	Z	G

L L L L L L L L L

L	L	L	L	L	L	L	L	L	L
SZG	SZG	SZG	SZG	SZG	SZG	SZG	SZG	SZG	SZG
L	L	L	L	L	L	L	L	L	L
SZG	SZG	SZG	SZG	SZG	SZG	SZG	SZG	SZG	SZG

Notes:

竖	折	弯	鉤
shù	zhé	wān	gōu
S	Z	W	G

ㄴ ㄴ ㄴ ㄴ ㄴ ㄴ ㄴ ㄴ

ㄴ	ㄴ	ㄴ	ㄴ	ㄴ	ㄴ	ㄴ	ㄴ	ㄴ	ㄴ
SZWG	SZWG	SZWG	SZWG	SZWG	SZWG	SZWG	SZWG	SZWG	SZWG

ㄴ	ㄴ	ㄴ	ㄴ	ㄴ	ㄴ	ㄴ	ㄴ	ㄴ	ㄴ
SZWG	SZWG	SZWG	SZWG	SZWG	SZWG	SZWG	SZWG	SZWG	SZWG

横	折	折

Notes:

(横折折, Héng Zhé Zhé, HZZ)

héng	zhé	zhé
H	Z	Z

HZZ	HZZ	HZZ	HZZ	HZZ	HZZ	HZZ	HZZ	HZZ	HZZ

HZZ	HZZ	HZZ	HZZ	HZZ	HZZ	HZZ	HZZ	HZZ	HZZ

353

横	折	弯	Notes:
héng	zhé	wān	(横折弯, Héng Zhé Wān, HZW)
H	Z	W	

HZW	HZW	HZW	HZW	HZW	HZW	HZW	HZW	HZW	HZW

HZW	HZW	HZW	HZW	HZW	HZW	HZW	HZW	HZW	HZW

横	折	提	Notes: (横折提, Héng Zhé Tí, HZT)
héng	**zhé**	**tí**	
H	**Z**	**T**	

㇊ ㇊ ㇊ ㇊ ㇊ ㇊ ㇊ ㇊ ㇊

㇊	㇊	㇊	㇊	㇊	㇊	㇊	㇊	㇊	㇊
HZT	**HZT**	**HZT**	**HZT**	**HZT**	**HZT**	**HZT**	**HZT**	**HZT**	**HZT**
㇊	㇊	㇊	㇊	㇊	㇊	㇊	㇊	㇊	㇊
HZT	**HZT**	**HZT**	**HZT**	**HZT**	**HZT**	**HZT**	**HZT**	**HZT**	**HZT**

横	折	鉤	Notes:
héng	zhé	gōu	(橫折鉤, **Héng Zhé Gōu,** **HZG**)
H	Z	G	

フ フ フ フ フ フ フ フ フ

フ	フ	フ	フ	フ	フ	フ	フ	フ	フ
HZG	HZG	HZG	HZG	HZG	HZG	HZG	HZG	HZG	HZG

フ	フ	フ	フ	フ	フ	フ	フ	フ	フ
HZG	HZG	HZG	HZG	HZG	HZG	HZG	HZG	HZG	HZG

横	斜	鉤
héng	xié	gōu
H	X	G

Notes:

(横斜鉤, Héng Xié Gōu, HXG)

HXG	HXG	HXG	HXG	HXG	HXG	HXG	HXG	HXG	HXG

HXG	HXG	HXG	HXG	HXG	HXG	HXG	HXG	HXG	HXG

横	折	折	折	Notes:
héng	zhé	zhé	zhé	
H	Z	Z	Z	

HZZZ	HZZZ	HZZZ	HZZZ	HZZZ	HZZZ	HZZZ	HZZZ	HZZZ	HZZZ
HZZZ	HZZZ	HZZZ	HZZZ	HZZZ	HZZZ	HZZZ	HZZZ	HZZZ	HZZZ

358

横	折	折	撇	Notes:
héng	zhé	zhé	piě	
H	Z	Z	P	

HZZP HZZP HZZP HZZP HZZP HZZP HZZP HZZP HZZP HZZP

HZZP HZZP HZZP HZZP HZZP HZZP HZZP HZZP HZZP HZZP

横 折 弯 鈎

héng	zhé	wān	gōu
H	Z	W	G

Notes:

HZWG	HZWG	HZWG	HZWG	HZWG	HZWG	HZWG	HZWG	HZWG	HZWG

HZWG	HZWG	HZWG	HZWG	HZWG	HZWG	HZWG	HZWG	HZWG	HZWG

横	撇	弯	鉤	Note:
héng	piě	wān	gōu	
H	P	W	G	

𝟛 𝟛 𝟛 𝟛 𝟛 𝟛 𝟛 𝟛 𝟛

𝟛	𝟛	𝟛	𝟛	𝟛	𝟛	𝟛	𝟛	𝟛	𝟛
HPWG	HPWG	HPWG	HPWG	HPWG	HPWG	HPWG	HPWG	HPWG	HPWG
𝟛	𝟛	𝟛	𝟛	𝟛	𝟛	𝟛	𝟛	𝟛	𝟛
HPWG	HPWG	HPWG	HPWG	HPWG	HPWG	HPWG	HPWG	HPWG	HPWG

竪	折	折	鉤	Notes:
shù S	**zhé** Z	**zhé** Z	**gōu** G	

ㄅ ㄅ ㄅ ㄅ ㄅ ㄅ ㄅ ㄅ

ㄅ	ㄅ	ㄅ	ㄅ	ㄅ	ㄅ	ㄅ	ㄅ	ㄅ	ㄅ
SZZG	SZZG	SZZG	SZZG	SZZG	SZZG	SZZG	SZZG	SZZG	SZZG

ㄅ	ㄅ	ㄅ	ㄅ	ㄅ	ㄅ	ㄅ	ㄅ	ㄅ	ㄅ
SZZG	SZZG	SZZG	SZZG	SZZG	SZZG	SZZG	SZZG	SZZG	SZZG

竖	折	折	弯	鉤
shù	zhé	zhé	wān	gōu
S	Z	Z	W	G

ㄅㄅㄅㄅㄅㄅㄅㄅㄅ

ㄅ	ㄅ	ㄅ	ㄅ	ㄅ	ㄅ	ㄅ	ㄅ	ㄅ	ㄅ
SZZWG	SZZWG	SZZWG	SZZWG	SZZWG	SZZWG	SZZWG	SZZWG	SZZWG	SZZWG

ㄅ	ㄅ	ㄅ	ㄅ	ㄅ	ㄅ	ㄅ	ㄅ	ㄅ	ㄅ
SZZWG	SZZWG	SZZWG	SZZWG	SZZWG	SZZWG	SZZWG	SZZWG	SZZWG	SZZWG

横	撇	折	弯	鉤
héng	piě	zhé	wān	gōu
H	P	Z	W	G

乙 乙 乙 乙 乙 乙 乙 乙

乙	乙	乙	乙	乙	乙	乙	乙	乙	乙
HPZWG	HPZWG	HPZWG	HPZWG	HPZWG	HPZWG	HPZWG	HPZWG	HPZWG	HPZWG

乙	乙	乙	乙	乙	乙	乙	乙	乙	乙
HPZWG	HPZWG	HPZWG	HPZWG	HPZWG	HPZWG	HPZWG	HPZWG	HPZWG	HPZWG

364

橫	折	折	弯	鈎
héng	zhé	zhé	wān	gōu
H	Z	Z	W	G

丩 丩 丩 丩 丩 丩 丩 丩

丩	丩	丩	丩	丩	丩	丩	丩	丩	丩
HZZWG	HZZWG	HZZWG	HZZWG	HZZWG	HZZWG	HZZWG	HZZWG	HZZWG	HZZWG

丩	丩	丩	丩	丩	丩	丩	丩	丩	丩
HZZWG	HZZWG	HZZWG	HZZWG	HZZWG	HZZWG	HZZWG	HZZWG	HZZWG	HZZWG

圈

quān
circle

Notes:

(圈, **quān**, **Q**) This is a very rare stroke. It is not seen in Chinese character sets.

O	O	O	O	O	O	O	O	O	O
Q	Q	Q	Q	Q	Q	Q	Q	Q	Q
quān	quān	quān	quān	quān	quān	quān	quān	quān	quān
O	O	O	O	O	O	O	O	O	O
Q	Q	Q	Q	Q	Q	Q	Q	Q	Q
quān	quān	quān	quān	quān	quān	quān	quān	quān	quān

Eight Principles of Yong

(永字八法, **Yǒngzì Bā Fǎ**, **Eternity Character Eight Method**)
There is a stream of explanation in classical Chinese literature that explains how to write the eight strokes common in Chinese characters. These strokes are all found in the one character (永, **yǒng**, **eternity**). It was believed that the frequent practice of these principles as a beginner calligrapher could ensure beauty in one's writing.

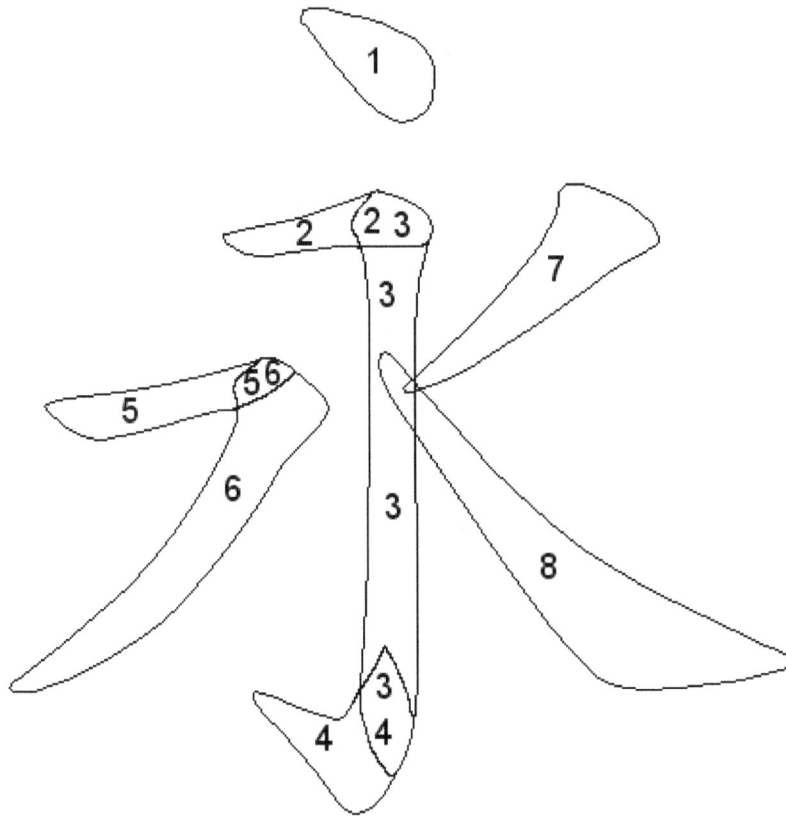

永

Yǒng

The direction and shape of these strokes originate from the use of a brush with soft hair bristles and black ink. The brush was held vertical between the first three fingers. Calligraphy is the art of drawing characters. Much can be learned from buying a bottle of ink and a brush. However, buy a large sheet of plastic to put under your work. I spent about two dollars in China for a large bottle of ink and a brush and did about $1,000.00 damage when I spilled it. There is a hotel owner in **Yuping** who is very angry. The ink will also penetrate most cheap paper so you may want to get a sheet of cardboard to put under your paper or a blotter sheet. If you can find a **Hero 99** pen or a refillable **Emporer Dragon 801**, they are excellent as they have a soft tapered synthetic tip. Also available but harder to find are fountain type pens with ink cartridges and similar soft tips that deform with pressure. They are mess free and the cartridges are inexpensive. Your Chinese friends may tell you to practice with a pencil. Forget it, they can alter the colour and the shape of the stroke by varying the pressure on the pencil or pen by moving it several thousandths of an inch. They have been doing it since they were infants, they have written millions of characters and they have better dexterity than you have.

1) (右点, **Yòu Diǎn**, **right dot**), the short downwards left to right convex stroke, is formed by drawing the brush toward the writer left to right in a downward arc. On the shortest strokes, it will look like a teardrop shape in which the brush is pushed into the page. The convex shape is hard to achieve with short strokes. On smaller characters, you simply push the brush down and pull it toward yourself with no draw of the tip.

2) (横, **Héng**, **horizontal**), the horizontal stroke is a varied stroke. The thickness is maintained by moving the wrist horizontally with no downward deflection. You will often see an ending flourish on various type fonts. This is a reflection of the history of **Hanzi** in which stamps

were carved in wood and the small notch at the end of the stroke kept the wooden block from splitting with repeated use.

3) (竖, **Shù**, **vertical**), the vertical down stroke, is a straight draw toward the writer. The thickness is varied by down pressure that comes at the beginning of the stroke. Any variations in down pressure result in uneven thickness of the line.

4) (鉤, **Gōu**, **hook**), the hook, exists as an addition to several strokes. It is formed by a flick of the writing instrument. The tip of the brush must be raised to get a sharp point. The direction of the stroke varies with the primary stroke it is attached to, either down or to the left.

5) (提, **Tí**, **to lift**), the left to right rising tapering stroke. This stroke is formed by a rising flick with a lift of the brush. This achieves the taper on the right tail of the stroke.

6) (弯, **Wān**, **bent**), describes a smooth curve. Although it is seen to exist standing alone in this classic character description, it is seldom seen in modern Hanzi. It is most often used to describe a curved transition.

7) (撇, **Piě**, **throw away**), the downwards right to left curved stroke is formed by drawing the brush initially down and to the left in a near flat rising arc at 45 degrees. A lift of the brush gives a tapered tail.

8) (捺, **Nà**, **press down firmly**), the downwards left to right up curved stroke is formed by drawing the brush toward and to the right of the writer. The brush follows a small flat rising arc to create a concave shape by pushing the brush away from the writer as it travels.

Guide to Pronunciation

If you become obsessed with the perfect pronunciation, grammar and tone of Standard Mandarin, your efforts will be in vain. You will be the only one in China and the world speaking it. A native English speaker from Hamilton, Ontario, where perfect English is spoken, can understand a man from England, Scotland, Australia, Newfoundland, East India and Nigeria. As long as you get close with Mandarin, an authentic Chinese friend can fine tune you. You will find that in China the pronunciation varies as much as the food and geography of China does. In fact you will find that as soon as you write a Hanzi character or speak Mandarin an enthusiastic smiling throng of proud Chinese will descend upon you to assist you. One of the more distressing things I have discovered is the inconsistency in different published books about the pronunciation of Pinyin.

Pinyin vowels are pronounced similarly to vowels in Roman alphabet languages and most consonants are similar to English. A pitfall for native English speakers is, however, the unusual pronunciation of *x*, *q*, *c*, *zh*, *sh* and *z* and sometimes *i* and the unvoiced portion of the pronunciation of *d*, *b*, *g*, and *j*. This will be detailed below.

The pronunciation of Pinyin is broken into Initials and Finals. Initials are initial consonants or vowels in a phoneme, while Finals are all possible combinations of consonants and vowels that form the ending of the word, hence the term ***Finals***.

What Defines a Chinese Word?

Words used to describe English grammar do not entirely work for Chinese grammar. A word in Hanzi / Hanyu is not necessarily one character. Some characters do not have a distinct meaning and must be bound to one or more other characters to give them meaning. These are described as ***Bound Morphemes***.

Morpheme

In English, a morpheme is the smallest unit of meaning. For example, the *s* added to a noun to make it plural is a morpheme. It has meaning and is indivisible. If a Chinese character does not have meaning, it is not a morpheme. However, Chinese language is all characters. There are no *s* equivalents to add to a character. Adding another stroke to a character creates a different character. A morpheme in Chinese grammar is thus enough characters to give meaning and cannot be broken down to give a different meaning. But it can be more than one character.

With this definition, many characters stand alone as having meaning and are thus morphemes and also words. Some words then are minimally two characters. A Chinese word is one or more characters combined to have meaning.

Phoneme

Pinyin is a system of assigning sounds or phonemes written with the Roman English alphabet to assign a standardized sound to each character. The sounds however are not unique. Each character has a unique appearance, defined by the placement of strokes that are used to make it. Each Pinyin sound word is assigned to many characters. It is more like assigning part numbers to inventory than it is a language. Because Pinyin does not have uniqueness of meaning, it is not a language; you cannot effectively communicate in Pinyin. You can use it to study the pronunciation of Chinese characters.

The compilation of phonemes of Pinyin parallels the words of Hanzi. If two characters are put together to create a Chinese word, then two Pinyin phonemes are put together to create a Pinyin sound word. If four characters are put together to create a Chinese word, then the four corresponding sound words are put together to create a Pinyin sound word. However, as Chinese characters are currently written, there are no space breaks between characters. Reading the Pinyin can help you determine which Chinese characters are compiled together to create multi-character words.

It is always important to remember the mathematical difficulty of writing a sentence using Pinyin. If you have 4 sound words that each are assigned to 10 different characters, you have 10,000 possible character combinations. If you think that you can write in Hanyu Pinyin as a language I assure you I can write a sentence in which it is necessary to use a computer to plot the multitude of different translations. This is why you will read about the difference in written versus spoken grammar and sentence construction. The choice of words used to speak is much less than the choice of words used to write due to the confusion of homophones.

Homophones

A homophone is a sound that is unique yet has more than one meaning. In English, eight-ate, great-grate and lie-lye are all paired homophones. Each pairing sounds the same but has different meanings. There are about 70,000 Chinese characters. Yet there are only about 1500 unique sounds to represent them. This means that one sound can represent many characters, dozens sometimes. This has many implications. Mandarin is a spoken representation of Chinese characters. It is spoken differently than it is written. Writing gives much greater opportunity to use a broad range of characters that spoken would be confused with others. One does not have to worry about chose of words when writing.

Speaking is another matter. Every spoken sound has different meanings. The context of the conversation and what has been spoken before gives great assistance to the listener. Of necessity, the vocabulary of speaking is limited. It is possible to say something that written would be easy to understand but spoken would be indecipherable.

The advantage of this is that you can learn to communicate with a very small number of spoken words in Mandarin. The difficulty is understanding someone who has a greater vocabulary. The mythical Standard Mandarin is precise but you can create grammatically correct sentences that just are not commonly used. This is why the most common expression in China may be;

请 写 下来
Qǐng xiě xiàlái.
Please write down.

Initials

(声母, shēng mǔ, initial sound)

Pronunciation of Initials

Initials are the consonants that form the beginning of Hanyu Pinyin words. Fine tuning can only occur in a region specific context. The *she bOO she* (是不是, **shì bù shì**, **is not is**) of Beijing becomes ***see buh see*** of Chengdu. While you are trying to get a Mandarin speaker to slow down you have to gauge their neutral tone, make adjustments for ethnic and geographic phonetic drift and figure out the dozens of meanings for each identical sounding word, good luck.

Just as an Englishman, an Australian and a Scotsman can understand each other, even though their accents vary, you will be able to adjust and understand various accents in Hanyu, eventually, maybe. In many books, you will find the Initial and Finals grouped according to where your tongue is in your mouth and whether you are leaking air up your nose. I encourage you to group the Initials as to how it makes most sense to you.

Pinyin	Explanation
b	As in English, un-aspirated *p*, as in *spit*. Examples *big*, *bad*, *bone*.
p	As in English, aspirated *p*, as in *pit*. Examples *pit*, *pathetic*, *portrait*.
m	As in English, examples *man*, *maw*, *mow*, *maul*.
f	As in English, examples *find*, *feel*, *ford*.
d	As in English, examples *dig*, *duffle*, *doubt*.
t	As in English, examples *time*, *tempo*, *tart*.
n	As in English, examples *no*, *night*, *never*.
l	As in English, examples *left*, *lime*, *lover*.
g	As in English, examples *gay*, *give*, *gore*.
k	As in English, examples *kill*, *kick*, *kiss*.
h	As in English, if followed by an *a*, otherwise, like the *ch* in *loch*.
j	As in English, almost, this exact sound is not used in English, the closest match is the *j* in *ajar*. Examples *jing*, *jittery*, *Jesus*.

q   Like the *ch* in *church*. Examples *church*, *chess*, *chest*.

x   Like the *sh* in *shy*. Examples *shower*, *shade*, *shiver*.

zh   As in English, with no aspiration, the tongue is curled back on the roof of the mouth, retroflexed. Examples *fudge*, *judge*, *grudge*.

ch   As in English as in *chin*, but with the tongue curled back on the roof of the mouth. Very similar to the *tu* of *nurture* but strongly aspirated.

sh   As in English, as in *shinbone*, but with the tongue curled back on the roof of the mouth, retroflexed, very similar to *undershirt*.

r   As in English as in *rank*, but with the lips spread and with the tongue curled back on the roof of the mouth, retroflexed. Examples, *pleasure*, *treasure*.

z   As in the English examples, *suds*, *buds*, *duds*.

c   As in English *cats*, examples *mats*, *bats*, *rats*.

s   As in English, examples *sun*, *sow*, *sung*, *song*.

w   As in English, examples *way*, *why*, *wind*.

y   As in English, examples *yes*, *yellow*, *yet*. Exception *yi* as *ēē*.

The only two-consonant Initials are *zh*, *sh* and *ch*. There are 11 pinyin with no Initial consonant. They are *a*, *ai*, *ao*, *an*, *ang*, *o*, *ou*, *e*, *ei*, *en*, and *er*. Please note that none of these start with *i*, *u*, or *ü*. There are special and unnecessary rules for these.

In this table above I have put 23 Initials. Many books would disagree with this and would not include *w* and *y*. Some books say there are 21 Initials and a *zero* Initial. The *zero* Initial is put in front of phonemes that begin with an *i*, *u* or *ü*. So you are to pretend that there is a silent and invisible letter in front of the phoneme because some anal linguist cannot stand the thought of a consonant and vowel having the same sound.

The almighty and great reference Li and Thompson (1981) says that there are 22 Initials yet their table shows 21 so they must attribute an invisible and silent consonant in absentia. Hopefully one day someone will logically reference the great and mighty (大毛猴子,**Dà Máo Hóuzi**, **Big Hairy Monkey**) and point out that there are 23.

Finals

(韵母, **yùn mǔ**, **final sound**)

Pronunciation of Finals

Finals are the vowels and vowel consonant combinations that are the ending of Pinyin phonemes. Several of these sounds do not correspond directly to sounds in English. If you agonize over a perfect pronunciation, you will find it varies immensely in China. The assumption is that you speak a neutral tone English such as would be spoken in the province of Ontario in Canada. If you have a highland Scottish brogue, are a Hungarian who speaks English as a second language, or are from East India, good luck with your background accent.

The only parts of *Finals* that are purely consonants in standard Hanyu are *n* and *ng*. (儿化, **érhuà**, **erhua**) is a phonetic regional window dressing with no meaning so I will avoid it here. The *Finals* take the form of;

single Vowel only (V),

two vowels (VV),

three vowels (VVV),

one vowel and a consonant (VC),

one vowel and two consonants (VCC),

two vowels and a consonant (VVC),

and two vowels and two consonants (VVCC).

In all these situations the single (C) is the letter *n* and the (CC) is always *ng*.

This is important to know as many *words* in Pinyin are composed from more than one character and the Pinyin is thus compiled together similarly. Knowing which combinations cannot go together helps you know where the break in a phoneme string or word is.

To find a given final, remove the initial consonant. For *zh*, *ch*, *sh*, both letters should be removed. They are the only Initial consonants spelled with two letters.

Many books show Finals beginning with *i as* a standalone Pinyin beginning with *y*. Example, *-ian* as *yan*. I do not see the utility of this confusion. This language is already confusing enough. These statements result from the conversionof older styles of Romanization such as Wade Gillis. The rule is simple, the Pinyin *y* is silent before the Pinyin *i*. In all other situations it is pronounced as the English letter *y*. When you see a character represented with *yan* there is no value to trying to remember it as really being represented as *–ian* with the letter *y* acting as a silent place holder.

Many books show Finals beginning with *u* as a standalone Pinyin beginning with *w*. Example, *-ua* as *wa*. The rule is simple, the Pinyin *u* is pronounced *w* when the Final stands alone. Same argument as above.

Many books show Finals beginning with *ü as* a standalone Pinyin beginning with *y*. Example, *- ün* as *yun*. Same argument as above.

Pinyin is not a language; it is a system that assigns a sound to each Chinese character.

This is the reason that many books do not show *w* and *y* as Initial consonants. This language is already confusing enough. There are in fact very few Pinyin that begin with a vowel as an Initial. The 11 combinations are *a*, *ai*, *ao*, *an*, *ang*, *o*, *ou*, *e*, *ei*, *en*, and *er*. I see little reason to learn complex rules about stand alone Finals as they never stand alone. Learn the combined sounds of the Initials and Finals and forget the *i-y*, *u-w* and, *ü-y*.

Learning from a chart, you will never get it right as there is no right. Race, height, age, alcohol, tobacco, many things affect your voice. There is so much variation in China that there is no perfect sounds. The other variable is that the transition from one phoneme to another affects the sound. Even within individual words the tone can have a great effect on the sound as you glide from one vowel to another.

(儿化, **érhuà**, **erhua**) adds another variable. Added to the neutral and first tone it is a continuation. Added to the second, third and fourth tone it can be an awkward addition.

Some books say that *zhi*, *chi*, *shi*, *ri*, *zi*, *ci* or *si* are pure consonant only sounds and that the *i* acts as a phonetic silent neutral place holder. Other books say that the *i* is sounded as a prolonged **zzzzzzz**. The **zzzzzzz** theory is definitely wrong. Mandarin is usually spoken so fast there are no prolonged sounds. Some lackey with a Master's degree trying to get his Ph.D. must have some Chinese undergrads wired up to an phonetic oscilloscope in a laboratory. The *i* theory is a little more credible but try making any of the pure consonant sounds and ending them just as they started.

If you take any sound and isolate it phonetically and analyze it it bears little resemblance to how it is used dynamically. I have great fun in China playing my language learning DVD's to my relatives and watch them howl with laughter as some guy sounds out each Pinyin in a slow dramatic fashion with gigantic ranges of tone. The third tone is particularly impressive under scrutiny. The phonemes are stretched to about 5 times their length and 3 times their tonal range.

Pinyin	Explanation
-i	Displayed as an *i* after: ***zh***, ***ch***, ***sh***, ***r***, ***z***, ***c*** or ***s***. The consonant is very dominant with very little sound effect from the *i*.
-i	After all other consonants it sounds as Ē.
-a	As in *father*, examples *saw, raw, law*.
-o	Occurring only in **bo**, **po**, **mo**, **wo**, and **fo**, it has a ***wahw*** like sound
-e	Similar to the English ***uh***, but not as open, *nut, mutt, but*.
-ê	As in *bet*. Only used in certain interjections.
-ai	As in English ***eye***, *sty*, *my*, *fly*, *die*.
-ei	As in English alphabetic *Ā* as in *lay, day, stay, bay*.
-ao	As in English in *cow*.
-ou	As in English *oh* or the long alphabetic *Ō*, examples *so, tow, mow*.
-an	As in English l**awn**. *Lawn, sawn, pawn*.
-en	As in English -***un***, as in *fun, done, run*.

-ang   As in English *ang*st.

-eng   As in English –*ung*, *b*ung, *s*ung, *st*ung.

er   As in English *are*. This word stands alone with no Initial.

-ia   As in English alphabetic *Ē* plus *awh*, ēēē-ahhh.

-io   As in English alphabetic *Ē* plus *Ō*.

-ie   As in English alphabetic *Ē* + **yuh**, but is short. The **yuh** is pronounced longer and carries the main stress. Ē-yyyuh

-iao   As in English alphabetic *Ē*, plus, as in English in c**ow**.

-iu   As in English alphabetic *Ē* plus *ewe*. As in English *knee-you*.

-ian   As in English alphabetic *Ē*, plus + *yawn*.

-in   As in English –*ēēn*, *bean*, *seen*, *mean*.

-iang   As in English alphabetic *Ē*, plus + **yawn-ggg**).

-ing   As in English *ing*. Examples are s*ing*, br*ing*, and st*ing*.

-u   As in English *ewe*, examples are *stew*, *do*, *crew*, *moo*.

-ua   As in English *w* plus the *a* in father, examples *wa*sh, *po*sh.

-uo   As in English *woe* or *wah*. **wo**re, **wo**rn.

-uai   As in English *why*.

-ui   As in English *way*.

-uan   As in English **wa**nder. **lawn**, **sawn**.

-un   As in English *un*. *fun*, *done*, *s*un.

-uang   As in English *wăng*.

-ong   Starts with the vowel sound in b'**oo**k and ends with the nasal sound in si**ng**. **ŏŏng**

-ü   As in German *üben* or French *lune*.

-ue   as **ü** + **ê**; the *ü* is short and light **üüuh**

-üan   as **ü** + *on*.

-ün   as **ü** + **n**.

-iong   as *y* + **ŏŏng**.

Explanations and Exceptions to General Rules

1)   *ü* is written as *u* after *j*, *q*, *x*, and **y**. *ü* is written as *u* when there is no ambiguity such as *j-u*, *q-u*, and *x-u*. These combinations of Initials and Finals do not phonetically exist. It is written as *ü* when there are corresponding Initial- *ü* syllables such as *lü* and *nü*) In such situations where there are corresponding *ü* syllables, it is often replaced with *v* on computer created correspondence, making it easier to type on a standard keyboard.

2)   *uo* is written as *o* after *b*, *p*, *m*, *w*, or *f*. Hanyu Pinyin that are actually pronounced as *buo*, *puo*, *muo*, *wuo*, and *fuo* are given a separate written representation as *bo*, *po*, *mo*, *wo*, and *fo*. The pronunciation remains as *buo*, *puo*, *muo*, and *fuo*.

3)   The Finals that would be phonetically arranged as, *iou*, *uei*, and *uen* are simplified as *iu*, *ui*, and *un*. This allows the following phonetic changes.

   -iu is pronounced as in English alphabetic $\bar{E}$ plus *ewe*. As in English *knee-you*.

   -ui is pronounced as in English *way*.

   -ün as **ü** + **n** similar to phonetic *nyun*.

Tones

To counter the effect of having so few combinations of *Initials* and *Finals*, Hanyu has distinct tones to give meaning to phonemes. Each *Initial Final* combination has a total of five possible tones. This has the effect of giving five times more distinct phonemes. What appears to be a small number of phonemes is amplified. However, each Initial Final combination does not always have all five tones.

The Pinyin system also incorporates markers to represent the four tones of Hanyu. Each tone is indicated by a mark above a non-medial vowel. Many books printed in China mix type fonts. This creates vowels with tone marks rendered in a different font than the surrounding text. This a practice that tends to give such Pinyin texts a typographically awkward appearance. This style originates from the limitations of the fonts made available to type setters printing literature. These limitations are overcome with electronic type fonts.

Fifth Tone / Zero Tone / Neutral Tone

轻声
Qīng shēng
Light tone

The tone that is neutral to a voice effort is called the *Fifth Tone*, *Zero Tone* or *Neutral Tone*. It is sometimes thought of incorrectly as a lack of tone. The *Neutral Tone* is particularly difficult for non-native speakers to master correctly because of its uncharacteristically large number of contours. The level of its pitch depends almost entirely on the tone carried by the syllable preceding it. It is not possible to end one phoneme without the effect of the *Final* influencing the neutral tone initiation of the next *Initial*. In the transition from one tone to another, there is in fact four short varied tones created that are not the named tones.

The only way to get around this is when you are learning to speak Hanyu, you can speak very slowly. This allows you to finish a word completely before you start the next word. This prevents the effect of the previous Final from influencing the coming Initial. This is not an efficient way to speak as it is so slow. However, you will learn to naturally acquire an understandable tone transition.

The learning curve will occur very naturally this way.

First Tone

阴平
Yīnpíng
High-level tone

The first tone is the *High Level Tone*. It is represented by a macron marker (ˉ) added to the Pinyin vowel or by adding a #1 at the end of the phoneme. To create this tone the speaker lifts his voice to a comfortable reproducible level.

Second Tone

阳平,
Yángpíng
High rising

The second tone is the *Rising Tone*. It is denoted by an French linguistic acute accent marker (´) or by adding a **#2** at the end of the phoneme. Second tone, or rising tone is a sound that rises from mid-level tone to high. Many books describe the tone raise as being similar to a hearing impaired person saying *What*? This tone rises from the neutral position to the *First Tone* position.

Third Tone

上声
Shǎngshēng
Up tone

The third tone is the ***Falling-Rising Tone***. It is symbolized by a grammatical marker caron (˘) or a **#3** added to the end of the phoneme. It has a mid-low to low descent, if at the end of a sentence or before a pause. It is then followed by a rising pitch. This tone is created by dropping the pitch from the Neutral Tone to a comfortable, reproducible and distinguishable lower tone.

Fourth Tone

去声
Qùshēng
Away tone

The fourth tone is the ***Falling Tone***. It is represented by a French grammatical grave accent (`) or by adding a **#4** at the end of the phoneme. Fourth tone or falling tone features a sharp downward accent dipping from high to low. It has a short sharp duration. Many books compare the sound to barking the command ***Stop***! This tone is created by quickly dropping the pitch from neutral tone to a tone near the depth of the downward deflection on the third tone.

Loud Tone

China has 1.5 billion people. You will seldom find yourself alone. With hundreds of people on any given bus or train conversation can get very loud. There is a tendency for cell phones to be ringing, music to be blasting and karaoke to being sung. At times like this it is very hard to discriminate tone. As a foreigner, you may find the volume uncomfortably loud. The context of the situation guides the listener as to what is being said. Usually in situations like this the topic is obvious and you will adjust to determine the tones, eventually. It is also difficult to whisper in tones.

Numbers in Place of Tone Marks

I totally cut and pasted and stole this page and table from the internet. So if you did not *get it* from the above discussion, read this. Numbers are useful in typing as the conversion to tone markers is often complex and requires more than one program on your computer. In the appendix I will include a chapter on modifying your computer to make in more useful for Chinese writing. Here is the paragraph I borrowed.

Since most computer fonts do not contain the accents, a common convention is to add a digit representing the tone to the end of individual syllables. For example, *tóng* is written *tong2*. The number used for each tone is as in the table below.

If you have Office 2007 with Word 2007 you can makc your computer type Pinyin with tone markers if you have the patience. You must add all the variations of Pinyin with the tone numbers into your dictionary as equivalents to the Pinyin with tone markers. The you set your document to auto correct. That way, when you type Pinyin with numbers you can auto correct to Pinyin with tone markers. You will find a document to help you with this on the included CD or at the website.

Tone	Tone Mark	Number added to end of syllable in place of tone mark	Example using tone mark	Example using number
First	(ˉ)	1	mā	ma1
Second	(´)	2	má	ma2
Third	(ˇ)	3	mǎ	ma3
Fourth	(`)	4	mà	ma4
Neutral or Fifth	No mark	*no number* *five* *or 0*	ma	ma ma5 ma0

Table above was borrowed from the internet without permission. (stolen)

Rules for Placing the Tone Mark

Tone markings always go above the Final. The rules for determining on which vowel the tone mark appears are as follows.

1. If there is one vowel the tone marker goes above this vowel.

2. If there is more than one vowel and the first vowel is *i*, *u*, or *ü*, then the tone mark appears on the second vowel.

3. In all other cases, the tone mark appears on the first vowel

The reasoning behind these rules is in the case of Finals of more than one vowel, the first vowel may be preserved for pronunciation of the Initial consonant. That is, in phoneme words such as (犬,**quǎn**, **dog**) the correct pronunciation is a two part syllable, similar to *chew on* not *chwan*. The tone change begins with the *ǎn* and the *qu* is preserved in the neutral tone.

There is another algorithm for determining the vowel on which the tone mark appears is as follows:

1. First, look for an *a* or an *e* If either vowel appears, it takes the tone mark. There are no possible Pinyin syllables that contain both an *a* and an **e**.
2. If there is no *a* or *e* look for an *ou*. If *ou* appears, then the *o* takes the tone mark.
3. If none of the above cases hold, then the last vowel in the syllable takes the tone mark.

Umlaut

An ***umlaut*** is placed over the letter *u* when it occurs after the initials *l* and *n* in order to represent the sound *you*. This distinguishes the *you* sound from the *ŏŏ* sound as in *boo*!

Examples:

(驴, **lü**, **donkey**)

versus

(炉, **lú**, **oven**)

Tonal markers can be added on top of the umlaut, as in *lǘ*. However, the *ü* is not used in other contexts where it represents a front high rounded vowel, namely after the letters *j*, *q*, *x* and *y*. For example, the sound of the word (鱼, *yú*, **fish**) is transcribed in Pinyin simply as *yú*, not as *yǘ*. Genuine ambiguities only happen with *nu* / *nü* and *lu* / *lü*, which are then distinguished by an umlaut diacritic marker.

Many fonts or input output methods do not support an umlaut for *ü* or cannot place tone marks on top of *ü*. Likewise, using *ü* in input methods is difficult because it is not present as a simple key on many keyboard layouts. Although a computer can be configured to type the umlaut, most do not know how to do it. For these reasons *v* is sometimes typed instead of *ü*.

Tonal Shift Patterns, or Tone Sandhi

As if learning tone is not complicated enough, there are addition rules and patterns of tone shift depending on the surrounding tones. The basis of tonal shift is that the preceding tone affects the following tone. These changes are of course not reflected in writing Chinese characters, the characters are unchanged. Neither are these changes reflected in Hanyu Pinyin. The diacritic tone markers remain unchanged. It is only the spoken presentation that changes. Many books alter the official rules to try and make it easier to understand. This is confusing, especially in books that do not provide written characters.

Sequential 1st Tone Rule

Sequential first tones are unchanged.
Example:

Sequential 2nd Tone Rule

Sequential second tones are unchanged.
Example:

Sequential 4th tone Rule

 Sequential fourth tones are unchanged.
Example:

Sequential 3rd Tone Rule

A single syllable third tone word preceding a single syllable third tone word changes to a second tone. If there are more than two 3rd tone words of a single syllable, the rules are more complex and not clear. If the sentence has a rhetoric pause between third tones, the first third tone is preserved. This is where a clear understanding of *word* becomes important.

Example: 老鼠, **lǎoshǔ**, becomes **lao2shu4**

Example: 我很好, **wǒ hěn hǎo**, is spoken **wo2 hen2 hao3**

In a character string with a polysyllabic word composed of two characters, each with a third tone, preceding a single syllable third tone word, the first two syllables become 2nd tones, the third syllable retains the 3rd tone.
Example: 保管好, **bǎoguǎn hǎo** is spoken **bao2guan2 hao3**

If the first word is one syllable, and the second word is two syllables, the first syllable becomes a 4th tone, the second syllable becomes 2nd tone, and the last syllable stays 3rd tone.
Example: 老保管, **lǎo bǎoguǎn** is spoken **lao4 pao2kuan3**

Tone Changes After the Third Tone

When a character that is assigned a 3rd tone and it is followed by a neutral, first, second or fourth tone, it usually becomes a 4th tone. This tone is oft described as a **half-third tone** in that it descends but does not rise. However, it does not fall as far as a full 4th tone. Variably, it may be described as a **low flat tone**, in that it does not descend but mirrors the first tone in tone profile. You will find dialectal and regional variations to these patterns. The speed of a conversation also affects these changes. There is no convention for assigning numbers or diacritic tone markers for this.

Example: 美妙, **měimiào** becomes mei4miao4

Rules for (一, yī, one)

(一, **yī**, **one**) has special rules which do not apply to other Chinese characters. When in front of a 4th tone syllable, (一, **yī**, **one**) becomes 2nd tone.

Example: (一定, **yīdìng**, **certainly**) becomes **yi2ding4**

When (一, **yī**, **one**) is in front of a 1st, 2nd, or 3rd tone syllable, (一, **yī**, **one**) becomes 4th tone.

Example: 1st tone (一天, **yītiān**) becomes **yi4 tian1**

Example: 2nd tone (一年, **yīnián**) becomes **yi4 nian2**

Example: 3rd tone (一起, **yīqǐ**) becomes **yi4 qi3**

When (一, **yī**, **one**) falls between two words, it becomes neutral tone.

Example: 不一样, **bù yī yáng** is spoken **bu4 yi yang2**

When used for numeric counting, and for all other situations, (一, **yī**, **one**) retains its value of 1st tone.

Rules for (不, bù, not)

(不, **bù**, **not**) has special rules which do not apply to other Chinese characters. (不, **bù**, **not**) becomes 2nd tone when followed by a 4th tone syllable.

Example: 不是, **bùshì** becomes bu2shi4

When (不, **bù**, **not**) comes between two words, it becomes neutral in tone.

Example: 是不是, **shìbùshì** becomes shi4 bushi4

Funny Stuff

Many books available to the learning student are written by people with numerous university degrees in language related fields. They use graphic pictures of human heads cut in cross section showing the position of the tongue inside the mouth. This is supposed to give you an idea as to how you are forming the sounds of Hanyu. If you just happen to have access to a human anatomy lab where you can look at heads cut in half, maybe this will help you, somehow. You will find it quicker and more useful if you just slosh your tongue around until the correct sound issues forth. Or buy a recording device to practice.

There is also a ton of words unique to those with Ph.D.'s that are specific to language sciences. Plosives, fricatives, labials, dental alveolars, bilabials, nasal something or another's. This is all just a barrier to learning how to speak. Toss them. Some guy even assigned numbers to the tone contours. Here they are, 55, 35, 214, 51. I have no idea what to do with them or what they mean. When I show this stuff to Chinese people they laugh heartily. The range of tones is variable on the situation. An MC in front of a crowd will make dramatic tonal ranges. An angry taxi driver will speak so fast that tone is near lost. There are many angry taxi drivers in China.

The most important hurdle to learning to speak is the acquisition of a Chinese friend. This is far better than books, tapes, MP3 players or DVD's. If you do not live in an area where there is a large Chinese population, say Antarctica, go to the local

Chinese restaurant, Laundromat or computer science department at a local university and put up a sign that says,

我教你英文你教我汉語

Wǒ jiāo nǐ Yīngwén, nǐ jiāo Wǒ Hànyǔ.
I teach you English, You teach me Han language.

Many of them will need to pass an English usage exam to stay in school or to improve their academic performance. You could also meet a seriously cute Chinese girl. Plus they usually can cook fantastic food. This sign is such a great idea I will include a tear out sign at the back of the book.

汉语 拼音

Hànyǔ Pīnyīn
Hanyu Pinyin

Pinyin, more formally *Hanyu Pinyin*, is the most commonly used system to assign standardized sounds to Chinese characters. From an English speakers perspective this may sound unusual. However, The Chinese characters represent a written language, not a spoken language. In fact, over the history of the many ethnic groups and regions that eventually became China, over two hundred spoken variants of the written language emerged.

History

The formation of the People's Republic of China (**PRC**) in 1948 lead to educational reforms to increase literacy. The people of the country were largely uneducated with 80% being illiterate. 57 ethnic groups spoke over 200 languages. In 1954, the Ministry of Education of the PRC struck a Committee for the Reform of the Chinese Written Language. This committee developed a unified system of sounds so that each Chinese character could be expressed the same throughout the different ethnic groups and regions of China.

This system was named Hanyu Pinyin. The (汉, **Hàn**, **Han**) are the ethnic majority group of China. Hanyu means the Han language from (汉, **Hàn**, **Han**) and (语, **yǔ**, **language**). Pinyin is formed from (拼, **pīn**, **spell**) and (音, **yīn**, **sound**).

Together, the characters (汉语 拼音, **Hànyǔ Pīnyīn**, **Hanyu Pinyin**) identify the language of the ethnic Han majority and the phonetics used to standardize it.

The pivotal work behind Hanyu Pinyin was done by Professor Zhou Youguang. Zhou was an American working in the New York banking system. With the end of the civil war in China in 1948, he decided to return to China to help rebuild the country. He became an economics professor in Shanghai. The government assigned him to help the development of a new Romanization system.

The Cultural Revolution began in 1957. Chairman Mao oversaw the execution of millions of literate Chinese. Doctors, lawyers, teachers, and the educated were all suspect. American trained economists were high on the list, however, Zhou was spared. The switch to language and writing largely saved him from the wrath of the Cultural Revolution of Mao Zedong.

The first draft was published on February 12, 1956. The first edition of ***Hanyu Pinyin*** was approved and adopted at the Fifth Session of the 1st National People's Congress on February 11, 1958. It was introduced to primary schools as a way to teach Standard Mandarin pronunciation. This made a major impact on literacy.

Romanization versus Anglisization

The Chinese characters are not phonetically driven. That is, you cannot determine the pronunciation from looking at the character, generally. This allowed different ethnic groups that adopted the written language to assign their own sounds to the characters. With the unification of China and increased migration within the country, this caused a biblical Babel.

Many efforts were made by the West to used the Roman based alphabet to assign sounds to the Chinese characters. Several systems evolved. The goal of Hanyu Pinyin was to forever create a standardized system developed by China that made use of the previous systems such as Wade and Wade-Gillis. Thus the rules and system of Hanyu Pinyin were struck.

Romanization refers to a method in which the English speaking world takes a non-alphabetic language that is composed of non-phonetically driven symbols or logograms and assign sounds using the Roman alphabet. The phonetics of Hanyu Pinyin generally follow the phonetics of the English alphabet, with some exceptions. Hanyu Pinyin is thus Romanized yet only partially Anglisized.

Pinyin replaced older Romanization systems such as Wade-Giles which was developed in 1859; modified Wade-Gillis in 1892 and the Chinese Postal Map system of Romanization.

The International Organization for Standardization (ISO) adopted Hanyu Pinyin as the standard Romanization for modern Chinese in 1982 as ISO 7098. This was superseded by ISO 7098 in 1991. The United Nations adopted it as an official and standardized Mandarin Romanization system in 1986. It has also been accepted by the government of Singapore, the Library of Congress, the American Library Association, and many other international institutions.

Hanyu Pinyin will also be the official ISO Romanization system in the Taiwan Republic of China starting in 2009.

In 2001, the Chinese Government issued the *National Common Language Law*, providing a legal basis for applying Hanyu Pinyin.

Rules of Pinyin

Pinyin differs from other Romanization in several aspects. However, since we are not studying the other systems such as Wade Giles, it does not matter. This is not a history of Romanization but rather the modern state of affairs. Many books take great freedom in including their own altered rules of Pinyin, usually at the beginning of the book. Since Pinyin was fabricated recently, it was put together by committees, not history and time. Thus, there are rules. This book will follow the rules.

Use of the Apostrophe

In a situation in which two characters form one word, the two Hanyu Pinyin are joined together. However, this can create a situation in which a Hanyu Pinyin ending in a vowel and a Hanyu Pinyin beginning with a vowel appear as another single Hanyu Pinyin. The apostrophe marker ' is thus used before *a*, *o*, and *e* to separate syllables in a word where ambiguity could arise.

Examples:

(皮袄, **pí'ǎo**, **fur quilted jacket**) versus (票, **piào**, **ticket**)

(西安, *Xī'ān*, **Xian**) versus (先, *xiān*, **before, first**)

Word Formation

Ambiguity can exist in partitioning words. Each character is a single syllable sound. However, many words, being composed of two or more characters hence form polysyllabic Hanyu Pinyin words. Spacing between words is based on separating Hanyu Pinyin words, not single syllables. Generally, the separation is based on taking character compilations that form words and separating them as distinct Hanyu Pinyin. Simply, words, not characters, stand alone. If the world could get China to do the same with characters, that is, separating words with a space, learning and identifying compound character words would be much easier.

However, there are often ambiguities in partitioning a word due to the alphabetic structure of Hanyu Pinyin. Orthographic rules were put into effect in 1988 by the;

National Educational Commission of China
(State Education Commission)
国家教育委员会
Guójiā Jiàoyù Wěiyuánhuì

 and the

National Language Commission of China
(National Language Writing Working Committee)
国家语言文字工作委员会
Guójiā Yǔyán Wénzì Gōngzuo Wěiyuánhuì

These above committee titles demonstrate the uninterrupted strings of Chinese characters, the Hanyu Pinyin words, and the literal versus common translation. Please note that in the first title, the word China does not appear in the character string but it appears in the translation. This is a good example of the randomness of some translations.

Single Meaning

Words that are created from Hanyu Pinyin that in combination or alone have a single meaning and are distinct recognizable combinations are written as one word and not capitalized.

Examples:

rén, 人, person	**niánqīng**, 年轻, young
pǎo, 跑, run	**zhòngshì**, 重视, takes
hǎo, 好, good	**wǎnhuì**, 晚会, party
hé, 和, and	**qiānmíng**, 签名, signature
hěn, 很, very	**shìwēi**, 示威, demonstration
fúróng, 芙蓉, cotton rose	**niǔzhuǎn**, 扭转, reverse
qiǎokèlì, 巧克力, chocolate	**chuánzhī**, 船只, ship
péngyou, 朋友, friend	**dànshì**, 但是, but
diànhuà, 电话, telephone	**fēicháng**, 非常, extremely
yuèdú, 阅读, reading	**diànshìjī**, 电视机, television
dìzhèn, 地震, earth quake	**túshūguǎn**, 图书馆, library

These above Hanyu Pinyin do not occur in the compiled format with the given tones for any other commonly spoken words.

Combined Meaning

Two And Three Character Words

Words created by combining two words or three words to have one meaning are written together.

Examples:

gāngtiě, 钢铁, steel and iron

wèndá, 问答, question and answer

hǎifēng, 海风, sea breeze

hóngqí, 红旗, Red Flag

dàhuì, 大会, congress

quánguó, 全国, nation

zhòngtián, 种田, farms

kāihuì, 开会, holds a meeting

dǎpò, 打破, to break

zǒulái, 走来, walks

húshuō, 胡说, nonsense

dǎnxiǎo, 胆小, timidly

qiūhǎitáng, 秋海棠, begonia

duìbuqǐ, 对不起, sorry

chīdexiāo, 吃得消, able to endure

àiniǎozhōu, 爱鸟周, to like bird week

Four Character Words

Words created by combining 4 or more characters are split up into constituent words with identified meaning. This rule is also used for compilations of more than 4 characters. Hanyu Pinyin words created by more than one character are separated in whole word units.

Examples:

wúfèng gāngguǎn, 无缝钢管, **seamless steel-tube**,

huánjìng bǎohù guīhuà, 环境保护规划, **environmental protection planning**,

jīngtǐguǎn gōnglǜ fàngdàqì, 晶体管功率放大器, **Transistor power amplifier**

Zhōnghuá Rénmín Gònghéguó, 中华人民共和国, **People's Republic of China**

Yánjiūshēngyuàn, 研究生院, **graduate school**

Hóngshízìhuì, 红十字会, **Red Cross**

Yúxīngcǎosù, 鱼腥草素, **cordate houttuynia element**

Gǔshēngwùxuéjiā, 古生物学家, **paleontologist**

Zhōngguó Shèhuì Kēxuéyuàn,
中国社会科学院,
China Academy Social Sciences

Duplicated Characters AA, AABB and ABAB

AA

When words are formed from characters that are duplicated in the form AA, they are written together.

Examples:

rénrén, 人人, **everybody**   **gègè**, 个个, **each one**

kànkàn, 看看, **to have a look**   **dàda**, 大大, **big**

niánnián, 年年, **yearly**   **shuōshuo**, 说说, **to say**

tiāntiān, 天天, **everyday**   **hónghóng de**, 红红的, **red**

ABAB

When two characters are duplicated in the form ABAB they are separated into two AB words repeated.

Examples:

yánjiū yánjiū, 研究研究, **to study, to research,**

xuěbái xuěbáide, 雪白雪白的, **snow-white**

chángshì chángshì, 尝试尝试, **attempts**

tōnghóng tōnghóngde, 通红通红的, **very red**

AABB

A hyphen is used with the schema AABB. The words are duplicated and separated with a hyphen.

Examples:

láilái-wǎngwǎng, 来来往往, **go back and forth**

qiānqiān-wànwàn, 千千万万, **numerous**

qīqī-bābā, 七七八八, **miscellaneous**

qīngqīng-chǔchǔ, 清清楚楚, **clear**

jiājiā-hùhù, 家家户户, **all families**, **each and every family**

shuōshuo-xiàoxiào, 说说笑笑, **chats**

wānwān-qūqū, 弯弯曲曲, **curving**

Abbreviations

For for ease of reading and understanding, the hyphen is used in certain situations. Words that are easily understood may be eliminated.

Examples:

huán-bǎo, 环保, **versus huánjìng bǎohù**, 环境保护, **environmental protection**

bā-jiǔ tiān, 八九天, **versus** 八十九天, **eighty-nine days**

rén-jī duìhuà, 人机对话, **versus** 人和机器的对话, **man-machine dialog**

lù-hǎi-kōngjūn, 陆海空军, **land-sea-air armed forces**

gōng-guān, 公关, **versus gōnggòng guānxì**, 公共关系, **public relations**

shíqī-bā suì, 十七八岁, **versus shíqī shíbā suì**, 十七十八岁, **17-18 years**

zhōng-xiǎoxué, 中小学, **versus zhōngxué-xiǎoxué**, 中学小学, **middle school-junior school**

Common Nouns and People Nouns

Common Nouns formed from multiple characters are written as one Hanyu Pinyin word.

Examples:

zhuōzi, 桌子, **table**

mùtou, 木头, **wood**

fùbùzhǎng, 副部长, **vice minister**

chéngwùyuán, 乘务员, **conductor**

háizimen, 孩子们, **children**

fēijīnshǔ, 非金属, **nonmetallic**

chāoshēngbō, 超声波, **ultrasonic wave**

zǒnggōngchéngshī, 总工程师, **chief engineer**

fēiyèwù rényuán, 非业务人员, **non-servicers**

fǎndàndào dǎodàn, 反弹道导弹, **antimissile missile**

chéngwùyuán, 乘务员, **train attendant**

kēxuéxìng, 科学性, **scientific nature**

yìshùjiā, 艺术家, **artist**

xiàndàihuà, 现代化, **modernization**

tuōlājīshǒu, 拖拉机手, **tractor driver**

Words of Position

Words of position acting as prepositions forming locative phrases are separated. Although standard Mandarin grammar is very similar to English, locative phrases are composed with the locative particle in the sentence final position.

Examples:

mén wàimiàn, 门 外面, door outside, outdoors,

hé lǐmiàn, 河里面, river inside, in the river

huǒchē shàngmiàn, 火车上面, train upon, on the train

Huáng Hé yǐnán, 黄河以南, Yellow River by south, south of Yellow River

shān shàngmiàn, 山上面, mountain upon, on mountain

Yǒngdìng Hé shàng, 永定河上, Yongding river on, on Yongdong River

shù xià, 树下, tree under, under the tree

xuéxiào pángbiān, 学校旁边, school nearby

Exceptions

Words traditionally connected continue to be connected in Hanyu Pinyin.

Examples:

tiānshàng, 天上, at the sky

kōngzhōng, 空中, in the air

dìxià, 地下, floor on, on the floor

hǎiwài, 海外, sea away, overseas

Chinese Personal Names

Family names are separated from the given name. If the given name consists of two syllables, they should be written together. All proper person names are capitalized.

Examples:

Lú XuéFèng, 卢 学凤   **Lǔ Xùn**, 鲁迅

Lǐ Huá, 李 花   **Zhāng Sān**, 张三

Name Titles

Titles names follow the Proper name. The title is separated and not capitalized.

Examples:

Wáng bùzhǎng, 王部长, **Wang minister**

Lǐ xiānshēng, 李先生, **Li Mister**

Tián zhǔrèn, 田主任, **Tian director**

Zhào tóngzhì, 赵同志, **Zhao comrade**

The honorific and respectful forms of addressing people with *Lǎo*, *Xiǎo*, *Dà* and *A* are capitalized: These forms of address come after the Proper Name.

Xiǎo Liú, 小刘, young Liu   **Lǎo Wú**, 老吴, senior Wu

Dà Lǐ, 大李, elder Li   **Lǎo Qián**, 老钱, elder Qian

A Sān, 阿三, honourable San

Exceptions are:

Kǒngzǐ, 孔子, **Master Confucius**

Bāogōng, 包公, **Bao Judge**

Xīshī, 西施, **Xishi**, **a historical person**

Mèngchángjūn, 孟尝君, **Mèngchángjūn, a historical person**

Geographical Names of China

Proper Noun location names are compounded together and any other designation is separated. Proper Nouns are capitalized as in English.

Examples:

Běijīng Shì, 北京市, **Beijing City**

Yālù Jiāng, 鸭绿江, **Yalu Stream**

Héběi Shěng, 河北省, **Hebei Province**

Tài Shān, 泰山, **Tai Mountain**

Dòngtíng Hú, 洞庭湖, **Donting Lake**

Táiwān Hǎixiá, 台湾海峡, **Taiwan Strait**

When a Proper Noun has additional characters that further define the location, each noun phrase is kept together as a single Hanyu Pinyin. Precision in location always works and thus locative words become entrenched into the Proper name.

Examples:

Xīliáo Hé, 西辽河, **Xiliao River**

Jǐngshān Hòujiē, 景山后街, **Jingshan Backstreet**

Cháoyángménnèi Nánxiǎojiē, 朝阳门内南小街, **Chaoyang Gate Inside, South Alley**

Many villages, towns and features are written as one Hanyu Pinyin with the usual capitalized geographic name joined to the location feature name.

Examples:

Wángcūn, 王村, **Wang Village**

Sāntányìnyuè, 三潭印月, **three pools reflecting the moon**

Jiǔxiānqiáo, 酒仙桥, **Jiuxian bridge**

Zhōukǒudiàn, 周口店, **Zhōukǒu store**

Non-Chinese Proper Nouns and Names

There is great creativity and confusion with the methodology in which the Chinese translate non-Chinese names into Hanyu Pinyin and Hanzi. Some Hanyu Pinyin are attempts to phonetically mirror the sounds of the non-Chinese Proper Nouns.

Examples:

Marx, 马克思, **Mǎkèsī**

Newton, 牛顿, **Niúdùn**

Washington, 华盛顿, **Huáshèngdùn**

London, 伦敦, **Lúndūn**

Others provide descriptives from a Chinese perspective.

Examples:

Dōngnányà, 东南亚, **east south Asia (South East Asia)**

Měiguó, 美国, **beautiful country (America)**

Dōngjīng, 东京, **east capital (Tokyo)**

Nánměi, 南美, **south beautiful (South America)**

The remainder are somewhat mystifying.

Examples:

Paris, 巴黎, **Bālí**

Akutagawa Ryunosuke, 芥川龙之介, **jiè chuān lóng zhī jiè**

Seypidin, 赛福鼎, **Sàifúdǐng**

Fēizhōu, 非洲, **evil continent (Africa)**

Déguó, 德国, **morality country (Germany)**

Verbs
Dòngcí
动词

Verbs and the characters affixed to them as grammatical particle suffixes such as (着, **zhe**), (了, **le**) and (过, **guo**) are written as one word.

(着, **zhe**, **durative grammatical particle**) is added to a verb to indicate and ongoing process. Functionally, it acts as *–ing* added to an English verb.

(了, **le**, **completed verb action particle**) is added to a verb to indicate the completion of the verb action.

(过, **guo**, **experiential verb particle**) is added to a verb to indicate initial exposure to an action.

Examples:

kànzhe, 看着, **seeing, looking**   **jìnxíngzhe**, 进行着, **to attempting**

kànle, 看 了, **saw, looked**   **jìnxíngle**, 进行了, **attempted**

kànguo, 看过, **seeing**   **jìnxíngguo**, 进行过, **attempt**

The sentence final particle 了, **le**, indicating a new state or immediacy, is written separately.

Example:

Huǒchē dào le, 火车到了, **train arrived**

Verbs Object Compounds

Verbs and their objects are separated:

Examples:

kàn xìn, 看信, **read letter**

chī yú, 吃 鱼, **eat fish**

kāi wánxiào, 开玩笑, **to be joking**

jiāoliú jīngyàn, 交流经验, **exchange experience**

In situations in which a Verb Object phrase word has numeric qualifiers, the quantitative adjectival phrase is inserted within the verb phrase following the appropriate rules.

Examples:

jūle gōng, 鞠了躬, **bowed body**

jūle yī gè gōng, 鞠了一个躬, bowed one body

lǐguo fà, 理过发, manages sent

lǐguo sān cì fà, 理过三次发, manages three times has sent

Verb Compliment Compounds

If one verb and it's complement verb are both monosyllabic and form a compound, they are written as one Hanyu Pinyin

Examples:

gǎohuài, 搞坏, causes to break down

jiànchéng, 建成, completes (such as a project)

shútòu, 熟透, thoroughly ripe

huàwéi, 化为, changes into

dǎsǐ, 打死, beat kill

If the verb or the compliment are polysyllabic they are written separately and two or more distinct Hanyu Pinyin are formed.

Examples:

zǒu jìnlái, 走进来, go forth enter come/go forth into

zhěnglǐ hǎo, 整理好, reorganizes well

jiànshè chéng, 建设成, construction becoming, constructs, builds

gǎixiě wéi, 改写为, rewrite for

Adjectives
Xíngróngcí
形容词

A one syllable adjective and its duplication are written as one and the complement is added to it to form one continuous Hanyu Pinyin.

Example:

mēngmēnglìang, 蒙蒙亮, (cover cover light), **dim**, **dawn**

lìangtāngtāng, 亮堂堂, **shining bright**

Complement of Size or Degree Adjectives

Complements of size or degree are written separated from the word they qualify. They are written after the involved verb. Duplication acts to increase the quality of the duplicated adjective. Duplicates are written continuously.

Example:

Yīdiǎndiǎnr, 一点点儿, is less than **yīdiǎnr**, 一点儿.

Examples:

xiē 些, **few, some**

yīxiē, 一些, **a few**

diǎnr, 点儿, **little**

yīdiǎnr, 一点儿, **a little**

yīdiǎndiǎnr, 一点点儿, **a little**

dà xiē, 大 些, **big some,**

dà yīxiē, 大一些, **big a little**

kuài yīdiǎnr, 快 一点儿, **fast a little**

kuài diǎnr, 快点儿, **fast a little**

Pronouns
Dàicí
代词

Personal Pronouns

(们, **men**, **plural suffix for pronouns and human nouns**), the plural suffix is compounded with the root noun or pronoun to form a compound Hanyu Pinyin word written continuously.

Examples:

wǒmen, 我们, we/us

tāmen, 他们, they

nǐmen, 你们, you (plural)

zánmen, 咱们, we / us

háizimen, 孩子们, children

lǎoshīmen, 老师们, teachers

nánshìmen, 男士们, gentlemen

nǚshìmen, 女士们, ladies

Demonstrative Pronouns
指示代词
Zhǐshì Dàicí

Demonstrative pronouns acting as definite articles are written separately from the target subject or object of a sentence. The grammatical affixes 些, 里, 儿, 边, and 个 are added continuously with the demonstrative pronouns.

Zhè / zhèi, 这, **this**

zhèxiē, 这些, **these**

zhèr, 这儿, **here**

nà / nèi, 那, **that**

nàxiē, 那些, **those**

nàli, 那里, **there**

gāi, 该, **this**

zhèli, 这里, **here**

zhèbian, 这边, **this side / here**

zhège / zheige, 这个, **this one**

nèige, 那个, **that one / that piece**

nàr, 那儿, **there**

běn, 本市, **this**

Examples:

zhè rén, 这 人, **this person**

zhèxiē rén, 这些人, **these person (s)**

dào zhèr lái, 到这儿来, **to here come**

dào nàr qù, 到那儿去, **to there go**

tā yào nàgè, 他要那个, **he want that one**

wǒ yào zhègè, 我要这个, **I want this one**

běn bùmén, 本部门, **this department**

nà cì huìyì, 那次会议, **that conference**

gāi kān, 该刊, **this publication**

gāi gōngsī, 该公司, **this company**

nàxiē cì huìyì, 那些次会议, **those conference(s)**

Quantitative Adjectives

Modifers of nouns that add a quantitative adjectival quality are written separate from the target noun. As these can modify countable nouns, the Countable Noun Indicator is also written separately.

gè, 各, **each**

měi, 每, **each**

mǒu, 某, **some, a certain**

Examples:

gè gè, 各个, **each**

gè guó, 各国, **each country**

měi nián, 每年, **every year**

mǒu rén, 某人, **somebody**

měi cì, 每次, **each time**

gè rén, 各人, **each person**

gè xuékē, 各学科, **various disciplines**

Numbers

For numbers between eleven and one hundred, write them continuously.

Examples:

shíyī, 十一, **eleven**　　　　　　**sānshísān**, 三十三, **thirty three**

shíwǔ, 十五, **fifteen**　　　　　　**jiǔshíjiǔ**, 九十九, **ninety nine**

For one hundred, one thousand, ten thousand, and one hundred million, the number in the first position is continuous with the larger number.

Examples:

jiǔbǎi, 九百, **900**

sānqiān, 三千, **3000**

liùwàn, 六万, **60,000**

sìyì, 四亿, **400,000,000**

Ordinal numbers are separated with a hyphen.

Examples:

dì-yī, 第一, **first**

dì-èrshíbā, 第二十八, **28th**

dì-shísān, 第十三, **13**[th]

dì-sānbǎi wǔshíliù, 第三百五十六, **356th**

Number, Countable Noun Indicator and Target Noun

Countable Nouns (**CN**) are preceded by a Quantitative Adjective (**QA**) and a Countable Noun Indicator (**CDI**). **CNI's** are variably called measure words or classifiers. The **QA**, **CNI** and **CN** are all separated. The **QA** can be an absolute number such as (两, **liǎng**, **two**) or can be a relative numeric indicator such as (多,**duō**, **many**), (几, **jǐ**, **several**) and (些, **xiē**, **a few**).

Examples:

liǎng gè rén, 两个人, two people

liǎng jiān bàn wūzi, 两间半屋子, two-and-a-half rooms

yī dà wǎn fàn, 一大碗饭, a large bowl food

wǔshísān réncì, 五十三人次, 53 people

yībǎi duō gè, 一百多个, 100 more, (more than one hundred)

jǐ jiā rén, 几家人, several family members

shí lái wàn rén, 十来万人, ten come ten thousand people

jǐ tiān gōngfu, 几天工夫, several day of free time

jǐshí, 几十, several dozen

shíjǐ gè rén, 十几个人, several people

jǐshí gēn gāngguǎn, 几十根钢管, several dozens steel pipes

Adverbs
副词
Fùcí

Adverbs are written separately from other words.

Examples:

hěn hǎo, 很好, *very good*

bù lái, 不来, not come

zuì dà, 最大, most big

fēicháng kuài, 非常快, very quick

dōu lái, 都来, always comes

gèng měi, 更美, more beautiful

Prepositions
介词
Jiècí

Prepositions are written separately.

Examples:

zài qiánmiàn, 在前面, **at frontside**

wèi rénmín fúwù, 为人民服务, **for people serves**

shēng yú 1940 nián, 生于 1940 年, **born in 1940 year**

xiàng dōngbiān qù, 向东边去, **toward eastside go**

cóng zuótiān qǐ, 从昨天起, **from yesterday**

guānyú zhègè wèntí, 于这个问题, **about this question**

Conjunctions
连词
Liáncí

Conjunctions are always written separately.

Examples:

gōngrén hé nóngmín, 工人和农民, **worker and farmer**

guāngróng ér jiānjù, 光荣而艰巨, **honorable and arduous**

bùdàn kuài érqiě hǎo, 不但快而且好, **not only quick moreover good**

Nǐ lái háishi bù lái, 你来还是不来, **you come or not come**

Structural Auxiliaries
结构助词
Jiégōu Zhùcí

的, **de**, **possessive, modifying, or descriptive particle, of**

地, **de**, **subordinate particle adverbial, -ly**

得, **dé**, **adverbial particle**

之, **zhī**, **literary equivalent of** 的 **as a subordinate particle**

Examples:

dàdì de nǔ' ér, 大地的女儿, **earth daughter**

zhè shì wǒ de shū, 这是我的书, **this is my book**

wǒmen guòzhe xìngfú de shēnghuó, 我们过着幸福的生活, **we happy life**

mài qīngcài luóbo de, 卖青菜萝卜的, **sells green vegetables radish**

tā mànman de zǒu, 他慢慢地走, **he walk slowly**

tǎnbái de gàosù nǐ ba, 坦白地告诉你吧, **tells you honestly**

dǎsǎo de gānjìng, 打扫得干净, **cleans cleanly**

hóng de hěn, 红得很, **red very**

xiě de bù hǎo, 写得不好, **writes not good**

lěng de fādǒu, 冷得发抖, **is cold trembles**

shàonián zhī jiā, 少年之家, **children's club**

zuì fādá de guójiā zhī yī, 最发达的国家之一, **one of most developed national**

Modal Particles
语气助词
Yŭqì Zhùcí

Particles indicating moods are written separately.

Examples:

Nĭ zhīdào ma?,你知道吗, **You know**?

Zěnme hái bù lái a?, 怎么还不来啊, **How yet not come**?

Kuài qù ba!, 快去吧!, **Quick go!**

Tā shì bù huì lái de.他是不会来的, **He is not able to come**.

Interjectives
叹词
Tàncí

Examples:

A! Zhēn měi!,啊!真美, **Really beautiful!**

Nnng, nĭ shuō shénme?, 嗯,你说什么, **what did you say?**

Hmmph!, zŏuzhe qiáo ba!, 哼走着瞧吧, **humph!, wait and see!**

Onomatopoeia
拟声词
Nǐshēngcí

pa!, 啪, **pa**!

jiji-zhazha, 叽叽喳喳, **chirp chirp**

huahua, 哗哗, **whish whish**

honglong, 轰隆一声, **yī shēng, bang**

Dà gōngjī wo-wo-tí., 大公鸡喔喔啼, **Big cockerel wo-wo cries.**

Dū, **qìdí xiǎng le.** 嘟,汽笛响了, **"du", the steam whistle made a sound.**

Idioms
成语
Chéngyǔ

Four word idioms are divided into two double syllables interpersed with a hyphen.

céngchū-bùqióng, 层出不穷, **emerges one after another incessantly**

àizēng-fēnmíng, 爱憎分明, **is clear about what to love and what to hate**

yángyáng-dàguān, 洋洋大观, **spectacular**

guāngmíng-lěiluò, 光明磊落, **frank**

fēngpíng-làngjìng, 风平浪静, **uneventful**

píngfēn-qiūsè, 平分秋色, **shares half and half**

diānsān-dǎosì, 颠三倒四, **disorderly**

There are four word idioms which are written continuously.

bùyìlèhū, 不亦乐乎, **delight**

àimònéngzhù, 爱莫能助, **wants to help but not be able**

húlihútu, 糊里糊涂, **bewildered**

diàoerlángdāng, 吊儿郎当, **careless**

zǒngéryánzhī, 总而言之, **in brief**

yīyīdàishuǐ, 一衣带水, **close**

hēibuliūqiū, 黑不溜秋, **swarthy**

Capital Letters
大写
Dàxiě

The first word in sentences and poetry each begin with a capital letter. Proper Nouns each begin with a capital letter.

Examples:

Běijīng, 北京, **Beijing**

Chángchéng, 长城, **Great Wall (long wall)**

Qīngmíng, 清明, **Pure Brightness (a city)**

For a Proper Noun which is composed of several words, each words first letter has a capital letter.

Examples:

Guójì Shūdiàn, 国际书店, **International Bookstore**

Guāngmíng Rìbào, 光明日报, **Guangming Daily**

Hépíng Bīnguǎn, 和平宾馆, **Peaceful Guesthouse**

When a Proper Noun forms a word with a Common Noun the word is written continuously. The Proper Noun is capitalized and the common noun is not.

Examples:

Zhōngguórén, 中国人, **Chinese person**

Míngshǐ, 明史, **Ming Dynasty history** (**Ming Dynasty is** 明朝, **Míng cháo**)

Guǎngdōnghuà, 广东话, **Cantonese** (**the spoken language of Guangdong province**)

There are some words that through common use have changed into common nouns. The first letter is therefore a small letter.

Examples:

guǎnggān, 广柑, **sweet orange**

zhōngshānfú, 中山服, **Chinese tunic**

chuānxiōng, 川芎, **rhizome of Ligusticum wallichii**

zàngqīngguǒ, 藏青果, **terminalia**

Dividing and Hyphenating Words

Dividing and hyphenating words to carry on to the next sentence must be done at the completion of a syllable. A hyphen is used between the two syllables.

Example:

(光明, **guāngmíng**, **bright**, **promising**)

Guāngmíng is split between the syllables forming the compound word, **guāng-míng**. The format **gu-āngmíng** cannot be used.

Tone Marker Placement

1. First, look for an *a* or an *e*. If either vowel appears, it takes the tone mark. There are no possible pinyin syllables that contain both an *a* and an *e*.
2. If there is no *a* or *e*, look for an *ou*. If *ou* appears, then the *o* takes the tone mark.
3. If none of the above cases hold, then the last vowel in the syllable takes the tone mark.

The reasoning behind these rules is in the case of diphthongs and triphthongs, *i*, *u*, and *ü* are considered medial glides rather than part of the syllable nucleus in Chinese phonology. The rules ensure that the tone mark always appears on the nucleus of a syllable.

Another way to find the vowel for a tone mark is to apply the tone mark in the following order: *a, e, o, i, u*, except for *iu*, in which case *u* takes the tone mark.

The Character Ü

An umlaut is placed over the letter *u* when it occurs after the initials *l* and *n*. This is necessary in order to distinguish the front high rounded vowel in *lü* from the back high rounded vowel in *lu*. Tonal markers are added on top of the umlaut, as in *lǘ*.

However, the *ü* is *not* used in other contexts where it represents a front high rounded vowel, namely after the letters *j*, *q*, *x* and *y*. Genuine ambiguities only happen with *nu / nü* and *lu / lü*, which are then distinguished by an umlaut diacritic.

Chinese Learning Websites

Cautionary Statement, Internet Rules

1) That which is on the internet today may not be there tomorrow.

2) The internet is the final resting ground for opinion, errors and misdirection.

3) Wikipedia is particularly unreliable as any enthusiast can edit it.

4) Self declared experts with grammar and spell check can seem very authoritative.

5) Some sites offering audio clips of Pinyin phonemes are particularly unreliable and entertaining.

6) University sites seem more reliable but less visually interesting.

7) It is far easier to find fee sites than free sites.

8) Much of what you need is there for free if you can find it but it is scattered across many sites.

9) Most sites you sign up for do not offer a simple cancellation, they will keep auto debiting your credit card.

10) The web site with pictures of me in a brothel with three girls in Chengdu was an interview I was doing.

How to Find the Ultimate Tools

There are many poor quality books, tapes, CD's, DVD's and flashcards on the market, many that I have bought. Learn from my mistakes. Some rules.

1) If it can fit in your pocket it is not good because the font is too small to read.

2) If it does not have English, Pinyin and Characters it is relatively useless.

3) If it gets too creative with translations it will impede your understanding of grammar.

4) If it is made of that super thin onion skin paper it makes excellent toilet paper. Which, when you go to China, you will always find a shortage of.

5) If you buy a character book and it does not have the characters for rice, eat, train and middle, the writer has never been to China and the book may be useless.

6) Nobody has cassette tape players anymore, why buy cassettes?

7) Big multi-coloured boxes can have surprisingly little in them. Open and inspect.

8) Eight CD sets often have enough information to be all fit onto one CD, with lots of room left over.

9) Do not assume that a position at a university or a Ph.D. makes the book better. The worst grammar books I have are written by grammar professors. Even my Chinese friends do not understand some of the grammar constructions.

10) Books written by Cantonese Chinese may have slightly different sentence constructions.

11) Introductory character writing or grammar books with sentences with more than five words or characters are too advanced for a beginner.

My Personal Favorite Web Sites

www.SpeakandWriteChinese.com

This is my website. It is in the building phase. I am going to try and gradually introduce everything that you will need. I am working on building a database that anyone can add to to add words, sentences and phrases. Ultimately I will write a program to write English, Hanzi and Pinyin at the same time. It will also have a review for books, CDs, DVDs, websites and other learning resources. You will be able to order any of my books, flash cards and CD's from this site. First I have to learn to use a computer.

www.mandarintools.com

This is hands down the best web site for character information in a dictionary format and it is free. Everything you need is there, dictionary, conversion utilities, the CEDICT database. There is even some useful grammar and sentence structure. The interface is a little awkward and unrevealing. If you delve into it and open everything it is a treasure of information and programs. They accept contributions. You can download their great stand alone program **DimSum** for free. You can also download the CEDICT database.

www.zhongwen.com

This is a great website for researching the Radicals and etymology of characters. The interface is easy to use. It also links to the Ocrat database, sometimes. The interface makes it easy to navigate quickly. The site is a no charge site. I feel that this is the best site for research and it shows the learner a fascinating look at how characters within a group evolved.

http://lost-theory.org/ocrat

This site has an easy to use interface and provides animated stroke order access. This side has common family names, P.R.C. provinces and other difficult to find but interesting characters. This site is a no charge site. Personally, I do not feel a great need to watch the stroke order of every character. I feel it is better to learn the rules of stroke order.

www.sexybeijing.tv

This website details the adventures of Su Fei, a hot Jewish girl from California who goes around creating adventure in Beijing. She takes her name from a brand name product line of women's sanitary pads. She is so funny and it is a great place to learn conversational Mandarin. Her videos are easiest to access at www.sexybeijing.tv. These videos give you a nice exposure to the real life for citizens of a big Chinese city.

www.chinesesavvy.com

This site has a nice profile of everything you need to learn to function in China. It is expensive and in some of the paid features the native Beijingers talk so fast it is hardly an introduction to spoken Mandarin. There is little English translation of these conversations. They have a great forum for discussing any issues in China. However, the moderator edits out any issues that are controversial in China.

www.chineselearner.com

This is a great website and is rapidly getting bigger and better. It is being updated often so sometimes is does not fire up immediately. The moderators are friendly and they respond to e-mails quickly. Most of what they offer is currently free. Oddly there are lessons offered in the Hanyu Pinyin section that are not translated from Hanzi.

http://www.csulb.edu/~txie/pinyin/pinyin.htm

This is a great website that has all you need to get your computer to type Pinyin and convert to Hanzi; in fact, it is more useful than the Microsoft embedded utility. If you have a bootleg Windows and cannot access Microsoft free downloads, this is the solution. I carry it on my USB wherever I go.

http://www.globechinese.com/

Chinese Character Bible or Hanzi Explorer 9.2 is an animated character writing program with pronunciation. It is a free shareware download. It has a colourful interface and is easy to use. Oddly, it does not show Pinyin when it demonstrates a character. So you are left to try and figure out the Pinyin or plug it into another program.

http://babelfish.yahoo.com/

This is a translator program that can interconvert Hanzi and English. Like all such programs the Hanzi to English and English to Hanzi is somewhat speculative.

http://xenomachina.com/toys/pinyin2hanzi.html

This site has a program that takes Pinyin and converts it to Hanzi to give you choices of characters.

http://technology.chtsai.org/

This is a great website for statistics of word frequency and links to useful word lists. There is also a hard to find list of Chinese names. These lists can save you hundreds of hours if you are writing a book. This is a must have site for the committed learner.

http://www.pinyin.info/

This website is full of useful tools for manipulating Pinyin. It has all the official rules of Pinyin along with conversion tools, spell checker and how to set up your computer for Chinese usage. There is also a comparison of the different Romanisation systems, which is very comprehensive

http://www.uni.edu/becker/chinese2.html

This website offers links to multitudes of other Chinese learning websites. The interface is easy and very colourful.

http://www.rci.rutgers.edu/~rsimmon/chingram/

This site has a good section on Mandarin Grammar but it lacks explanation. It appears to be a slide presentation that served as highlights to the speaker. It does cover all the relevant areas of Mandarin Chinese grammar.

http://www.askbenny.cn

Benny, the world's most famous Chinese teacher, is a great site that introduces very useful sentence constructions and vocabulary. He is very personable and has more energy than is possible. This site is free!!!!, but please donate. I would rank this site number one in ease of access, utility and fun for a speaking tool.

http://www.chinese-tools.com/

This website has a good dictionary and a translator that converts characters to Hanyu Pinyin with tone markers. There is also a idiom dictionary with 30,000 idioms.

http://chinesepod.com/

This website is a audio video site based on progressive learning of Standard Mandarin. There are various levels of membership and the price is very reasonable at the beginner level. The higher priced long winded explanations are too complex for learners. Some of the speakers speak far too fast to make it a learning experience. However, the transcripts in English and Hanyu Pinyin available with the sound files are excellent. The moderator *Ken* gives some very incorrect grammatical translations. These can be a huge barrier to learning Mandarin Grammar as he mixes up both word order and word usage.

Using a Computer in China

Using a computer in China at an internet café is full of risk. First, they are common sites for thieves and I have had young boys crawl on their hands and knees and try and unplug my USB, take by backpack, wallet, passport etc. Often the computers are set up with keystroke copy programs and will copy your credit card, bank account and e-mail passwords. I have had bank accounts emptied twice and charge cards emptied twice.

If you bring your own computer it is a target for thieves and you cannot fall asleep on a bus or train without risk. To safely prepare a computer for use is no short or simple task. I always carry a USB with *CCleaner* on it from www.ccleaner.com, a free registry cleaner. I clean the registry both before and after I use the computer.

I also carry the free download *Counter Spy* from www.sunbelt-software.com and I run the program to find viruses and spyware. Chinese computers can be very slow and it can take from 20 minutes to 2 hours to make a computer safe. Many Chinese chat programs open the IP address and will take whatever information you have to steal. *QQ* is the most popular chat program in China. Chinese people do not realize that the purpose of the program is to take your information for marketing purposes and sell it to advertisers. The chat utility is a cover. So I remove it.

Programs such as *Windows Password Reset* will allow you to bypass security functions and remove malicious programs. I always remove *QQ* and the entire *Tencent* family of programs. I install my registry cleaner and spyware program and sometimes take out dozens of Trojans and viruses. I have found that most computers in China are not secured and they have no administrator passwords anyhow.

It is very important to have *Skype* on your USB, a headset and a *Skype* account. Calling out of China can be a real challenge in remote areas. **www.Skype.com**

How to Spend Your Money Wisely

If you have money to spend I would highly recommend;

1) My books, CD's and website. www.SpeakandWriteChinese.com

2) Beginner's Chinese by Yong Ho. 1977   ISBN 0-7818-0566-X

There are multitudes of introductory books on the market but this book has more useful methods to learn in this book of 174 pages than a huge pile of other books I have. I carried this book in China for a long time.

3) Chinese Grammar by Claudia Ross. 2004   ISBN 0-07-137764-6

I have all the classic grammar texts, Chao, Li, etc. but this book has all the relevant grammar in it. If you master this book you do not need any other grammar to speak Mandarin. The book is structured in a very practical way.

4) Wenlin DVD available at www.languageworld.com

Of the multitude of Chinese learning DVD's I have, this replaces them all. You can learn everything here in an easy interface, stroke order, Radicals, Words versus characters. You can search specific Radicals within characters and words. For the beginner or researcher this is the best bang for the buck. Rather than randomly buy 10 different tools, buy this one.

5) e-Stroke available at www.eon.com

This program allows you to cut, paste, and drop a character into their tool and it gives you an animated stroke order, Pinyin and definition. It is indispensible for identifying obscure characters.

Cut these out or photocopy them and put your phone number in the columns and get these babies plastered all over China Town or the Faculty of Computer Science at your local university.

我 教 你 英 文 你 教 我 汉 語

Wǒ jiāo Nǐ Yīngwén, Nǐ jiāo Wǒ Hànyǔ.

I teach you English, You teach me Han language.

我 教 你 英 文 你 教 我 汉 語

Wǒ jiāo Nǐ Yīngwén, Nǐ jiāo Wǒ Hànyǔ.

I teach you English, You teach me Han language.

Notes: